NAVIGATING MICROFINANCE: Insights and Implementation

Management Students and MFI Pros Must Read for Self Development

PRADEEP KUMAR SINGH

INDIA • SINGAPORE • MALAYSIA

ISBN 979-8-89133-685-8

NAVIGATING MICROFINANCE: INSIGHTS & IMPLEMENTATION

Navigating Microfinance: "Insights and Implementation" is a valuable resource for students of Management and professionals in Microfinance, NBFCs, Banks, SFBs, and Payment Banks with a keen interest in microfinance in India and globally, including its historical context

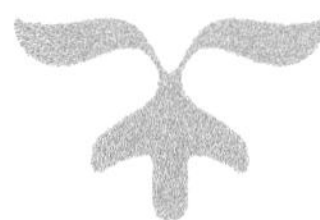

Dedication

With love and gratitude to All the people in the World who have contributed to Microfinance in any way, I dedicate this book.

To My Parents: Shri Jay Prakash Singh & Smt. Subhadra Devi, for your unwavering support and encouragement have been my guiding light throughout this journey.

To My Wife: Sanju for Your love, patience, and sacrifice have been the bedrock of my aspirations.

To My lovely Daughters: Pari, Vartika & Shristi, for your understanding and unconditional support during this endeavour mean the world to me.

To Nephew Abhishek to your support and assistance have been invaluable.

To All the Teachers: For imparting knowledge and wisdom.

To Seniors: Mr. Vivek Tiwari, Mr. Shirish Chandra Panda, Mr. Anirban Sinha, Mr. Vinod Pandey Sir, Mr. Abin Mukhopadhyay Sir and Mr Rajesh Kumar for your invaluable mentorship.

To Friends: Rakesh, Sanjay, Manish, Kishor, Krishna, Nishant and Amit for your unwavering support.

To All the Subordinates: For following and standing by me, giving me the courage to pursue this path.

This book is a tribute to the collective efforts of all those who have contributed to the world of Microfinance in countless ways. Your dedication and support have made this journey possible.

With Regards
Pradeep Kumar Singh

Table of Contents

Foreword

As I stand on the threshold of introducing "Navigating Microfinance: Insights and Implementation," I am profoundly moved by the dedication and passion that Pradeep Kumar Singh brings to this transformative field. This book is a testament to his unwavering commitment and over two decades of experience in the world of Microfinance, Insurance & Banking.

Microfinance has always held a special place in my heart, given its ability to uplift communities and empower individuals. It's more than just financial transactions; it's about creating a more inclusive and equitable world. In "Navigating Microfinance," Pradeep Kumar Singh beautifully encapsulates the essence of this sector.

One of the remarkable features of this book is its accessibility. It caters to a diverse audience, whether you're a student eager to learn about Microfinance, a professional in the field, or simply someone with a curiosity about its impact on our world.

This book is more than just theory; it's a practical guide that brings together insights and real-world perspectives. Each chapter provides a window into the complex world of Microfinance, offering a holistic view of its history, challenges, and triumphs.

As you delve into the narratives within these pages, you will encounter real-life stories of individuals whose lives have been transformed by Microfinance. These stories are a testament to the resilience and determination of those who, with a little financial support and guidance, have achieved remarkable success.

What sets this book apart is its commitment to staying current with the evolving landscape of Microfinance. The authors have diligently incorporated the latest trends and best practices, ensuring that readers are equipped with the most up-to-date knowledge.

I commend Pradeep Kumar Singh for his tireless efforts in the Microfinance sector. His two decades of experience have been instrumental in shaping this book and ensuring its relevance.

As you embark on this journey through "Navigating Microfinance: Insights and Implementation," I hope you find it as enlightening and inspiring as I have. May it encourage you to engage more deeply with Microfinance, whether as a practitioner, student, or advocate, and may you become a catalyst for positive change in the lives of those who need it most.

Sincerely,
Editor

Preface

Introduction

This book is a testament to the incredible journey of Microfinance and its profound impact on the world. It is dedicated to the unwavering support of every individual contributing to the field of Microfinance and to all management students eager to delve into the practices of Microfinance, both in India (India) and around the globe.

Microfinance, with its roots firmly planted in the idea of financial inclusion, has emerged as a powerful instrument of change, lifting communities out of poverty and empowering individuals to build better lives. It is a field that transcends boundaries, reaching the far corners of the world and touching the lives of countless people.

In the pages that follow, you will embark on a journey through the intricate workings of Microfinance, exploring its diverse models, delivery methods, and profound implications. This book is designed to provide insights and real-world perspectives that will not only benefit the practitioners of Microfinance but also serve as a valuable resource for aspiring management students eager to learn about the practical intricacies of this field.

The world of Microfinance is ever-evolving, and this book is a guide to navigating its complexities. It brings together the experiences, knowledge, and dedication of countless individuals who have contributed to the growth and development of Microfinance. It pays homage to their relentless efforts and commitment to financial inclusion.

Whether you are a seasoned professional in Microfinance or a student with a thirst for knowledge, this book is here to equip you with the insights you need to understand Microfinance's role in shaping communities, transforming lives, and creating a more inclusive and empowered world.

Thank you for joining us on this journey of discovery and learning. Together, we will explore the dynamic landscape of Microfinance and uncover the insights and implementations that drive positive change in the lives of millions.

Welcome to "Navigating Microfinance: Insights and Implementation."

Acknowledgments

In the vast landscape of Microfinance, countless individuals and organizations have played pivotal roles in shaping and enriching this field. It is with immense gratitude that I acknowledge their contributions and support.

To the world of Microfinance, I extend my heartfelt appreciation. It is your dedication to financial inclusion and empowerment that continues to inspire and drive positive change in our communities. Your unwavering commitment to making a difference is the cornerstone of this transformative industry.

I would also like to express my gratitude to the Indian Institute of Bank and Finance (IIBF), MFIN, Sa-Dhan, and the Reserve Bank of India (RBI) for their invaluable contributions to the Microfinance sector. Your guidance, policies, and initiatives have been instrumental in fostering the growth and stability of Microfinance in India.

To the Tata Institute of Social Sciences (TISS), I offer my thanks for providing a platform for education and research in agriculture and Agri-input management, a vital aspect of Microfinance that contributes to the welfare of rural communities.

I extend my special appreciation to Mr. Shirish Panda Sir, Mr. Vinod Pandey Sir, Mr. Anirban Sinha Sir, Mr. Vipin Pandey Sir, Mr. Sanjay Kumar, Mr. Kishor Kumar, Mr. Amit Dubey, Mr. J. K. Pandey Sir, Mr. Abin Mukhopadhyay Sir and Mr. Indrajeet Verma Sir for their support and insights. Your guidance has been instrumental in shaping this book and ensuring its relevance to the Microfinance community.

I am also thankful to all the creators and publishers of information on the internet. Your vast wealth of knowledge has been an invaluable resource in the research and development of this book.

To all those who have contributed to the field of Microfinance, directly or indirectly, your efforts have not gone unnoticed. Your dedication to financial inclusion and empowerment is a beacon of hope for countless individuals and communities.

Thank you for your unwavering support and commitment to making the world a better place through Microfinance.

Background

In the realm of Microfinance, the clock never stops ticking. Microfinance institutions are engines of financial inclusion, tirelessly working to uplift underserved communities by providing access to credit and financial services. In this dynamic and ever-evolving sector, the efficient management of time is of paramount importance.

This book, "Navigating Microfinance: Insights and Implementation," emerges from the profound need to equip Microfinance professionals and borrowers with the essential knowledge and understanding required to thrive in the world of Microfinance. Time waits for no one, and it is crucial that all stakeholders, from field force to management, are well-prepared to navigate the intricacies of this transformative field.

Microfinance companies and their dedicated staff are at the forefront of addressing economic disparities and empowering individuals and communities. However, the success of these endeavours' hinges on comprehensive and accessible knowledge. This book endeavours to bridge that knowledge gap, providing a foundation upon which Microfinance professionals can build, grow, and excel in their roles.

Furthermore, this book is not just for Microfinance professionals; it is for everyone who has ever been touched by the impact of Microfinance. Whether you are a seasoned practitioner or someone who has benefited from Microfinance services, this book aims to provide a comprehensive understanding of the industry.

In the pages that follow, we will embark on a journey through the world of Microfinance, exploring its core concepts, global perspectives, and the unique landscape of Indian Microfinance. It is my hope that this book will serve as a valuable resource, enabling all those involved in Microfinance to make informed decisions, drive positive change, and contribute to financial inclusion and empowerment.

The clock is ticking, and the world of Microfinance waits for no one. Let us embark on this journey together, armed with knowledge and a shared commitment to create a more inclusive and equitable financial landscape.

Objectives:

The primary objectives of this book are twofold: to empower Microfinance ground staff and to provide valuable insights to management students seeking a comprehensive understanding of Microfinance. This book aspires to elevate the knowledge and skills of those actively involved in the field of Microfinance while serving as a practical guide for aspiring professionals.

For Microfinance Ground Staff:

Empowerment: One of the central aims of this book is to empower Microfinance ground staff with the knowledge and tools they need to excel in their roles. Microfinance professionals working directly with borrowers are the lifeblood of the industry, and their effectiveness is critical to the success of financial inclusion efforts.

Knowledge Enhancement: By offering a holistic view of Microfinance, including its principles, models, and global best practices, this book seeks to enhance the knowledge base of Microfinance ground staff. It equips them with a deeper understanding of the field's nuances, allowing them to better serve their clients and communities.

For Management Students:

Comprehensive Learning: This book serves as a comprehensive resource for management students who are eager to delve into the world of Microfinance. It combines theoretical knowledge with practical insights, offering a well-rounded education on the subject.

Knowledge Label: The book's objective is to help management students achieve a "knowledge label" in Microfinance. By gaining expertise in this field, students can enhance their career prospects and contribute effectively to the Microfinance sector, aligning theory with real-world practice.

Practical Application: Beyond theoretical concepts, this book emphasizes practical aspects of Microfinance, providing students with valuable tools they can apply in their future careers. It bridges the gap between classroom learning and real-world application, preparing students for the challenges and opportunities in Microfinance management.

"Navigating Microfinance: Insights and Implementation" seeks to be a catalyst for empowerment and knowledge enhancement. It aims to elevate both Microfinance ground staff and management students, fostering a deeper understanding of this transformative field. With a perfect blend of theory and practicality, this book aspires to equip individuals with the skills and insights needed to drive positive change, promote financial inclusion, and contribute to the betterment of society.

Scope:

This book, "Navigating Microfinance: Insights and Implementation," is designed to provide readers with a comprehensive understanding of the

Microfinance sector, encompassing a wide range of topics and areas of interest. The scope of this book is broad, aiming to cover various facets of Microfinance while bridging the gap between theory and practical application.

Specific Topics and Areas Covered:

Foundational Concepts: The book starts by introducing readers to the core principles, objectives, and methodologies of Microfinance. It offers a solid foundation for those new to the field.

Global Perspective: Readers will embark on a global journey, exploring diverse Microfinance models from around the world. This section showcases innovative approaches to promoting financial inclusion.

Delivery Mechanisms: The book delves into the various delivery methodologies employed by Microfinance institutions. It discusses the roles of banks, non-banking financial companies (NBFCs), and microfinance institutions (MFIs) in reaching underserved populations.

Indian Microfinance Landscape: A significant portion of the book is dedicated to the Indian Microfinance sector. It offers insights into its evolutionary path, notable characteristics, legal and governance framework, and recent developments.

Financial Inclusion: The concept of financial inclusion and its profound impact on addressing economic disparities is explored in detail. Readers will gain an understanding of how it can uplift marginalized communities.

Business Correspondence Model: The critical business correspondence model within the Indian banking system is investigated, shedding light on collaborative efforts to expand financial services.

Impact Assessment: The book evaluates the implications and impact of Microfinance on individuals and communities, emphasizing its role in economic empowerment and improved livelihoods.

Emerging Trends: Readers will gain insights into the recent evolution and emerging trends within the Indian Microfinance sector, including innovations and challenges faced by Microfinance institutions.

Profiles and Entities: Profiles of prominent figures in the Microfinance industry and an overview of Microfinance companies, NBFCs, SFBs, and banks in India are included as a reference guide.

Limitations and Exclusions:

While this book aims to provide a comprehensive overview of Microfinance, it's important to acknowledge its limitations. The following areas are excluded from the book's scope:

Advanced Financial Modelling: In-depth financial modelling and advanced quantitative analysis are beyond the scope of this book. Readers seeking specialized financial modelling techniques may need to refer to additional resources.

Country-Specific Regulations: The book primarily focuses on the Indian Microfinance landscape. While it offers a global perspective, it does not delve into country-specific regulations in detail.

Microfinance Case Studies: While practical insights are provided, extensive case studies of specific Microfinance institutions are not included due to space constraints.

"Navigating Microfinance: Insights and Implementation" covers a wide array of topics within the Microfinance sector, offering a holistic understanding of the field. However, readers should be aware of the book's limitations, especially in areas requiring advanced financial analysis and detailed country-specific regulations.

Audience:

This book, "Navigating Microfinance: Insights and Implementation," is crafted to cater to a diverse audience, each finding value and relevance within its pages. The target audience encompasses a wide spectrum of individuals and professionals who can benefit significantly from the knowledge and insights provided.

1. Microfinance Professionals:

Field Staff: Ground-level Microfinance practitioners, including loan officers, field agents, and branch managers, will find this book invaluable. It equips them with a deeper understanding of Microfinance concepts, enabling them to serve clients more effectively.

Management: Mid-level and senior managers within Microfinance institutions can use this book to enhance their strategic thinking and operational efficiency. It provides a holistic view of the industry, aiding in decision-making and policy formulation.

Executives: CEOs, directors, and executives of Microfinance institutions can gain fresh perspectives on global trends, emerging practices, and innovative approaches to furthering the mission of financial inclusion.

2. Management Students:

Business and Management Students: Aspiring management professionals, especially those specializing in finance or seeking careers in Microfinance, will benefit from the practical insights and real-world examples presented in this book. It bridges the gap between classroom theory and industry practice.

Microfinance Researchers: Researchers and academics interested in Microfinance will find this book a valuable resource for understanding industry dynamics, regulatory frameworks, and impact assessment.

3. Policy Makers and Regulators:

Government Officials: Policymakers and government officials involved in shaping financial inclusion policies will gain insights into the Microfinance sector's nuances and its role in addressing economic disparities.

Regulatory Authorities: Regulatory bodies, such as the RBI in India, can use this book to better understand the challenges and opportunities in regulating Microfinance effectively.

4. NGOs and Development Practitioners:

Non-Governmental Organizations: NGOs and development practitioners working in the field of financial inclusion can leverage the book's knowledge to design more impactful programs and initiatives.

Social Entrepreneurs: Individuals and organizations committed to creating social impact through innovative financial services will find inspiration and practical guidance in this book.

5. General Readers:

Financial Enthusiasts: General readers interested in finance and economics can explore the Microfinance landscape, gaining a broader perspective on global financial inclusion efforts.

Students and Educators: Educational institutions can use this book as a reference for courses related to Microfinance, financial inclusion, and development economics.

Relevance to the Audience:

This book's relevance lies in its ability to bridge the gap between theory and practice in the Microfinance sector. It offers actionable insights, real-world examples, and a holistic understanding of Microfinance's role in promoting financial inclusion and empowerment. Whether you're a Microfinance professional seeking to enhance your skills, a management student aspiring to enter the industry, a policymaker shaping financial inclusion strategies, or simply someone interested in the field, this book provides a comprehensive guide to navigate the world of Microfinance effectively.

Structure:

"Navigating Microfinance: Insights and Implementation" is structured meticulously to offer readers a comprehensive journey through the diverse landscape of Microfinance. The book is divided into two volumes, each catering to specific aspects of the Microfinance ecosystem.

Volume 1: Microfinance Insights

This volume comprises twelve enlightening chapters that unravel the intricacies of Microfinance:

Chapter 1: Rural Credit and Financial Inclusion: This chapter explores the pivotal role of rural credit and financial inclusion in alleviating economic deprivation, shedding light on the challenges faced by rural populations.

Chapter 2: Microfinance Concepts: Laying the foundation, this chapter introduces Microfinance concepts, offering a solid understanding of its principles, objectives, and methodologies.

Chapter 3: Global Microfinance Models: Readers embark on a global tour in this chapter, showcasing diverse Microfinance models from around the world, highlighting innovative approaches to promoting financial inclusion.

Chapter 4: Delivery Methodologies: Delving into the various delivery methodologies of Microfinance services, this chapter explores the roles of banks, non-banking financial companies (NBFCs), and Microfinance institutions (MFIs) in reaching underserved populations.

Chapter 5: Indian Microfinance: Providing an in-depth look at the evolutionary path and unique characteristics of Indian Microfinance, this chapter offers a comprehensive overview of its growth.

Chapter 6: Legal and Governance Framework: Venturing into the legal and governance framework that governs Microfinance, this chapter covers regulations, policies, and governance structures shaping the industry.

Chapter 7: Financial Inclusion: Exploring the concept of financial inclusion and its profound impact on addressing economic disparities, this chapter showcases how it uplifts marginalized communities.

Chapter 8: Business Correspondence Model: This chapter investigates the critical business correspondence model within the Indian banking system, revealing how banks, NBFCs, and MFIs collaborate to expand financial services in India.

Chapter 9: Impact of Microfinance: Evaluating the implications and impact of Microfinance on individuals and communities, this chapter emphasizes its role in economic empowerment and improved livelihoods.

Chapter 10: Emerging Trends: Providing up-to-date insights, this chapter discusses the recent evolution and emerging trends within the Indian Microfinance sector, including innovations and challenges faced by Microfinance institutions.

Chapter 11: Tribute to Leaders: Paying tribute to the veterans of Microfinance and Indian Microfinance leaders, this chapter highlights their pivotal contributions and inspiring leadership.

Chapter 12: Reference Guide: Serving as a comprehensive reference guide, this chapter offers an overview of Microfinance companies, NBFCs, Small Finance Banks (SFBs), and banks in India.

Recurring Themes and Concepts:

Throughout both volumes of the book, readers will encounter recurring themes and concepts such as financial inclusion, rural development, regulatory frameworks, innovative models, and the transformative impact of Microfinance. These themes are interwoven to provide a holistic understanding of the Microfinance sector, catering to the diverse needs of our readership.

Unique Features:

"Navigating Microfinance: Insights and Implementation" stands out in the realm of Microfinance literature due to its distinctive features and contributions:

Holistic Exploration: Unlike many publications that focus solely on theory or practice, this book offers a holistic exploration of Microfinance by seamlessly blending theoretical concepts with real-world applications. It provides a 360-degree view of the Microfinance landscape, catering to both academic and practical interests.

Comprehensive Coverage: With twelve in-depth chapters, the book covers a wide spectrum of topics, from the fundamentals of Microfinance to emerging trends and innovations. It is designed to be a one-stop resource for readers seeking a deep and comprehensive understanding of the field.

Global Perspective: While rooted in the context of Indian Microfinance, the book takes readers on a global tour, showcasing diverse Microfinance models and approaches from around the world. This global perspective offers valuable insights for readers interested in Microfinance beyond India's borders.

Practical Insights: The book goes beyond theoretical concepts to provide practical insights and case studies, making it a valuable resource for Microfinance professionals, practitioners, and students. It bridges the gap between theory and practice by offering real-world examples and scenarios.

Reference Guide: Chapter 12 serves as a comprehensive reference guide, offering a detailed overview of Microfinance companies, Non-Banking Financial Companies (NBFCs), Small Finance Banks (SFBs), and traditional banks operating in India. This reference section simplifies access to critical information for industry professionals.

Tribute to Leaders: Chapter 11 pays tribute to the veterans and leaders of Microfinance, showcasing their pivotal contributions to the industry. This unique feature provides historical context and honours those who have played a significant role in Microfinance's growth.

Engaging and Accessible: The book is written in an engaging and accessible manner, making complex concepts understandable to a wide audience. Whether you are a seasoned Microfinance professional or a newcomer to the field, the book caters to your level of expertise.

Author's Perspective: Pradeep Kumar Singh, with over two decades of experience in Microfinance, offers a unique authorial perspective. His insights, experiences, and dedication to the field enrich the content and provide practical wisdom.

"Navigating Microfinance: Insights and Implementation" distinguishes itself through its comprehensive coverage, global perspective, practical insights, and unique reference guide. It is a valuable resource for anyone interested in gaining a profound understanding of Microfinance and its transformative role in financial inclusion and empowerment.

Use of Sources:

The content presented in "Navigating Microfinance: Insights and Implementation" is the result of a meticulous approach that draws from various sources to provide a comprehensive and well-informed perspective on Microfinance. The book's foundation is rooted in a blend of the following:

Original Research: The book incorporates original research conducted by the author, Pradeep Kumar Singh, who brings over 21 years of hands-on experience in Microfinance, Banking & Insurance to the table. This practical knowledge has been instrumental in shaping the content and ensuring its relevance to the real-world challenges and opportunities faced by Microfinance professionals.

Extensive Literature Review: To provide readers with a well-rounded understanding of the field, the book relies on an extensive literature review of scholarly articles, reports, and publications related to Microfinance.

This review serves as a basis for presenting theoretical concepts, global perspectives, and emerging trends.

Case Studies: The inclusion of case studies offers readers practical insights into Microfinance operations, showcasing real-world scenarios and success stories. These case studies are sourced from a variety of industry reports and documented experiences, adding depth and authenticity to the book.

Author's Experiences: The author's experiences and observations as a Microfinance professional have significantly influenced the content. His on-the-ground involvement in Microfinance operations has contributed to the book's practical orientation and relevance.

Secondary Research: Information and data from reputable sources such as the Indian Institute of Bank and Finance (IIBF), Microfinance Institutions Network (MFIN), Sa-Dhan, and the Reserve Bank of India (RBI) have been referenced to ensure accuracy and credibility.

Acknowledgment of Online Resources: The book acknowledges the role of online resources, including websites, research papers, and publications, as valuable sources of information. It recognizes the contributions of individuals and organizations in sharing knowledge and insights related to Microfinance.

By drawing from these diverse sources, "Navigating Microfinance: Insights and Implementation" aims to provide readers with a well-rounded, evidence-based, and practical understanding of Microfinance. It is a testament to the collaborative nature of knowledge-sharing in the field of Microfinance and the importance of integrating various sources to offer a comprehensive resource for readers.

Personal Connection:

As I embarked on the journey of writing "Navigating Microfinance: Insights and Implementation," I couldn't help but reflect on the profound personal connection I have with the subject matter. My passion for Microfinance is deeply rooted in my upbringing and the values instilled in me by my parents, Jay Prakash Singh and Subhadra Devi.

Growing up in the serene village of Patehara Kalan in Mirzapur, Uttar Pradesh, I witnessed firsthand the challenges faced by rural communities. My parents, who hail from a lower-middle-class farming background, instilled in me the importance of empathy, community, and financial inclusion. Their unwavering commitment to providing for our family, despite limited resources, left an indelible mark on my understanding of economic disparities and the need for change.

My personal journey from those humble beginnings to a career spanning over two decades in the financial and Microfinance sectors has been a testament to the power of dedication and resilience. This book is not just a culmination of my professional experiences but a tribute to the values and lessons I learned from my parents.

Additionally, my wife, Sanju, and our three daughters, Pari, Vartika, and Shristi, have been pillars of support throughout this writing endeavour. Their sacrifice, encouragement, and unwavering belief in the importance of this project have been a driving force behind its completion.

As I share the insights, knowledge, and experiences within these pages, I hope to convey the essence of Microfinance not just as an industry but as a means of empowering individuals and communities. This personal connection fuels my commitment to financial inclusion and the betterment of underserved populations.

I invite you, the reader, to join me on this journey through the world of Microfinance. May this book not only impart knowledge but also inspire positive change and a deeper understanding of the transformative potential of Microfinance in the lives of millions.

Closing Remarks:

As I conclude this preface, I am filled with immense excitement and anticipation about sharing "Navigating Microfinance: Insights and

Implementation" with you, our readers. This book represents a labor of love, dedication, and a profound belief in the power of Microfinance to transform lives and uplift communities.

I invite you to delve into the pages that follow, where you will find a comprehensive exploration of the world of Microfinance, its principles, its global perspectives, and the dynamic landscape of Indian Microfinance. Whether you are a seasoned professional in the field or a management student eager to learn, this book has been meticulously crafted to provide you with valuable insights and practical knowledge.

Microfinance isn't just an industry; it's a catalyst for change. It has the potential to break the chains of economic deprivation, empower individuals, and foster financial inclusion. With the dedication and support of many, I have endeavoured to create a resource that not only imparts information but also inspires action.

I encourage you to approach this book with an open heart and a curious mind. Explore its contents, engage with its concepts, and consider the profound impact that Microfinance can have on society. Together, we can navigate the intricate landscape of Microfinance, gaining a deeper understanding of its nuances and its potential to drive positive change.

Thank you for embarking on this journey with me. I am excited to be your guide as we navigate the transformative world of Microfinance, one page at a time.

Pradeep Kumar Singh

07th September 2023

About the Author

Pradeep Kumar Singh

Mobile/WhatsApp: +91 92639 00275;
Phone: +91 612 – 3137627;
E-mail: pradeepcreditexpert@gmail.com
https://in.linkedin.com/in/pradeepsingh5
https://www.facebook.com/Pradeepcredit
https://youtube.com/@PradeepCreditExpert
https://instagram.com/pradeepcredit?igshid=ZDdkNTZiNTM=
https://www.threads.net/@pradeepcredit
https://whatsapp.com/channel/0029VaBv4jULdQeZW25eiK0b
https://www.kooapp.com/profile/PradeepCredit

- A dynamic professional with more than 21+ years' experience in MSME, Microfinance, Farmer Finance Operations, Strategic Planning, Branch Operations, Businesses Development, Team Management, Micro Insurance along with Cross Sell management.

- Sales and Operational experience of Microfinance in various States like Uttar Pradesh West & East, Uttarakhand, Madhya Pradesh, Punjab, Rajasthan, Bihar, West Bengal, Chhattisgarh, Maharashtra and Gujarat.
- Expertise in Retail Microfinance, Team Handling, Portfolio management, Business Correspondence relationship, Business Facilitator relationship, Farmer Credit and Agri Business Partner Credit.
- Deft in supporting Operations, Inclusive conceptualizing & implementing short- and long-term business plan.
- Managing teams with focus on excelling business targets.
- Expertise in driving the sales of various Loan products Like Micro Credit, MSME Loans, Farmer Credit & Cross selling of various types of products like house hold goods, Electronic Goods, Micro Insurance, Solar light, By-Cycle, Agriculture Asperses and Agri Input's.
- Steering Branch Operations with major focus on implementing industry solutions to drive more value from business processes, reviewing high impact processes and delivering proven solutions to improve coverage of key business attributes and operational effectiveness.
- An effective communicator with good presentation, negotiation, relationship and leadership skills.
- Strong organizer, motivator, team player and a decisive leader with successful track record in directing from original concept through implementation to handle diverse market dynamics.
- Specialist in Microfinance, Farmer Finance, B to B Finance, B to C Finance; Sales & Marketing, Business Development, Managing Quality Portfolio, Relationship Management, Channel Management & Frontline Leader of Financial Sector.

Volume: 1 Microfinance Insights

Chapters:

"Yoga is mandatory for every professional. Dedicate at least 30 minutes daily to unleash your full potential and achieve a balanced life."

Chapter - 1

Economic Deprivation Rural Credit and Financial Inclusion

1.1. Introduction to Microfinance:

Microfinance is a financial concept and practice that aims to provide financial services, including small loans, savings, insurance, and payment services, to low-income individuals and marginalized communities who lack access to traditional banking facilities. It emerged as a response to the challenges faced by those excluded from the formal financial sector due to factors like limited collateral, low credit history, and living in remote or underserved areas.

The concept of microfinance gained significant momentum in the late 20th century, particularly with the work of Nobel laureate Muhammad Yunus and the establishment of Grameen Bank in Bangladesh. The success of microfinance in empowering impoverished individuals and promoting entrepreneurship led to its expansion worldwide.

Microfinance institutions (MFIs) or microfinance banks are the key players in this field. They offer financial products and services tailored to the needs of low-income clients, enabling them to manage their finances effectively, start or grow small businesses, and improve their economic well-being.

Microfinance has proven to be a powerful tool in poverty alleviation, as it allows people to break the cycle of poverty by providing them with opportunities to generate income and improve their livelihoods. It also promotes financial inclusion, empowering those on the fringes of society to be part of the formal economy and benefit from various financial services.

With its focus on financial literacy and capacity building, microfinance empowers clients to make informed financial decisions and builds a path toward economic self-sufficiency. Furthermore, microfinance often targets women, recognizing their pivotal role in households and communities, and aims to foster gender equality and women's empowerment.

1. Microfinance is a financial service that provides small loans, savings, and other financial products to low-income individuals or entrepreneurs who lack access to traditional banking services. It aims to empower the underserved population, particularly in developing countries, by promoting financial inclusion and supporting their business ventures.

2. From a social perspective, microfinance has been praised for reducing poverty, improving living standards, and empowering women, as it often reaches those who are excluded from the formal financial sector.

3. However, there have been critiques too. Some argue that high-interest rates on microloans can lead to a cycle of debt for borrowers. Additionally, the impact of microfinance on poverty reduction has been debated, with some studies showing mixed results.

4. From an economic perspective, microfinance can stimulate economic growth by fostering entrepreneurship and small businesses. It can also contribute to financial system stability by reducing the reliance on informal lenders.

Microfinance continues to evolve and adapt to address the unique financial needs of underserved populations, contributing significantly to socio-economic development and financial inclusion on a global scale.

1.2. Poverty:

Poverty is a social issue that affects millions of people worldwide. It stems from various factors such as unemployment, hunger, lack of education, and lack of access to basic rights. Addressing poverty involves implementing appropriate government schemes, social programs, and development projects. Microfinance plays a crucial role in reducing poverty by providing small loans and financial services to individuals, enabling them to start businesses and increase their income.

1.3. Rural Credit:

In rural areas, many individuals in the agricultural and cooperative sectors often require financial assistance. Rural credit helps raise awareness about financial inclusion and provides them with access to loans and other financial services. It encourages entrepreneurial activities in rural areas and contributes to economic prosperity.

1.4. Financial Inclusion:

Financial inclusion is a comprehensive concept that aims to extend financial services to all segments of the population. It enables everyone to be part of the financial system, availing themselves of banking facilities, insurance, pensions, and other financial services. Financial inclusion contributes to poverty reduction, economic growth, and overall development.

By understanding and addressing these three issues, and implementing relevant solutions, positive changes can be fostered in society, benefiting a larger population and promoting prosperity for all.

1.5. Objective of Microfinance:

The primary objective of microfinance is to promote financial inclusion and provide access to financial services to low-income individuals, especially those in underserved and marginalized communities. Microfinance aims to empower the economically disadvantaged population by offering them affordable and convenient financial products such as small loans, savings accounts, insurance, and payment services.

1.5.1. The key objectives of microfinance include:

1. **Poverty Alleviation:** By providing access to credit and other financial services, microfinance seeks to alleviate poverty and improve the living standards of the poor. It enables them to invest in income-generating activities, start or expand small businesses, and ultimately improve their economic conditions.

2. **Financial Inclusion:** Microfinance aims to bring the financially excluded individuals into the formal financial system. Many low-income individuals do not have access to traditional banking services due to various reasons like lack of collateral or a credit history. Microfinance institutions fill this gap and enable them to participate in the formal economy.

3. **Empowerment:** Microfinance promotes financial literacy and capacity building among its clients. Through financial education and training, it empowers individuals to make informed financial decisions, manage their resources better, and build a pathway towards economic self-sufficiency.

4. **Women's Empowerment:** Microfinance often targets women as they are disproportionately affected by poverty and financial exclusion. By extending financial services to women, microfinance has the potential to improve gender equality and empower women to be active contributors to their households and communities.

5. **Sustainable Development:** Microfinance contributes to sustainable development by fostering entrepreneurship, creating job opportunities, and promoting economic growth in local communities. It encourages small-scale economic activities, which can have positive ripple effects on the overall economy.

6. **Social Impact:** Microfinance programs also have positive social impacts. They can lead to improvements in health, education, and overall well-being, as increased financial stability allows families to invest in their children's education and healthcare.

The objective of microfinance is to uplift the underserved population and help them break free from the cycle of poverty by providing them with the necessary financial tools and resources for their economic and social advancement.

1.6. Poverty & its forms along with extent:

Poverty is a social issue that exists in various forms and can be found in both developed and developing countries. It arises from several factors, such as economic disparities, unequal distribution of resources, social and economic policies, population growth, and environmental changes.

1.6.A. Different forms of poverty include:

1. **Absolute Poverty:** It refers to the lack of essential resources needed for survival, such as food, clean water, shelter, and basic healthcare. People living in absolute poverty struggle to meet their basic needs.

2. **Relative Poverty:** This type of poverty is based on a comparison with the average living standards of society. It relates to the social and economic disparities between different groups or individuals within a society.

3. **Multidimensional Poverty:** Multidimensional poverty considers various dimensions of deprivation, including health, education, standard of living, and access to basic services. It provides a more comprehensive understanding of poverty beyond just income levels.

The extent of poverty varies from country to country and region to region. Developed countries generally have a lower poverty rate compared to developing countries. Poverty is measured by different indicators, including income levels, access to education and healthcare, and living conditions.

Governments and non-governmental organizations work together to combat poverty and improve social justice and welfare. Poverty alleviation strategies include implementing social welfare programs, promoting sustainable development, and addressing the root causes of poverty to create a more equitable and inclusive society.

1.7. Role of Credit in Poverty Alleviation:

The role of credit in poverty alleviation is crucial and has been widely recognized as an effective tool in empowering the economically disadvantaged. Access to credit enables individuals and households living in poverty to improve their financial situation and work towards breaking the cycle of poverty. Here are some key aspects of the role of credit in poverty alleviation:

1. **Income Generation:** Credit allows the poor to invest in income-generating activities, such as starting a small business, purchasing productive assets, or expanding existing ventures. This additional income can lift them out of poverty and provide a sustainable source of livelihood.

2. **Entrepreneurship Promotion:** Credit helps foster entrepreneurship among the poor. It enables them to explore their business ideas, take calculated risks, and seize economic opportunities that they may not have had otherwise. Successful entrepreneurial ventures can create jobs and stimulate local economies.

3. **Smoothing Consumption:** Credit can be utilized during periods of financial hardship, helping poor households to smooth consumption and meet urgent needs, especially during emergencies or seasonal fluctuations in income.

4. **Human Capital Investment:** Credit can be utilized for investing in education, healthcare, or vocational training, enhancing the human capital of the poor. Improved skills and health contribute to better employability and economic mobility.

5. **Empowerment:** Access to credit empowers individuals by giving them control over their finances and fostering a sense of ownership and responsibility. This empowerment often leads to better financial decision-making and increased participation in economic activities.

6. **Financial Inclusion:** Credit facilities provided by microfinance institutions (MFIs) and other financial organizations contribute to financial

inclusion. Many poor individuals lack access to formal banking services due to the absence of collateral or a credit history. Microfinance fills this gap and integrates them into the formal financial system.

7. Women's Empowerment: Credit programs often target women, recognizing their significant role in households and communities. Providing credit to women can lead to gender equality, as they tend to invest more in the well-being of their families and communities.

However, it's essential to ensure that credit programs are designed and implemented responsibly to avoid over-indebtedness among the poor. Sustainable credit initiatives that offer fair interest rates, adequate financial literacy training, and appropriate monitoring mechanisms can have a positive impact on poverty alleviation and lead to more inclusive and resilient societies.

1.8. State Initiative in Rural Credit in India:

In India, rural credit plays a crucial role in supporting the agricultural and rural development sectors. The government of India has undertaken several state initiatives to promote rural credit and ensure financial inclusion in rural areas. Some of the prominent state initiatives in rural credit are:

1. National Bank for Agriculture and Rural Development (NABARD): NABARD is a key institution established by the Indian government to promote sustainable rural development and provide financial assistance to agricultural and rural sectors. NABARD provides refinance support to rural financial institutions like Regional Rural Banks (RRBs), Cooperative Banks, and Microfinance Institutions (MFIs), facilitating the flow of credit to farmers and rural entrepreneurs.

2. Priority Sector Lending (PSL) Norms: The Reserve Bank of India (RBI) mandates banks to allocate a specified percentage of their total lending to priority sectors, which includes agriculture and allied activities, micro and small enterprises, and other weaker sections of society. This ensures that a significant portion of bank credit reaches the rural and agricultural sectors.

3. Kisan Credit Card (KCC) Scheme: The KCC scheme was introduced to provide easy and timely access to formal credit for farmers. It enables farmers to avail themselves of credit for crop production, post-harvest expenses, working capital, and other agricultural needs without the need for multiple loan applications. The KCC also comes with flexible repayment options and interest subvention schemes to benefit farmers.

4. Self-Help Group (SHG)- Bank Linkage Program: This initiative aims to provide credit to rural women by promoting the formation of Self-Help Groups. Banks extend micro-credit to SHGs, which, in turn, provide loans to their members for income-generating activities. This program has been successful in empowering rural women and improving their socio-economic status.

5. Regional Rural Banks (RRBs): RRBs are financial institutions set up to cater exclusively to the banking needs of rural areas. They are jointly owned by the central government, the concerned state government, and the sponsor bank. RRBs play a crucial role in extending rural credit and financial services to remote and underprivileged areas.

6. Pradhan Mantri Jan Dhan Yojana (PMJDY): Launched in 2014, this scheme aims to provide access to financial services, including credit, to all households in India. Under this initiative, bank accounts are opened for unbanked individuals, enabling them to avail various financial services, including credit facilities.

These state initiatives have been instrumental in increasing rural credit penetration, empowering farmers and rural entrepreneurs, and fostering agricultural and rural development in India. The government continues to implement new measures to enhance the effectiveness of rural credit delivery and promote inclusive growth in rural areas.

1.9. Emergence of Microfinance:

The emergence of microfinance can be traced back to the mid-20th century, with its roots in several experimental and innovative initiatives aimed at providing financial services to low-income and marginalized populations. Here are some key points in the emergence of microfinance:

1. **Experimental Beginnings:** The concept of microfinance took shape through various experimental programs and pilot projects in different parts of the world. In the 1960s and 1970s, Dr. Mohammad Yunus, a Bangladeshi economist and Nobel laureate, played a significant role in pioneering microfinance through his experiments with providing small loans to impoverished communities in Bangladesh.

2. **The Grameen Bank Model:** In 1983, Dr. Yunus founded the Grameen Bank, a specialized microfinance institution, which became a groundbreaking model for providing microcredit to the poor, especially rural women. The Grameen Bank focused on group-based lending, emphasizing social collateral (joint liability of group members) rather than traditional collateral.

3. **Growth of Microfinance Institutions (MFIs):** Inspired by the success of the Grameen Bank, microfinance institutions started emerging in various countries to address the financial needs of the unbanked and underserved populations. These MFIs adopted various innovative approaches, such as village banking and peer lending, to make financial services accessible to the poor.

4. **Advancements in Microfinance Practices:** Over time, microfinance expanded its scope beyond credit and started offering other financial services, such as savings, insurance, and remittances. It also embraced technology to improve outreach and operational efficiency.

5. **Recognition and Support:** The impact of microfinance on poverty alleviation and women empowerment gained international recognition and support from governments, international organizations, and development agencies. This led to the creation of favourable policy environments and funding support for microfinance initiatives.

6. **Microfinance and Financial Inclusion:** Microfinance played a crucial role in promoting financial inclusion by extending formal financial services

to those excluded from the traditional banking system. It helped millions of low-income individuals and households access credit and savings facilities to improve their livelihoods and build assets.

7. Challenges and Innovations: While microfinance has been successful in many ways, it has also faced challenges, such as over-indebtedness and high-interest rates. To address these issues, the industry has seen continuous innovations, including the integration of digital technology and the development of responsible lending practices.

Today, microfinance continues to evolve and expand globally, with a growing focus on ensuring sustainability, social impact, and client protection. It remains an essential tool in the fight against poverty and promoting inclusive economic growth.

Summary:

1. Poverty, its forms, and extent: Poverty refers to the state of being extremely poor, lacking the basic necessities of life. It can take various forms, such as absolute poverty (lack of basic needs) and relative poverty (compared to others in society). Poverty's extent varies across regions and countries, affecting billions of people worldwide.

2. Role of Credit in Poverty Elevation: Credit plays a crucial role in poverty alleviation by providing financial resources to the poor to invest in income-generating activities, education, healthcare, and other essential needs. Access to credit empowers individuals and communities to break the cycle of poverty and improve their economic conditions.

3. State Intervention in Rural Credit in India: The Indian government has undertaken several initiatives to promote rural credit and financial inclusion. Programs like NABARD, Priority Sector Lending, Kisan Credit Card, Self-Help Group (SHG)-Bank Linkage, and Regional Rural Banks (RRBs) have been implemented to enhance rural credit penetration and support agricultural and rural development.

4. Emergence of Microfinance: Microfinance emerged in the mid-20th century through experimental programs and pilot projects. Dr. Mohammad Yunus and the Grameen Bank in Bangladesh played a significant role in pioneering microfinance by providing small loans to the poor, especially rural women. Microfinance institutions (MFIs) expanded globally, offering not just credit but also savings, insurance, and remittance services.

The combination of these factors contributes to the overall efforts to alleviate poverty, promote rural development, and ensure financial inclusion, with microfinance serving as an essential tool in the fight against poverty. State interventions play a crucial role in providing institutional support and creating an enabling environment for financial services to reach the underserved and marginalized sections of society, ultimately contributing to the goal of inclusive economic growth and sustainable development.

Chapter - 2

Introduction to Microfinance Concepts

Microfinance is a financial concept that aims to provide small-scale financial services, such as loans, savings accounts, and insurance, to low-income individuals and underserved communities. It is designed to empower people who lack access to traditional banking systems and help them improve their economic situations. Microfinance institutions, often known as microfinance banks, microcredit organizations, or NGOs, play a crucial role in disbursing these small-scale financial services to the target population. The goal is to promote financial inclusion, poverty reduction, and sustainable development in various regions around the world.

2.1. Objective of Microfinance:

The main objective of microfinance is to promote financial inclusion and improve the socio-economic conditions of low-income individuals and underserved communities. Some key objectives of microfinance include:

1. Financial Inclusion: To provide access to basic financial services, such as credit, savings, insurance, and remittances, to those who are excluded from the formal banking sector.

2. Poverty Alleviation: To help alleviate poverty by enabling individuals to invest in income-generating activities, create livelihood opportunities, and build assets.

3. Empowerment: To empower women and marginalized groups by offering them financial resources and opportunities for economic participation.

4. Sustainable Development: To contribute to sustainable development by fostering entrepreneurship, enhancing productivity, and promoting responsible financial practices.

5. Social Impact: To improve the overall well-being and living standards of the target population, leading to positive social outcomes in education, health, and housing.

6. Financial Education: To provide financial literacy and education to clients, promoting responsible borrowing, saving, and money management.

By achieving these objectives, microfinance seeks to create a positive impact on the lives of the economically vulnerable and contribute to the broader goal of inclusive and sustainable development.

2.2. Introduction of Microfinance:

Microfinance is a financial concept that emerged to address the needs of individuals who lack access to traditional banking services due to their low income and limited collateral. It involves providing small-scale financial services, such as microloans, micro savings, micro insurance, and money transfers, to empower the underserved population and promote financial inclusion. The goal of microfinance is to uplift impoverished communities by enabling them to start or expand small businesses, manage financial risks, and build a pathway towards economic self-sufficiency. Microfinance institutions, often non-profit organizations or specialized banks, play a vital role in delivering these services to those in need, aiming to foster sustainable development and reduce poverty in various regions worldwide.

2.3. Financial Needs of the Poor:

The poor have various financial needs that are critical for their well-being and economic empowerment. Some of the key financial needs of the poor include:

1. **Access to Credit:** The poor often lack access to formal credit sources, making it difficult for them to invest in income-generating activities or cope with emergencies. Access to microloans and small-scale credit can help them start or expand small businesses and improve their livelihoods.

2. **Savings and Insurance:** Building a financial safety net is essential for the poor to protect themselves from unforeseen events such as illness, natural disasters, or other emergencies. Access to micro savings accounts and microinsurance products can provide them with the necessary financial resilience.

3. **Financial Literacy:** Many poor individuals may not have adequate knowledge about financial concepts, budgeting, and responsible financial management. Financial literacy programs can empower them to make informed decisions about money, savings, and investments.

4. **Access to Banking Services:** The poor often lack access to basic banking services, such as savings accounts, which limits their ability to save money securely and gain access to formal financial systems.

5. **Remittances and Money Transfers:** For those living in rural areas or migrant workers, the ability to send and receive money efficiently and at low costs is crucial for supporting their families and communities.

6. **Access to Technology:** Leveraging technology and digital financial services can enhance financial inclusion for the poor, enabling them to access financial services conveniently and at lower costs.

7. **Skills Development and Education:** Enhancing skills and education opportunities is essential for the poor to improve their employability and income-generating potential, thus addressing their long-term financial needs.

Meeting these financial needs is vital to uplift the poor from poverty, foster sustainable development, and promote economic and social progress in underserved communities. Microfinance and various other financial inclusion initiatives play a significant role in addressing these needs and empowering the economically vulnerable population.

2.4. Why Microfinance?

Microfinance plays a crucial role in addressing financial inclusion and empowering the economically vulnerable population. Here are some key reasons why microfinance is essential:

1. **Financial Inclusion:** Microfinance provides access to financial services to those who are excluded from traditional banking systems due to their low income and lack of collateral. It brings the unbanked and underserved population into the formal financial sector.

2. **Poverty Reduction:** By providing small-scale loans and financial resources, microfinance helps individuals invest in income-generating activities and small businesses, which can lead to poverty alleviation and improved livelihoods.

3. **Empowerment:** Microfinance empowers women and marginalized groups by giving them the means to take control of their financial lives and participate in economic activities.

4. **Sustainable Development:** By promoting entrepreneurship and productivity in local communities, microfinance contributes to sustainable economic development.

5. **Financial Resilience:** Access to micro savings and microinsurance products enables the poor to build a financial safety net, protecting them from unexpected expenses and risks.

6. **Job Creation:** Microfinance can stimulate job creation and self-employment opportunities, particularly in rural and underserved areas, thus contributing to economic growth and reduced unemployment.

7. **Social Impact:** Improved financial well-being and access to resources can lead to positive social outcomes, such as better education and healthcare for families.

8. Microenterprise Support: Microfinance supports small-scale businesses, microenterprises, and informal sectors, which are crucial components of many developing economies.

9. Reduced Dependence on Informal Moneylenders: Microfinance offers an alternative to exploitative informal moneylenders, reducing the debt burden on the poor and providing them with fair and transparent financial services.

Microfinance promotes inclusive economic growth, empowers individuals and communities, and fosters sustainable development, making it an essential tool in the fight against poverty and financial exclusion.

2.5. Microfinance: Definition, Meaning and Scope:

2.5.1. Definition of Microfinance:

Microfinance refers to the provision of small-scale financial services, such as micro loans, micro savings, micro insurance, and money transfers, to low-income individuals and underserved communities who do not have access to traditional banking services. It aims to promote financial inclusion, empower the economically vulnerable population, and alleviate poverty through the provision of tailored financial products and services.

2.5.2. Meaning of Microfinance:

Microfinance is a financial concept that focuses on addressing the financial needs of the poor and marginalized by offering them access to basic financial services. It recognizes that even small amounts of money can have a significant impact on the livelihoods of the economically vulnerable, allowing them to invest in income-generating activities, manage risks, and build financial resilience.

2.5.3. Scope of Microfinance:

The scope of microfinance extends to various aspects of financial services targeted at the financially excluded population. It encompasses the following:

1. **Microcredit:** Providing small-scale loans to individuals or groups for income-generating purposes, often without the need for collateral.

2. **Micro savings:** Offering savings accounts with low minimum deposit requirements and easy access to encourage regular savings among the poor.

3. **Micro insurance:** Providing affordable insurance products that protect against various risks, such as health, crop failure, or natural disasters.

4. **Money Transfers**: Facilitating secure and affordable money transfers, particularly for migrant workers or those living in remote areas.

5. **Financial Education:** Offering financial literacy programs to enhance the financial knowledge and skills of clients, promoting responsible financial practices.

6. **Microenterprise Support:** Supporting the growth and development of small-scale businesses and microenterprises, often run by individuals or small groups.

The scope of microfinance goes beyond merely providing financial services; it also emphasizes the social impact, empowerment, and sustainable development of the targeted communities. Microfinance institutions, such as microfinance banks, credit unions, and non-governmental organizations, play a vital role in delivering these services and driving positive change in the lives of the economically vulnerable population.

2.6. Importance of Microfinance:

The importance of microfinance lies in its ability to address the financial needs of the economically vulnerable population and promote financial inclusion. Here are some key reasons highlighting its significance:

1. **Financial Inclusion:** Microfinance enables the unbanked and underserved population to access basic financial services, thus bringing them into the formal financial system. It provides a pathway for individuals who have limited access to traditional banking services to become financially included and participate in the economy.

2. **Poverty Alleviation:** By providing small-scale loans and financial resources, microfinance empowers the poor to invest in income-generating activities and small businesses. This, in turn, helps in poverty reduction, as individuals are able to enhance their economic prospects and improve their livelihoods.

3. **Empowerment:** Microfinance empowers women and marginalized groups by giving them control over their financial lives. It fosters economic self-sufficiency and increases their decision-making power within households and communities.

4. **Sustainable Development:** By promoting entrepreneurship and productivity in local communities, microfinance contributes to sustainable economic development. It strengthens the local economy and fosters a sense of ownership and responsibility among borrowers.

5. **Financial Resilience:** Access to micro savings and microinsurance products enables the poor to build a financial safety net, protecting them from unexpected expenses and risks. This helps in reducing vulnerability to economic shocks and crises.

6. **Job Creation:** Microfinance can stimulate job creation and self-employment opportunities, particularly in rural and underserved areas. It supports microenterprises and small-scale businesses, contributing to economic growth and reduced unemployment.

7. **Social Impact:** Improved financial well-being and access to resources through microfinance can lead to positive social outcomes. It can result in better access to education and healthcare for families, ultimately leading to improved living standards.

8. Reduced Dependence on Informal Moneylenders: Microfinance offers an alternative to exploitative informal moneylenders, reducing the debt burden on the poor and providing them with fair and transparent financial services.

9. Financial Education: Microfinance institutions often provide financial literacy programs, empowering borrowers with essential financial knowledge and skills to make informed decisions about money management and investments.

Microfinance plays a vital role in promoting inclusive economic growth, reducing poverty, and fostering sustainable development. It empowers individuals, strengthens communities, and contributes to a more equitable and prosperous society.

2.7. Assumptions of microfinance:

Microfinance operates based on certain assumptions that form the foundation of its approach and effectiveness. Some key assumptions of microfinance include:

1. Creditworthiness of the Poor: Microfinance assumes that even individuals with low income and limited assets can be creditworthy borrowers. It believes that providing them with small loans can help them generate income and repay the borrowed amount.

2. Group Lending: Group lending assumes that forming small borrower groups can create a sense of collective responsibility and mutual support. By lending to groups, the risk of default is reduced, as group members are incentivized to ensure timely repayment.

3. Income-Generating Activities: Microfinance assumes that the poor can use borrowed funds effectively to engage in income-generating activities, such as starting or expanding a small business. It believes that these activities will generate sufficient income to cover loan repayments and improve the borrower's financial situation.

4. Social Capital: Microfinance relies on the notion of social capital, which refers to the social relationships, networks, and trust within a community. It assumes that leveraging social capital can enhance the success of microfinance interventions.

5. Financial Sustainability: Microfinance institutions assume that they can achieve financial sustainability by charging interest rates and fees that cover their operational costs. This assumption is critical to ensure the long-term viability and expansion of microfinance services.

6. Women's Empowerment: Microfinance often assumes that providing financial services to women can lead to greater empowerment, as women tend to invest in their families' well-being and education when given access to financial resources.

7. Repayment Discipline: Microfinance assumes that clients, especially in group lending models, will have a strong incentive to repay their loans promptly to maintain their creditworthiness and access future loans.

8. Positive Social Impact: Microfinance assumes that providing access to financial services can have positive social outcomes, including poverty reduction, improved education, and better healthcare, among others.

2.8. Microfinance Lesson from International Experiences:

International experiences in microfinance have provided valuable lessons that can guide the development and implementation of microfinance programs worldwide. Some key lessons include:

1. Client-Centric Approach: Successful microfinance initiatives prioritize the needs and preferences of their clients. Understanding the unique financial requirements of the target population and offering tailored products and services is crucial for building trust and ensuring long-term sustainability.

2. Diverse Product Offerings: Effective microfinance institutions offer a range of financial products beyond microcredit, such as microsavings, microinsurance, and remittances. This diversity allows clients to access a comprehensive suite of services that address their various financial needs.

3. Social Performance Metrics: Microfinance institutions should consider social performance metrics alongside financial indicators. Measuring the impact on clients' lives, such as poverty reduction, women's empowerment, and education outcomes, helps assess the true success of microfinance interventions.

4. Technology Integration: Embracing technology, such as mobile banking and digital platforms, can significantly enhance the outreach and efficiency of microfinance services. Digitization facilitates faster transactions, reduces costs, and increases accessibility, particularly in remote areas.

5. Partnerships and Collaboration: Successful microfinance programs often collaborate with various stakeholders, including governments, NGOs, and private sector entities. Partnerships can enhance outreach, access to funding, and technical expertise, leading to more effective and sustainable microfinance initiatives.

6. Financial Education and Training: Offering financial literacy programs and capacity-building initiatives is essential to empower clients to make informed financial decisions, manage their resources effectively, and become more financially resilient.

7. Responsible Finance Practices: Microfinance institutions must adhere to responsible lending practices, including transparent pricing, ethical collection practices, and adequate client protection mechanisms. Treating clients fairly fosters trust and helps prevent over-indebtedness.

8. Graduation Models: Graduation programs aim to move the extreme poor out of poverty by providing comprehensive support, including financial services, livelihood training, and social protection. These models have shown promising results in promoting sustainable livelihoods for vulnerable populations.

9. Impact Evaluation: Conducting rigorous impact evaluations is crucial to understand the effectiveness and social impact of microfinance interventions. Evaluations help identify strengths, weaknesses, and areas for improvement in microfinance programs.

10. Adaptation to Local Context: Microfinance programs should be tailored to the specific cultural, economic, and social context of the target population. Understanding local norms and preferences can enhance acceptance and participation in microfinance initiatives.

International experiences in microfinance highlight the importance of client-centricity, social impact measurement, innovation, and responsible practices for achieving sustainable and meaningful financial inclusion for the poor and underserved communities.

Summary:

Summary of Microfinance:

Microfinance aims to provide financial services to the poor and underserved population, helping them meet their financial needs, access credit, and engage in income-generating activities. It involves offering small loans, savings, insurance, and other financial products tailored to the needs of vulnerable individuals, including women, farmers, and marginalized communities.

Introduction of Microfinance:

Microfinance is a financial service that caters to the needs of the economically disadvantaged. It offers small loans, savings, and insurance services to help them improve their economic well-being and achieve financial inclusion.

Financial Needs of the Poor:

The poor face various financial challenges due to their low income and limited access to resources. Microfinance addresses these needs by providing them with affordable financial services, fostering economic growth, and promoting self-reliance.

Why Microfinance?

Microfinance plays a vital role in promoting financial inclusion for the poor by providing them with access to credit, savings, and insurance. It empowers them to engage in income-generating activities, break the cycle of poverty, and improve their livelihoods.

Definitions Meaning and Scope of Microfinance:

Microfinance refers to the provision of financial services, such as small loans, savings, and insurance, to low-income individuals and vulnerable communities. Its scope extends to promoting financial inclusion, poverty alleviation, social progress, and development.

Importance of Microfinance:

Microfinance is crucial as it empowers the economically marginalized, particularly women, to become financially self-sufficient. It promotes entrepreneurship, supports small businesses, and facilitates economic growth in underserved regions.

Assumptions of Microfinance:

Microfinance operates on the assumptions that the poor can be creditworthy borrowers, group lending fosters accountability, income-generating activities can improve their financial situation, and social capital enhances program success. It also assumes that financial sustainability, women's empowerment, and positive social impact can be achieved through responsible finance practices.

Microfinance Lessons from International Experience:

International experiences in microfinance emphasize a client-centric approach, diverse product offerings, social performance measurement, technology integration, partnerships, financial education, and responsible lending practices. These experiences highlight the importance of adapting microfinance interventions to the local context for greater impact and sustainability.

Microfinance has been a crucial tool in promoting financial inclusion and poverty reduction worldwide. Some key lessons from international experience include:

1. **Client- Cantered Approach:** Successful microfinance institutions prioritize understanding the needs of their clients and designing appropriate financial products and services tailored to their specific requirements.

2. **Diverse Product Offerings:** Offering a range of financial products beyond microcredit, such as savings accounts, insurance, and remittance services, helps meet various client needs and enhances the impact of microfinance.

3. **Social Performance Management:** Ensuring positive social outcomes alongside financial sustainability is essential. Measuring and tracking social performance indicators help maintain the focus on the social mission of microfinance institutions.

4. **Responsible Lending:** Striking a balance between responsible lending and avoiding over-indebtedness is critical. Transparent and fair lending practices protect borrowers and foster long-term financial stability.

5. **Technology Adoption:** Embracing digital technologies can increase efficiency, reduce costs, and expand outreach, enabling easier access to financial services in remote areas.

6. **Building Trust and Community Ties:** Successful microfinance initiatives often build trust within the community they serve. This trust is essential for fostering a sense of ownership and cooperation among clients.

7. **Capacity Building and Financial Literacy:** Providing financial education and training empowers clients to make informed decisions and manage their finances more effectively.

8. **Collaborations and Partnerships:** Establishing partnerships with NGOs, governments, and other stakeholders can help leverage resources and expertise to reach a broader client base.

9. Monitoring and Evaluation: Regularly assessing the impact and effectiveness of microfinance programs is crucial for making data-driven improvements and measuring success.

10. Adaptability to Local Context: Microfinance models need to be flexible and adapted to the specific socio-economic, cultural, and regulatory context of each region or country.

By learning from these lessons and continuously improving microfinance practices, we can further enhance its positive impact on poverty alleviation and economic development globally. Microfinance is a powerful tool that aims to address the financial needs of the poor and promote financial inclusion. It offers a range of financial products and services tailored to the specific requirements of its clients, with a client-cantered approach being essential. The main goal of microfinance is to provide access to financial resources for those who are traditionally excluded from formal banking systems.

In conclusion, microfinance addresses the financial needs of the poor by providing tailored financial services. Its definition and scope encompass various offerings, and its importance lies in promoting financial inclusion and poverty reduction. Assumptions of microfinance focus on the capabilities of the poor and the pursuit of social and financial goals. International experience has provided valuable lessons that can improve the effectiveness and impact of microfinance initiatives globally.

Chapter – 3

Diverse Microfinance Models Around the Globe

3.1. Models of Microfinance across the World:

Microfinance models vary across the world, but some common ones include Grameen Bank's group lending in Bangladesh, Self-Help Groups in India, Village Savings and Loan Associations in Africa, and online peer-to-peer lending platforms globally. Each model has its unique features and serves to provide financial services to low-income individuals and small entrepreneurs who lack access to traditional banking systems.

3.2. Objective of models of microfinance across the world:

The objective of microfinance models across the world is to provide financial services to low-income individuals, small entrepreneurs, and underserved communities who lack access to traditional banking systems. These models aim to empower the economically disadvantaged by offering them opportunities to borrow small amounts of money, save, and access other financial products like insurance and remittances. The ultimate goal is to alleviate poverty, foster entrepreneurship, and promote economic development in these communities. By offering inclusive financial services, microfinance models strive to enable people to improve their livelihoods and break the cycle of poverty.

3.3. Introduction of models of microfinance across the world:

Microfinance models, implemented across the world, are innovative financial systems designed to cater to the needs of low-income individuals and marginalized communities. These models aim to provide access to basic financial services such as credit, savings, insurance, and remittances, which are typically unavailable through traditional banking channels to these underserved populations. By adopting various approaches like group lending, peer-to-peer networks, community-based organizations, and online platforms, microfinance models seek to empower people economically and promote financial inclusion. These initiatives have shown promising results in poverty reduction, women's empowerment, and fostering local entrepreneurship, making them a significant force in the global effort to alleviate poverty and improve livelihoods.

3.4. Models of microfinance across the world in detail:

Let's dive into the details of some common models of microfinance across the world:

3.4.1. Grameen Bank Model (Bangladesh):

Developed by Nobel laureate Muhammad Yunus, the Grameen Bank model is one of the pioneering microfinance models. It emphasizes group lending, were small groups of individuals, mostly women, form borrowing groups. Each member of the group is jointly responsible for the repayment of loans taken by any member. The model promotes social collateral and encourages a strong sense of community support. Grameen Bank also provides other financial services, such as savings accounts and insurance, to its members.

Grameen Bank and the Bangladesh Rural Advancement Committee (BRAC) are two prominent organizations in Bangladesh that have made significant contributions to microfinance and rural development.

3.4.1.A. Grameen Bank: Grameen Bank was founded by Nobel laureate Muhammad Yunus in 1983. It is renowned for pioneering the concept of microcredit and microfinance. Grameen Bank provides small loans, known as microloans or microcredits, to impoverished individuals, particularly women, in rural areas of Bangladesh. These loans are given without collateral and are used to support various income-generating activities, such as farming, small businesses, and handicrafts.

The bank's approach emphasizes financial inclusion and social development. It has empowered millions of poor individuals, helping them escape poverty and improve their economic conditions. The Grameen Bank model has been replicated in many countries worldwide and has had a transformative impact on poverty alleviation and women's empowerment.

3.4.1.B. Bangladesh Rural Advancement Committee (BRAC): BRAC is a large non-governmental organization (NGO) based in Bangladesh. Established in 1972, BRAC's mission is to alleviate poverty and improve the lives of disadvantaged communities. While BRAC is not a bank, it has been actively involved in microfinance and various development projects.

BRAC's microfinance program provides small loans and financial services to poor households, especially women, to engage in income-generating activities and improve their livelihoods. In addition to microfinance, BRAC runs a wide range of development programs, including education, healthcare, agriculture, and social empowerment initiatives.

Both Grameen Bank and BRAC have played crucial roles in the development and expansion of microfinance in Bangladesh. Their efforts have contributed significantly to poverty reduction, women's empowerment, and overall rural development in the country.

3.4.1.C. Key features of the Grameen Bank model include:

1. Group-Based Lending: Borrowers are organized into small groups, typically of five members, who collectively guarantee each other's loans. This group-based lending approach fosters social cohesion, mutual support, and a sense of responsibility among the borrowers.

2. Focus on Women: The model places a strong emphasis on lending to women, as research has shown that empowering women economically leads to positive outcomes for families and communities.

3. No Collateral: Grameen Bank does not require conventional collateral for its microloans. Instead, it relies on the group guarantee system, where borrowers support each other in the repayment process.

4. Gradual Increase in Loan Size: Borrowers start with small loan amounts, and as they demonstrate reliable repayment behaviour, they become eligible for larger loans. This approach encourages responsible borrowing and financial discipline.

5. Socio-Economic Development: The Grameen Bank model aims to not only provide financial services but also offer other support, such as financial literacy training, healthcare, and social development programs, to improve the overall well-being of the borrowers and their communities.

The success of the Grameen Bank model has been recognized globally, and it has inspired the establishment of many microfinance institutions worldwide, promoting financial inclusion and poverty reduction. The Grameen Bank and its model have had a significant impact on lifting millions of people out of poverty in Bangladesh and served as a blueprint for many other microfinance initiatives around the world.

3.4.2. Self-Help Groups (SHGs) (India):

SHGs are community-based microfinance models widely used in India. Women from similar socio-economic backgrounds come together and form self-managed groups. They pool their savings and can access loans from the group's fund. The success of SHGs is based on regular meetings, collective decision-making, and peer support. SHGs also engage in social development activities and capacity-building initiatives.

The Self-Help Group (SHG) model is an important grassroots-level microfinance initiative in India. It was introduced in the early 1990s as part of poverty alleviation and women empowerment efforts. The SHG model aims to provide financial services and support to marginalized communities, particularly women, in rural and semi-urban areas.

Here's how the SHG model works:

3.4.2.1. Formation of Self-Help Groups: A small group of 10 to 20 individuals from the same socio-economic background come together to form an SHG. The members usually belong to a similar geographical location or community.

3.4.2.2. Savings and Internal Lending: Each member contributes a regular amount as savings to the SHG. These collective savings form a common fund, which is then utilized to provide small loans to group members based on their financial needs.

3.4.2.3. Regular Meetings and Decision Making: SHG members meet regularly, usually on a monthly basis, to discuss financial matters, make collective decisions, and address any issues affecting the group or its members.

3.4.2.4. Access to Credit: Once the group has built up sufficient savings, it can start providing small loans to its members at a reasonable interest rate. These loans are often used for income-generating activities, small businesses, or emergencies.

3.4.2.5. Capacity Building and Skill Training: SHGs also focus on capacity building and skill development of their members. They conduct training sessions on financial literacy, entrepreneurship, and other relevant topics to enhance the members' knowledge and capabilities.

3.4.2.6. Linkages with Banks: As SHGs mature and demonstrate financial discipline, they can establish linkages with formal financial institutions like banks. These linkages enable SHGs to access larger loans and more extensive financial services beyond their internal savings.

The SHG model has been successful in empowering women, promoting financial inclusion, and fostering community development in India. It has played a vital role in poverty reduction and improving the socio-economic status of its members. Many government and non-governmental organizations have actively supported the expansion and sustainability of SHGs throughout the country.

3.5. In India the Joint Liability Group (JLG) model:

In India, the Joint Liability Group (JLG) model is a popular and effective microfinance initiative to provide financial services to small and marginalized groups. It was introduced as a way to expand microcredit and enhance financial inclusion for rural and underprivileged communities. The JLG model is commonly used by microfinance institutions (MFIs) and banks to extend credit to individuals who lack collateral or formal credit history. Here's how the JLG model works in detail:

3.5.1. Formation of Joint Liability Group (JLG):

The JLG model involves the formation of a group of 4 to 10/20 individuals who come together to apply for a loan. These individuals usually have similar socio-economic backgrounds, live in the same area, and are engaged in similar income-generating activities.

3.5.2. Group Responsibility:

In the JLG model, the group members share collective responsibility for each other's loans. The group acts as a guarantor for each member's loan, making sure that all members repay their loans promptly. This joint liability reduces the risk for lenders, as the peer pressure within the group encourages timely repayment.

3.5.3. Group Recognition and Trust:

MFIs or banks carefully assess and recognize JLGs based on factors like the members' willingness to support each other, trustworthiness, and the viability of their income-generating activities. Trust and mutual support among group members are critical elements for the success of the JLG model.

3.5.4. Loan Disbursement:

Once the JLG is formed and recognized, the microfinance institution or bank disburses loans to the group. The loan amount is distributed among individual members according to their respective financial requirements.

3.5.5. Utilization of Loan:

Each member utilizes their portion of the loan for their specific income-generating activities, such as agriculture, livestock, trade, or small businesses. The loans are generally small, short-term, and intended to meet the immediate financial needs of the members.

3.5.6. Loan Repayment:

Repayment schedules are set based on the members' cash flow and income-generating cycles. Group members are required to make regular repayments, and failure to do so affects the creditworthiness of the entire group.

3.5.7. Monitoring and Support:

MFIs or banks provide ongoing support, training, and financial literacy programs to the JLG members. Regular monitoring is done to ensure compliance with repayment schedules and to address any challenges faced by the group.

The JLG model has been successful in expanding access to credit and improving the livelihoods of rural communities in India. It encourages financial discipline, fosters group cohesion, and reduces the risk for lenders, making it an effective and sustainable microfinance approach.

3.6. Village Savings and Loan Associations (VSLAs) (Africa)

VSLAs are popular in various African countries. In this model, community members voluntarily come together to save money regularly in a communal fund. Members can take small loans from this fund and repay with interest. The model is simple, cost-effective, and managed by the community itself, which fosters a sense of ownership and sustainability.

Village Savings and Loan Associations (VSLAs) are community-based microfinance groups commonly found in various countries across Africa. VSLAs are a grassroots-level initiative that empowers rural communities by providing access to financial services and fostering a culture of savings and credit. The VSLA model is based on the principles of self-help, mutual trust, and collective decision-making. Here's an overview of how VSLAs work:

3.6.1. Formation of VSLAs:

VSLAs are formed by a group of individuals within a village or community who come together voluntarily to pool their savings and create a common fund. The group typically consists of around 15 to 25 members, usually women, although men may also be part of the groups.

3.6.2. Regular Savings:

Members of the VSLA make regular contributions to the common fund. They gather at regular meetings, often weekly or monthly, to make their savings deposits. The amount contributed by each member is flexible and can be adjusted based on their financial capacity.

3.6.3. Collective Fund Management:

The common fund is managed collectively by the VSLA members. Simple and transparent bookkeeping systems are used to record individual contributions and track the overall balance of the fund.

3.6.4. Internal Lending:

Once the common fund grows, VSLA members can access small loans from the fund. These loans are provided at reasonable interest rates and are typically used for income-generating activities, emergencies, or personal needs.

3.6.5. Repayment and Interest:

Loan repayments are made at regular intervals, and the interest earned from loans is added to the common fund. The interest earned benefits all members, contributing to the overall growth of the VSLA's financial resources.

3.6.6. Social Support and Community Development:

Beyond financial transactions, VSLAs foster a strong sense of community and mutual support. Members share knowledge, experiences, and challenges, and they often provide each other with advice and encouragement in various aspects of life, including business, health, and education.

3.6.7. Capacity Building:

VSLAs often receive support from non-governmental organizations (NGOs) or development agencies, which provide training and capacity-building programs. These programs focus on financial literacy, entrepreneurship, and other relevant skills to empower VSLA members and enhance their decision-making abilities.

The VSLA model has proven to be a successful approach to promote financial inclusion, community development, and poverty alleviation in rural Africa. By encouraging a culture of savings and self-reliance, VSLAs empower individuals and communities to improve their livelihoods and build a more sustainable future.

3.7. Online Peer-to-Peer (P2P) Lending Platforms:

With advancements in technology, online P2P lending platforms have gained popularity globally. These platforms connect individual lenders with borrowers, eliminating the need for traditional financial intermediaries. P2P platforms enable people to lend and borrow money directly, often at more flexible terms compared to traditional banking systems.

Online Peer-to-Peer (P2P) lending platforms are digital marketplaces that connect individual lenders (investors) directly with borrowers, cutting out traditional financial intermediaries like banks. These platforms enable individuals or small businesses to borrow money from a pool of lenders, often at competitive interest rates, and offer an alternative investment opportunity for individuals looking to earn a return on their money.

Here's how P2P lending platforms generally work:

3.7.1. Registration:

Borrowers and lenders register on the P2P lending platform, providing their personal and financial information.

3.7.2. Loan Application and Screening:

Borrowers submit loan applications detailing the amount they need, the purpose of the loan, and their creditworthiness. The platform typically assesses the borrowers' credit risk using various criteria and credit scoring methods.

3.7.3. Listing:

Approved loan applications are listed on the platform, visible to potential lenders. Lenders can review the borrower's profiles and decide whether to fund a portion of the loan.

3.7.4. Funding:

Lenders have the option to invest small amounts in multiple loans, diversifying their risk. Once enough lenders commit to funding the loan, it becomes fully funded, and the borrower receives the loan amount.

3.7.5. Repayment:

Borrowers make regular loan repayments, typically on a monthly basis, including both principal and interest. The platform facilitates the collection of repayments from borrowers and distributes the payments to lenders accordingly.

3.7.6. Risk:

Management: P2P lending platforms may employ risk management tools, such as credit assessments, diversification strategies, and collections processes, to reduce the risk of default for lenders.

Benefits of P2P Lending Platforms:

For Borrowers: P2P lending platforms offer an alternative source of financing with potentially lower interest rates and faster loan processing compared to traditional banks. It can be accessible to individuals or businesses with limited credit history or difficulties in obtaining loans from traditional sources.

For Lenders: P2P lending provides an opportunity for individual investors to earn interest income and diversify their investment portfolio. They can choose to invest in various loans based on their risk appetite and investment goals.

However, it's important to note that P2P lending carries certain risks, including the potential for loan defaults and lack of regulatory protections compared to traditional banking. As with any investment, it's essential for both borrowers and lenders to thoroughly research and understand the risks and benefits associated with P2P lending before participating in such platforms.

3.8. Microfinance Institutions (MFIs):

MFIs are specialized financial institutions that provide microfinance services to the underserved population. They can operate in various models, such as non-profit organizations, cooperatives, or for-profit entities. MFIs typically offer microloans, savings accounts, and other financial services tailored to the specific needs of their target clientele.

Microfinance Institutions (MFIs) in India play a significant role in providing financial services to the unbanked and underprivileged segments of society. These institutions aim to promote financial inclusion, alleviate poverty, and empower individuals by offering a range of financial products and services tailored to the needs of low-income and marginalized communities. Here are some key points about MFIs in India:

3.8.1. Background:

Microfinance gained prominence in India in the 1990s and has since grown rapidly. MFIs were established to address the lack of formal financial services for the poor and to cater to the financial needs of individuals who are unable to access credit from traditional banking sources.

3.8.2. Legal Structure:

MFIs in India can operate as non-banking financial companies (NBFCs) or as section 8 companies under the Companies Act. Some MFIs also operate as self-help groups (SHGs) and provide financial services at the community level.

3.8.3. Target Customers:

MFIs primarily target individuals and microenterprises with limited access to formal credit due to their low-income status, lack of collateral, or inadequate credit history.

3.8.4. Products and Services:

MFIs offer a range of financial products, including microloans, savings accounts, insurance, and remittance services. Microloans are typically small, short-term loans extended to support income-generating activities or meet emergency needs.

3.8.5. Group Lending Model:

Many MFIs in India follow a group lending model, where loans are provided to self-help groups (SHGs) or joint liability groups (JLGs). In this model, group members act as guarantors for each other's loans, fostering peer support and collective responsibility for repayment.

3.8.6. Technology Integration:

In recent years, technology has played a crucial role in advancing the microfinance sector in India. Many MFIs have adopted digital channels to deliver services efficiently, improve outreach, and lower operational costs.

3.8.7. Regulation:

The Reserve Bank of India (RBI) regulates NBFC-MFIs and has introduced guidelines to ensure responsible lending practices, protect borrower interests, and promote sustainable growth of the microfinance sector.

3.8.8. Impact:

MFIs have played a vital role in poverty reduction and women's empowerment in India. By providing access to financial services, they have helped individuals build livelihoods, create businesses, and improve their standard of living.

It's important to note that while MFIs have had a positive impact, there have also been instances of over-indebtedness and debt distress among borrowers. The industry continues to evolve, with a focus on balancing financial inclusion with responsible lending practices to ensure the sustainable development of microfinance in India.

3.9. Islamic Microfinance:

This model adheres to the principles of Islamic finance, avoiding interest-based transactions and focusing on profit-sharing and ethical financial practices. Islamic microfinance institutions offer Sharia-compliant financial services to cater to the needs of Muslim populations.

Islamic microfinance is a financial system that adheres to the principles of Islamic finance while providing microloans and financial services to low-income individuals or small businesses. It operates in compliance with Sharia law, which prohibits the payment or receipt of interest (riba) and engages in socially responsible investments. Instead of interest, Islamic microfinance uses profit-sharing arrangements, leasing contracts, and other innovative mechanisms to facilitate financial transactions without violating Islamic principles. This approach aims to promote financial inclusion and empower disadvantaged communities while ensuring ethical practices in the financial industry.

3.10. SACCOS (Savings and Credit Cooperative Organizations):

Commonly found in East Africa, SACCOS are member-owned cooperative societies that provide financial services to their members. They encourage savings and offer credit facilities at competitive rates, catering to the financial needs of their members.

These are just a few examples of the diverse microfinance models that exist worldwide. Each model addresses the unique challenges and opportunities within the specific context it operates, contributing to the goal of promoting financial inclusion and poverty reduction.

SACCOS stands for "Savings and Credit Cooperative Organizations." They are member-owned financial institutions that operate on a cooperative basis. SACCOS are formed by individuals or communities who pool their savings to provide affordable credit and other financial services to their members.

The main objectives of SACCOS are to encourage savings among members and provide them with access to credit facilities. Members contribute their savings to the cooperative, and these savings are then used to provide loans to members at reasonable interest rates. The interest earned on loans and other financial activities is distributed among the members as dividends or used to improve the cooperative's services.

SACCOS play a significant role in promoting financial inclusion, especially in areas where traditional banking services may not be easily accessible. They empower members to save, invest, and access credit, thereby contributing to the economic development of their communities. Additionally, SACCOS often prioritize the social and economic well-being of their members, making them valuable tools for financial empowerment and community development.

3.11. ROSCAs (Rotating Savings and Credit Associations):

ROSCAs are informal microfinance models found in many cultures. In a ROSCA, a group of individuals agrees to contribute a fixed amount regularly, and each member takes turns receiving the pooled sum. This rotation continues until all members have received their share. ROSCAs provide a source of interest-free credit and encourage savings.

ROSCAs, which stands for "Rotating Savings and Credit Associations," are informal financial arrangements that exist in many cultures and communities around the world. In a ROSCA, a group of individuals agree to contribute a fixed amount of money regularly to a common fund, and each member takes turns receiving the entire fund as a lump sum.

The cycle continues until each member has received the lump sum once. ROSCAs can operate with different variations and names in different regions. Some common names for ROSCAs include "chit funds" in India, "tandas" in Mexico, "hagbad" in Somalia, and "tontines" in West Africa.

ROSCAs serve various purposes, such as providing interest-free loans, helping members save for specific goals, or supporting community-based financial needs. They are based on trust and social cohesion among the participants, as there are no formal contracts or legal obligations involved.

While ROSCAs can be a valuable financial tool for those without access to formal banking services, they also come with certain risks, such as the possibility of default by a member or disputes arising within the group. Nonetheless, they continue to play a significant role in enhancing financial inclusion and fostering mutual support within communities.

A credit union is a type of financial cooperative that is owned and operated by its members, who are also its customers. It operates under the principle of "people helping people" and is focused on providing financial services to its members at competitive rates.

Credit unions offer a wide range of financial products and services, similar to traditional banks, including savings accounts, checking accounts, loans (such as personal loans, auto loans, and mortgages), credit cards, and other financial products.

One of the key differences between credit unions and banks is their ownership structure. In a credit union, members are both customers and partial owners of the institution. This means that profits generated by the credit union are often returned to the members in the form of dividends, lower interest rates on loans, and fewer fees.

Credit unions are known for their community-oriented approach, and they typically serve specific groups of members based on common characteristics, such as where they live, work, or their affiliation with certain organizations or industries.

Because of their cooperative nature, credit unions often prioritize personalized customer service and can be a good option for individuals seeking a more community-focused and member-centric financial institution.

3.12. International Commercial Banks with Microfinance Initiatives:

Some commercial banks have incorporated microfinance initiatives to cater to the financial needs of underserved populations. They offer smaller loan amounts and more flexible terms compared to regular banking products.

Many international commercial banks have recognized the importance of financial inclusion and have introduced microfinance initiatives to cater to the needs of low-income individuals and underserved communities. These initiatives aim to provide access to financial services and credit to those who may not have access to traditional banking services. Some well-known commercial banks with microfinance initiatives include:

3.12.1. Citibank:

Citibank has various microfinance initiatives to support financial inclusion, particularly in developing countries.

3.12.2. Standard Chartered Bank:

Standard Chartered has a Microfinance program that focuses on providing financial services to small and medium-sized enterprises (SMEs) and individuals in underserved markets.

3.12.3. HSBC:

HSBC has microfinance programs and partnerships in several countries to promote financial inclusion and support micro and small businesses.

3.12.4. Barclays Bank:

Barclays has implemented microfinance initiatives to support entrepreneurship and financial inclusion in different regions.

3.12.5. Bank of America:

Bank of America has undertaken microfinance initiatives in collaboration with nonprofit organizations to provide credit and financial services to low-income entrepreneurs and small businesses.

3.12.6. BNP Paribas:

BNP Paribas has engaged in microfinance initiatives to foster social and economic development in underserved communities.

3.12.7. Deutsche Bank:

Deutsche Bank has been involved in microfinance initiatives to support small and medium-sized enterprises and social enterprises in various countries.

It's important to note that the scope and reach of microfinance initiatives may vary among commercial banks and across different regions. The goal of these initiatives is to empower disadvantaged communities, promote financial inclusion, and foster economic development through responsible lending and financial services. Several Indian commercial banks have implemented microfinance initiatives to promote financial inclusion and support underserved communities. Here are some well-known Indian commercial banks with such initiatives:

3.12.A.1. State Bank of India (SBI): SBI, being one of the largest banks in India, has various microfinance initiatives to reach out to low-income individuals and small businesses in rural and semi-urban areas.

3.12.A.2. ICICI Bank: ICICI Bank has been actively involved in microfinance programs, providing financial services and credit to micro and small enterprises.

3.12.A.3. HDFC Bank: HDFC Bank has initiated microfinance programs to cater to the financial needs of underserved sections of the society, especially in rural regions.

3.12.A.4. Axis Bank: Axis Bank has implemented microfinance initiatives to empower economically weaker sections and promote entrepreneurship.

3.12.A.5. IDBI Bank: IDBI Bank has undertaken microfinance programs to address the financial needs of individuals and small businesses in rural and remote areas.

3.12.A.6. Yes Bank: Yes Bank has been engaged in microfinance initiatives to enhance financial inclusion and support micro and small enterprises.

3.12.A.7. Kotak Mahindra Bank: Kotak Mahindra Bank has also participated in microfinance efforts to extend financial services to marginalized communities.

It's worth noting that the landscape of microfinance initiatives in India is continually evolving, and more banks may have introduced such programs or expanded their existing initiatives since my last update. For the latest and most comprehensive information, I recommend checking the official websites or contacting the respective banks directly to inquire about their current microfinance initiatives.

3.13. The Business Correspondence (BC) model of microfinance in India:

The Business Correspondence (BC) model of microfinance in India is a financial inclusion strategy that allows banks to extend their services to underserved and remote areas by partnering with third-party agents or intermediaries. These agents, known as Business Correspondents (BCs), act as a bridge between the bank and the customers in areas where the bank does not have a physical presence.

The BC model was introduced by the Reserve Bank of India (RBI) to enhance financial inclusion and provide banking services to the unbanked population, especially in rural and semi-urban regions. Here's how the BC model works:

3.13.1. Appointment of Business Correspondents:

Banks appoint individuals, entities, or organizations as BCs after conducting due diligence and ensuring their credibility. These BCs can be local grocery shop owners, post offices, NGOs, self-help groups, or other entities with a community presence.

3.13.2. Banking Services Delivery:

BCs are authorized to provide certain basic banking services on behalf of the bank they are associated with. These services may include account opening, deposit collection, cash withdrawal, fund transfer, loan application processing, and other financial transactions.

3.13.3. Outreach and Customer Acquisition:

BCs act as a touchpoint for the bank in remote areas, promoting financial literacy and encouraging people to open bank accounts. They also help in completing necessary documentation and formalities for the customers.

3.13.4. Technology and Infrastructure:

BCs use technology, such as point-of-sale (PoS) devices, biometric authentication, or mobile banking apps, to conduct transactions securely and efficiently.

3.13.5. Compensation and Incentives:

Banks provide commissions or incentives to BCs based on the volume of transactions and other performance indicators, as a way to encourage them to expand their outreach and deliver quality services.

The BC model has been instrumental in expanding the reach of formal banking services in India, especially to those who were previously excluded from the banking system. It has contributed significantly to financial inclusion, allowing more people to access banking facilities and avail themselves of various financial products and services. Moreover, this model has also helped reduce the burden on the physical branch network of banks, making banking services more cost-effective and accessible to a broader population.

3.14. Microfinance through NGOs and Charities:

Non-governmental organizations (NGOs) and charitable organizations often provide microfinance services to vulnerable communities. These organizations use funds from donors and grants to offer microloans, financial literacy training, and other support services.

Microfinance through NGOs (Non-Governmental Organizations) and charities is an important approach to extending financial services to underserved and economically disadvantaged communities. NGOs and charities often play a significant role in promoting financial inclusion by offering microfinance programs that cater to the specific needs of vulnerable populations. Here's how microfinance through NGOs and charities works:

3.14.1. Targeted Outreach:

NGOs and charities have a strong presence in communities with limited access to formal financial institutions. They identify and target individuals and groups in need of financial services, such as low-income entrepreneurs, women, and marginalized communities.

3.14.2. Microcredit and Savings:

These organizations provide microcredit, which involves offering small loans to borrowers who may not qualify for loans from traditional banks. Additionally, they encourage and facilitate savings among their beneficiaries to promote financial discipline and build a safety net for emergencies.

3.14.3. Financial Literacy:

NGOs and charities also focus on promoting financial literacy and education. They conduct workshops and training sessions to help beneficiaries understand financial concepts, manage their finances, and make informed decisions regarding loans and savings.

3.14.4. Social Development:

Apart from financial services, NGOs and charities often integrate social development components into their microfinance initiatives. They address other critical needs of the community, such as healthcare, education, and skill development, to improve the overall well-being of the beneficiaries.

3.14.5. Responsible Lending:

Microfinance programs run by NGOs and charities typically follow responsible lending practices. They assess borrowers' repayment capacity, avoid over-indebtedness, and ensure transparency in loan terms and conditions.

3.14.6. Group-Based Lending:

Many NGOs and charities adopt a group-based lending approach, where borrowers form self-help groups or small cooperatives. These groups provide social collateral and mutual support, which helps in reducing the risk of default and strengthens community ties.

3.14.7. Impact Measurement:

NGOs and charities often conduct impact assessments to evaluate the effectiveness of their microfinance initiatives in improving the lives of the beneficiaries and the community as a whole.

Microfinance through NGOs and charities has proven to be an effective way to empower disadvantaged communities, especially in areas where formal banking services are scarce. By combining financial services with social development efforts, these initiatives contribute to poverty alleviation, women empowerment, and overall community development.

3.15. Mobile Banking and Digital Financial Services:

With the widespread use of mobile phones, mobile banking and digital financial services have gained popularity in microfinance. Digital platforms enable easier access to financial services, such as mobile wallets, mobile-based loans, and payment systems.

Mobile banking and digital financial services have played a transformative role in the microfinance sector, revolutionizing the way financial services are delivered to underserved populations. Here's how mobile banking and digital financial services have impacted microfinance:

3.15.1. Increased Accessibility:

Mobile banking and digital financial services have extended the reach of microfinance institutions to remote and rural areas, where physical branches are often scarce. With the widespread use of mobile phones, even people in far-flung regions can access financial services conveniently.

3.15.2. Cost-Effective Operations:

Digital financial services have reduced operational costs for microfinance institutions. By leveraging technology, these institutions can streamline processes, reduce paperwork, and offer services at a lower cost, benefiting both the institutions and the customers.

3.15.3. Enhanced Customer Experience:

Mobile banking and digital platforms offer a user-friendly interface, making financial transactions easier and more convenient for clients. Customers can check their account balance, make payments, and apply for loans with just a few taps on their mobile devices.

3.15.4. Financial Inclusion:

Mobile banking and digital financial services have played a crucial role in promoting financial inclusion. Individuals who were previously excluded from formal banking services now have access to savings accounts, credit, and other financial products tailored to their needs.

3.15.5. Quick Loan Disbursements:

Digital financial services enable faster loan disbursements. Once a loan application is approved, funds can be disbursed directly to the borrower's mobile wallet or bank account, eliminating the need for physical cash transactions.

3.15.6. Mobile Wallets:

Mobile wallets have become popular tools for microfinance customers, allowing them to store and manage their funds securely. These wallets offer a cashless payment option, reducing the reliance on physical cash and promoting a more formal financial ecosystem.

3.15.7. Data Analytics and Risk Assessment:

Digital financial services provide valuable data insights that help microfinance institutions make informed decisions. They can assess creditworthiness and manage risks more effectively, leading to better-targeted financial solutions.

3.15.8. Financial Literacy:

Mobile banking and digital platforms often include financial education modules, empowering customers with knowledge about managing finances and making sound financial decisions.

While mobile banking and digital financial services have significantly improved access to financial services, it's important to address challenges related to digital literacy, connectivity, and data security to ensure that the benefits of these innovations are accessible to all, especially in underserved communities. Nonetheless, the continued evolution of digital technologies holds great promise for the growth and sustainability of microfinance initiatives worldwide.

3.16. Micro leasing:

Micro leasing involves providing equipment or assets on lease to small entrepreneurs who cannot afford to purchase them. This model helps small businesses access essential assets for their operations without the burden of high upfront costs.

Micro-leasing, also known as microfinance leasing or micro asset leasing, is a financial service that allows individuals and small businesses to access assets and equipment through a lease agreement. It is a form of microfinance that caters to the specific needs of low-income individuals and micro-entrepreneurs who may not have access to traditional financing options.

In micro-leasing, a leasing company or microfinance institution (MFI) provides the client with the use of an asset, such as agricultural equipment, machinery, vehicles, or tools, for a predetermined period. The client pays regular lease payments, which are typically more affordable than the upfront cost of purchasing the asset outright.

3.16.A. Key features of micro-leasing:

3.16.A.1. Asset-Centric: Micro-leasing is focused on providing access to assets rather than offering monetary loans. This allows clients to use the asset to generate income and improve their livelihoods.

3.16.A.2. Income Generation: Micro-leasing is often used for income-generating purposes, enabling clients to start or expand small businesses, engage in agricultural activities, or enhance their productivity.

3.16.A.3. Flexible Terms: Micro-leasing agreements usually come with flexible terms to suit the needs of the clients. The lease period, payment frequency, and end-of-lease options may be tailored to the client's financial capacity and usage requirements.

3.16.A.4. Risk Mitigation: Micro-leasing reduces the risk for both the client and the leasing company. The leasing company retains ownership of the asset, which serves as collateral, reducing the risk of default.

3.16.A.5. Asset Maintenance: The leasing company is responsible for maintaining the leased asset during the lease period, ensuring that it remains in good working condition.

Micro-leasing has been particularly beneficial for micro-entrepreneurs and smallholder farmers in developing countries, enabling them to access essential equipment and tools to improve their productivity and income-generating capabilities. It promotes financial inclusion and economic empowerment by providing a viable alternative to outright asset ownership for those who lack the financial means for significant upfront investments.

3.17. Green Microfinance:

Green microfinance focuses on providing financial services to support environmentally sustainable initiatives and businesses. It promotes eco-friendly practices and projects that contribute to environmental conservation.

Green microfinance, also known as eco-friendly microfinance or sustainable microfinance, is a specialized form of microfinance that focuses on promoting environmentally friendly and sustainable practices among micro-entrepreneurs and small businesses. It aims to integrate environmental considerations into the financial services provided to clients, encouraging them to adopt eco-friendly initiatives and contribute to environmental conservation.

3.17.A. Key features of Green Microfinance:

3.17.A.1. Sustainable Projects: Green microfinance supports projects that have positive environmental impacts. These projects may include renewable energy initiatives (such as solar panels or biogas plants), sustainable agriculture practices, waste management, and energy-efficient technologies.

3.17.A.2. Environmental Education: Green microfinance institutions often provide environmental education and training to their clients, raising awareness about sustainable practices and their benefits. This helps clients understand the importance of adopting green solutions and how it can improve their long-term financial stability.

3.17.A.3. Green Products and Services: Green microfinance institutions offer financial products and services specifically designed for eco-friendly projects. These may include green loans, eco-friendly savings accounts, and financial incentives for adopting sustainable practices.

3.17.A.4. Environmental Impact Assessment: Before funding a project, green microfinance institutions may conduct environmental impact assessments to ensure that the proposed initiatives align with sustainability goals and do not harm the environment.

3.17.A.5. Monitoring and Evaluation: Green microfinance institutions monitor the progress and impact of funded projects to assess their environmental effectiveness and make data-driven decisions for future financing.

3.17.B. Benefits of Green Microfinance:

3.17.B.1. Environmental Conservation: Green microfinance plays a vital role in encouraging environmentally friendly practices, contributing to conservation efforts and mitigating the impacts of climate change.

3.17.B.2. Poverty Alleviation: Sustainable projects supported by green microfinance can help lift people out of poverty by providing income-generating opportunities and reducing vulnerability to environmental risks.

3.17.B.3. Enhanced Resilience: By adopting sustainable practices, micro-entrepreneurs and small businesses can build resilience against environmental shocks and adapt to changing environmental conditions.

3.17.B.4. Community Development: Green microfinance initiatives often foster community development by promoting cooperation among local stakeholders and fostering sustainable economic growth.

3.17.B.5. Global Sustainable Development: Green microfinance aligns with broader global goals, such as the United Nations Sustainable Development Goals (SDGs), particularly those related to environmental sustainability and poverty reduction.

Green microfinance showcases the potential for finance to become a force for positive change, supporting both economic development and environmental conservation in a balanced and sustainable manner.

3.18. Microfinance through Remittances:

In some cases, remittances sent by migrant workers back to their home countries can serve as a form of microfinance. Families may use remittances for income-generating activities or to start small businesses.

Microfinance through remittances is an innovative approach that leverages the flow of remittances to provide financial services and promote financial inclusion among recipient households in developing countries. Remittances are the funds sent by migrant workers working abroad back to their families in their home countries. By integrating microfinance services with remittances, various financial institutions and service providers facilitate access to credit, savings, insurance, and other financial products for remittance-receiving households.

3.18.A. Here's how microfinance through remittances works:

3.18.A.1. Remittance Channels: Migrant workers send money to their families using formal remittance channels like banks, money transfer operators (MTOs), or digital remittance platforms.

3.18.A.2. Linking with Microfinance Institutions (MFIs): Microfinance institutions or other financial service providers collaborate with remittance service providers to create linkages between remittance transfers and microfinance services.

3.18.A.3. Mobile Money and Digital Wallets: In some cases, remittances are directly deposited into recipients' mobile money or digital wallets, facilitating easy access to microfinance services through digital platforms.

3.18.A.4. Remittance-Backed Loans: Recipients of remittances, particularly women and small entrepreneurs, may be eligible for microloans backed by the regular remittance flow they receive. These loans can be used for business development, education, or other productive purposes.

3.18.A.5. Remittance-Savings Linkage: Recipients of remittances are encouraged to save a portion of the remitted funds through savings accounts or other financial instruments offered by microfinance institutions. This promotes financial resilience and helps build assets over time.

3.18.A.6. Financial Education: Microfinance institutions often provide financial literacy and education to remittance-receiving households to empower them with better financial management skills.

3.18.B. Benefits of Microfinance through Remittances:

3.18.B.1. Enhanced Financial Inclusion: Integrating microfinance services with remittances helps extend financial services to remittance-receiving households, including those in remote areas with limited access to traditional banking.

3.18.B.2. Empowerment and Entrepreneurship: Microfinance provided through remittances empowers recipients to engage in income-generating activities, leading to economic growth and entrepreneurship.

3.18.B.3. Risk Mitigation: For microfinance institutions, the regular inflow of remittances acts as a form of collateral, reducing the risk of default on loans.

3.18.B.4. Lower Transaction Costs: The integration of remittances and microfinance can lead to cost-effective and efficient financial services for both the sender and receiver.

3.18.B.5. Positive Social Impact: Microfinance through remittances contributes to poverty reduction, improved living standards, and increased investment in education and healthcare.

Microfinance through remittances demonstrates the potential for innovative financial solutions to bridge gaps in financial access and create positive socio-economic impacts for migrant workers and their families.

3.19. Microfinance in Conflict-Affected Areas:

In regions affected by conflict or displacement, microfinance models are adapted to support livelihoods and economic recovery. These models aim to provide stability and empowerment to vulnerable communities.

Microfinance in conflict-affected areas is a challenging but essential approach to promote economic stability, financial inclusion, and social resilience among vulnerable populations living in regions impacted by conflicts, wars, or political unrest. While providing microfinance services in such areas comes with unique risks and obstacles, it also offers significant opportunities for positive impact. Here are some key considerations and strategies for implementing microfinance in conflict-affected areas:

3.19.1. Contextual Understanding:

It is crucial for microfinance institutions to have a deep understanding of the local context, including the dynamics of the conflict, cultural norms, and socio-economic challenges. This understanding helps design appropriate financial products and services that cater to the specific needs of the affected communities.

3.19.2. Safety and Security:

Ensuring the safety and security of both clients and microfinance staff is paramount in conflict zones. Microfinance institutions must establish robust risk management protocols and adapt operations to minimize exposure to danger.

3.19.3. Flexibility and Adaptability:

Conflict situations are highly dynamic, and microfinance institutions must be flexible and adaptable in responding to changing circumstances. This may involve adjusting loan terms, repayment schedules, or providing alternative channels for service delivery.

3.19.4. Targeting Vulnerable Groups:

Microfinance initiatives in conflict-affected areas should prioritize serving vulnerable groups, such as internally displaced persons (IDPs), refugees, and women-headed households, who often face heightened financial challenges during conflicts.

3.19.5. Collaborations and Partnerships:

Engaging with local organizations, NGOs, or humanitarian agencies can facilitate the effective delivery of microfinance services and extend support to the affected communities.

3.19.6. Holistic Approach:

In conflict-affected areas, microfinance should be combined with social support programs that address various aspects of vulnerability, including access to healthcare, education, and psychosocial support.

3.19.7. Building Trust:

Establishing trust with clients is crucial in conflict-affected areas, where people may be wary of formal financial institutions due to past negative experiences or uncertainties. Building trust may involve community engagement, transparent practices, and strong customer service.

3.19.8. Economic Recovery:

Microfinance can play a vital role in supporting post-conflict economic recovery by providing access to credit and capital for entrepreneurship and livelihood activities.

3.19.9. Monitoring and Evaluation:

Regular monitoring and evaluation of microfinance projects in conflict-affected areas are essential to assess the impact, effectiveness, and potential challenges of the interventions.

By addressing the unique challenges and leveraging the opportunities, microfinance in conflict-affected areas can contribute to economic stability, poverty alleviation, and social resilience, helping communities rebuild and recover from the devastating effects of conflicts. It requires a patient and long-term commitment from microfinance institutions and other stakeholders to foster sustainable development amidst adversity.

3.20. Microfinance through Agricultural Cooperatives:

In rural areas, agricultural cooperatives sometimes extend microfinance services to farmers and agricultural workers. They provide loans for agricultural inputs, equipment, and other farming-related needs.

Microfinance through agricultural cooperatives is a powerful mechanism to support smallholder farmers and rural communities in developing countries. Agricultural cooperatives are organizations formed by farmers who come together to pool their resources and collectively address their financial, social, and economic needs. By integrating microfinance services within these cooperatives, farmers gain access to financial products and services tailored to their specific agricultural requirements. Here's how microfinance through agricultural cooperatives works:

3.20.1. Group-Based Lending:

Agricultural cooperatives act as a collective platform for farmers to access microloans. Group-based lending is a common approach, where members of the cooperative collectively guarantee each other's loans. This mutual support reduces the risk for lenders and allows farmers with limited collateral to access credit.

3.20.2. Savings and Deposits:

Microfinance services within agricultural cooperatives often include savings and deposit accounts. Farmers can save their surplus income in these accounts, enabling them to build financial reserves for investment in agricultural inputs or other productive activities.

3.20.3. Insurance:

Agricultural cooperatives may also offer microinsurance products tailored to the specific risks faced by farmers, such as crop failure due to adverse weather conditions or livestock diseases. Insurance provides a safety net and protects farmers' livelihoods.

3.20.4. Technical Assistance and Training:

Microfinance through agricultural cooperatives goes beyond just providing financial services. These cooperatives often offer technical assistance and training to improve farming practices, increase productivity, and enhance farmers' income-generating capabilities.

3.20.5. Market Access:

Some agricultural cooperatives also facilitate market linkages for their members, helping them sell their produce at fair prices and access better market opportunities.

3.20.A. Benefits of Microfinance through Agricultural Cooperatives:

3.20.A.1. Increased Access to Finance: By leveraging the collective strength of the cooperative, individual farmers gain access to microfinance services that they might not have qualified for individually.

3.20.A.2. Reduced Transaction Costs: Group-based lending and savings within the cooperative help reduce transaction costs for both farmers and microfinance providers.

3.20.A.3. Enhanced Bargaining Power: As a unified entity, agricultural cooperatives can negotiate better terms with microfinance institutions and other stakeholders, increasing the benefits for their members.

3.20.A.4. Social Cohesion: Microfinance through agricultural cooperatives fosters social cohesion and community development among farmers, promoting cooperation and mutual support.

3.20.A.5. Sustainable Agriculture: By offering financial products along with technical assistance, agricultural cooperatives contribute to sustainable agricultural practices and rural development.

Microfinance through agricultural cooperatives not only addresses the financial needs of smallholder farmers but also strengthens their capacity to cope with challenges and seize opportunities in the agricultural sector. It plays a pivotal role in empowering farmers, promoting food security, and supporting rural economic growth.

3.21. Microfinance for Artisans and Craftsmen:

Some microfinance initiatives focus on supporting artisans and craftsmen by providing them with access to credit for raw materials, tools, and marketing support to improve their businesses.

Microfinance for artisans and craftsmen is a specialized form of microfinance that caters to the financial needs of individuals engaged in traditional artisanal and craft activities. Artisans and craftsmen often belong to economically vulnerable communities and may face challenges in accessing formal financial services. Microfinance initiatives tailored to their needs can empower them economically, preserve traditional craftsmanship, and contribute to local economic development. Here's how microfinance for artisans and craftsmen works:

3.21.1. Customized Financial Products:

Microfinance institutions design financial products that suit the specific requirements of artisans and craftsmen. These may include microloans for purchasing raw materials, tools, and equipment, working capital loans, and income-smoothing products to manage seasonal fluctuations.

3.21.2. Group-Based Lending:

Artisans and craftsmen often form self-help groups or cooperatives to access microfinance. Group-based lending allows them to collectively guarantee each other's loans, reducing individual risk and strengthening their borrowing capacity.

3.21.3. Skill Enhancement and Training:

Microfinance initiatives for artisans and craftsmen may include skill enhancement and training programs. These programs help artisans improve their craft, innovate their designs, and enhance the marketability of their products.

3.21.4. Marketing Support:

Some microfinance programs offer marketing support to artisans, helping them promote and sell their products in local and international markets.

3.21.5. Access to Markets:

Microfinance institutions may collaborate with other organizations or platforms to facilitate access to wider markets for artisans' products, enabling them to reach a broader customer base.

3.21.6. Financial Inclusion:

Microfinance for artisans and craftsmen promotes financial inclusion by offering them formal financial services and bringing them into the mainstream financial system.

3.21.A. Benefits of Microfinance for Artisans and Craftsmen:

3.21.A.1. Economic Empowerment: Microfinance enables artisans and craftsmen to access capital and financial resources to invest in their craft, expand their businesses, and improve their livelihoods.

3.21.A.2. Preserving Traditional Crafts: By supporting artisans, microfinance contributes to preserving traditional crafts and cultural heritage, which can be at risk of decline in the face of modernization.

3.21.A.3. Poverty Alleviation: Providing financial services to artisans and craftsmen helps alleviate poverty by creating income-generating opportunities and improving their socio-economic conditions.

3.21.A.4. Community Development: Microfinance initiatives for artisans often have a positive impact on the entire community by stimulating economic activities, creating jobs, and fostering local entrepreneurship.

3.21.A.5. Social Inclusion: Microfinance promotes social inclusion by providing opportunities for marginalized artisans and craftsmen, including women and members of disadvantaged communities.

Microfinance for artisans and craftsmen not only supports their economic well-being but also plays a role in preserving cultural heritage and promoting sustainable development. It empowers artisans to thrive in their traditional crafts and contribute to the cultural richness of their societies.

3.22. Microfinance for Education:

Microfinance models have been adapted to support access to education. They offer loans or financial assistance to students and their families to cover educational expenses, enabling them to pursue higher studies and skill development.

Microfinance for education is a specialized financial service that aims to promote access to education and address financial barriers to learning. It involves providing loans, savings, and other financial products specifically tailored to support students, parents, and educational institutions in their pursuit of education. Here's how microfinance for education works in more detail:

3.22.1. Student Loans:

Microfinance institutions offer student loans to cover educational expenses such as tuition fees, books, uniforms, and other school-related costs. These loans enable students to pursue primary, secondary, tertiary, or vocational education.

3.22.2. Education Savings Accounts:

Microfinance institutions may offer education savings accounts, allowing parents or guardians to save money regularly for their children's education. These accounts help build funds for future educational expenses, ensuring that parents have the necessary resources to support their children's education.

3.22.3. School Improvement Loans:

Microfinance for education can extend to educational institutions as well. Microfinance institutions may provide loans to schools or colleges for infrastructure development, improvement of facilities, or to purchase educational materials.

3.22.4. Flexible Repayment Options:

Microfinance for education often offers flexible repayment options, taking into account the borrower's financial capacity. This can include deferred payments until after graduation or income-sensitive repayment plans.

3.22.5. Financial Literacy and Training:

Microfinance institutions may provide financial literacy training to students and their families, helping them make informed decisions about managing educational expenses and planning for the future.

3.22.A. Benefits of Microfinance for Education:

3.22.A.1. Increased Access to Education: Microfinance for education helps bridge the financial gap and allows individuals from low-income backgrounds to access education, improving overall educational attainment.

3.22.A.2. Empowerment and Socio-Economic Mobility: Access to education empowers individuals with knowledge and skills, enhancing their employability and economic opportunities.

3.22.A.3. Poverty Reduction: Education is a key factor in breaking the cycle of poverty by providing individuals with the means to improve their living standards and prospects for the future.

3.22.A.4. Human Capital Development: Investing in education through microfinance contributes to the development of a skilled and educated workforce, which positively impacts economic growth and development.

3.22.A.5. Gender Equality: Microfinance for education can help promote gender equality by supporting girls and women in accessing education and reducing gender disparities in education.

Microfinance for education plays a crucial role in promoting educational equity and social development. By providing financial services tailored to the specific needs of students and educational institutions, microfinance helps create a more inclusive and educated society, fostering long-term economic and social progress.

3.23. Microfinance for Healthcare:

Healthcare microfinance programs aim to address healthcare-related expenses. They provide loans for medical treatments, health insurance, or support for healthcare facilities in underserved communities.

Microfinance for healthcare is a financial service that aims to improve access to quality healthcare services and address healthcare-related financial barriers for individuals and communities, especially those in low-income or underserved areas. It involves providing financial products and services that help individuals afford healthcare expenses and support the development of healthcare facilities. Here's how microfinance for healthcare works:

3.23.1. Medical Loans:

Microfinance institutions offer medical loans to individuals to cover healthcare expenses, including hospitalization costs, medical treatments, surgeries, medications, and medical equipment.

3.23.2. Health Savings Accounts:

Microfinance institutions may offer health savings accounts that allow individuals to save money regularly for future healthcare needs. These accounts help build a fund to cover medical expenses as they arise.

3.23.3. Financing Healthcare Facilities:

Microfinance can extend to healthcare providers, supporting the development and improvement of healthcare facilities, clinics, and hospitals in underserved areas.

3.23.4. Health Insurance:

Microfinance institutions may collaborate with insurance providers to offer health insurance products to individuals or families. Health insurance helps individuals access medical services without facing a significant financial burden.

3.23.5. Community Health Initiatives:

Microfinance for healthcare can also support community-based health initiatives, such as preventive health programs, maternal and child health projects, and disease prevention campaigns.

3.23.A. Benefits of Microfinance for Healthcare:

3.23.A.1. Improved Access to Healthcare: Microfinance for healthcare expands access to medical services and treatments for individuals who would otherwise face financial obstacles in seeking medical care.

3.23.A.2. Better Health Outcomes: Timely access to healthcare through microfinance can lead to improved health outcomes and a better quality of life for individuals and communities.

3.23.A.3. Financial Protection: Microfinance for healthcare provides a safety net, protecting individuals from falling into poverty due to unexpected medical expenses.

3.23.A.4. Health Infrastructure Development: By supporting healthcare facilities, microfinance contributes to the development of health infrastructure in underserved areas, increasing the availability of medical services.

3.23.A.5. Health Awareness and Prevention: Community health initiatives foster health awareness and preventive measures, promoting healthier lifestyles and reducing the burden of preventable diseases.

Microfinance for healthcare plays a crucial role in promoting health equity and addressing disparities in healthcare access. By providing financial solutions tailored to healthcare needs, microfinance helps ensure that everyone has the opportunity to receive essential medical services and leads to healthier and more resilient communities.

3.24. Micro franchising:

Micro franchising is a business model that offers low-income entrepreneurs the opportunity to run a small franchise with the support and guidance of a larger franchising organization. This model helps individuals start and manage a business with an established brand and business model.

Micro franchising is a business model that adapts the principles of traditional franchising to create smaller and more affordable franchise opportunities for aspiring entrepreneurs, especially those in low-income or underserved communities. It aims to promote entrepreneurship, economic development, and social impact by enabling individuals to start and run their own businesses with the support and branding of an established franchise system. Here's how micro franchising works:

3.24.1. Simplified Franchise Model:

Micro franchising simplifies the traditional franchise model to make it more accessible and affordable for individuals with limited financial resources. It often involves smaller-scale businesses and reduced initial investment requirements.

3.24.2. Standardized Business Model:

The micro franchise model offers a standardized business model that includes pre-designed products or services, operational procedures, marketing strategies, and training materials. This standardization ensures consistency and replicability across multiple micro franchise units.

3.24.3. Training and Support:

Micro franchisors provide training and ongoing support to micro franchisees. This includes training on business operations, product knowledge, customer service, and marketing techniques to help them run successful businesses.

3.24.4. Branding and Marketing:

Micro franchisees benefit from the brand recognition and marketing efforts of the franchisor, which can help attract customers and build trust in the local community.

3.24.5. Community Impact:

Micro franchising often targets underserved communities, providing income-generating opportunities and fostering local economic development.

3.24.A. Examples of Micro franchising:

Micro franchising can be found in various industries, including food and beverage, retail, healthcare, and social services. Examples of micro franchising initiatives include:

3.24.A.1. Food Carts: Micro franchising food cart businesses that offer simple and affordable food options in busy areas or communities with limited dining choices.

3.24.A.2. Mobile Health Clinics: Micro franchise models that deploy mobile health clinics to provide essential healthcare services in remote or underserved areas.

3.24.A.3. Clean Energy Solutions: Micro franchising initiatives that distribute and install clean energy products, such as solar lamps or clean cookstoves, to improve energy access in rural communities.

3.24.A.4. Water Purification: Micro franchising businesses that sell and distribute water purification systems to provide safe drinking water in areas with limited access to clean water.

3.24.B. Benefits of Micro franchising:

3.24.B.1. Entrepreneurial Opportunities: Micro franchising empowers individuals with limited resources to become entrepreneurs and own their businesses.

3.24.B.2. Reduced Risk: Micro franchising offers a proven business model and ongoing support, reducing the risk of business failure compared to starting an independent venture.

3.24.B.3. Social Impact: Micro franchising can lead to positive social impact by creating job opportunities, improving local economies, and addressing community needs.

3.24.B.4. Scalability: Micro franchising allows franchisors to rapidly scale their business while extending the benefits of entrepreneurship to more individuals.

Micro franchising is an innovative approach that combines the advantages of traditional franchising with social impact, making entrepreneurship accessible to a broader segment of the population and driving economic development in underserved areas.

3.25. Microfinance for Clean Energy:

This model promotes access to clean energy solutions, such as solar lamps and clean cookstoves, by providing microloans to households and small businesses to purchase these environmentally friendly products.

Microfinance for clean energy is a specialized form of microfinance that aims to promote the adoption of clean and renewable energy solutions among individuals, households, and small businesses. It enables access to affordable financing for clean energy products and services, such as solar panels, clean cookstoves, energy-efficient appliances, and other sustainable energy technologies. Here's how microfinance for clean energy works:

3.25.1. Financing Clean Energy Products:

Microfinance institutions offer loans or credit facilities specifically for the purchase and installation of clean energy technologies. These loans are tailored to the affordability and income levels of the borrowers.

3.25.2. Energy Savings:

Microfinance for clean energy often takes into account the potential energy savings achieved by using renewable and energy-efficient technologies. The savings in energy costs can offset the loan repayments, making the investment financially viable for borrowers.

3.25.3. Pay-As-You-Go (PAYG) Models:

Some microfinance initiatives adopt pay-as-you-go models, where borrowers make small and frequent payments for clean energy products until the full cost is covered. PAYG models are especially suitable for those with irregular incomes.

3.25.4. Group-Based Approaches:

Microfinance institutions may implement group-based lending approaches, where communities or self-help groups collectively access clean energy loans. This reduces the risk for the lender and builds social support for clean energy adoption.

3.25.5. Training and Education:

Microfinance for clean energy often includes training and education for borrowers on the benefits and effective use of clean energy technologies. This enhances the borrowers' capacity to maximize the benefits of their investment.

3.25.A. Benefits of Microfinance for Clean Energy:

3.25.A.1. Increased Clean Energy Adoption: Microfinance for clean energy expands access to financing, making clean energy solutions more affordable and accessible to a broader population.

3.25.A.2. Environmental Impact: By promoting the use of clean and renewable energy technologies, microfinance contributes to reducing greenhouse gas emissions and combating climate change.

3.25.A.3. Energy Access: Microfinance for clean energy enhances energy access, particularly in remote and underserved areas where access to traditional energy sources may be limited.

3.25.A.4. Cost Savings: The adoption of clean energy technologies can lead to long-term cost savings for borrowers by reducing their dependence on expensive and polluting energy sources.

3.25.A.5. Socio-Economic Development: Access to clean energy contributes to socio-economic development by improving living conditions, supporting income-generating activities, and fostering community development.

Microfinance for clean energy aligns with global sustainability goals and addresses the dual challenges of energy poverty and environmental conservation. By facilitating the transition to cleaner and more sustainable energy sources, microfinance plays a critical role in promoting a greener and more inclusive future.

3.26. Microfinance for Women's Empowerment:

Several microfinance initiatives specifically target women, recognizing their significant role in household finances and community development. These models often incorporate financial literacy training and women-focused support services.

Microfinance for women's empowerment is a powerful tool that uses financial services and resources to promote gender equality, economic independence, and social empowerment among women. It provides women, particularly those in low-income or marginalized communities, with access to credit, savings, insurance, and other financial products and services. Here's how microfinance for women's empowerment works:

3.26.1. Access to Credit:

Microfinance institutions offer small loans to women entrepreneurs and self-employed women to start or expand businesses. These loans enable women to invest in income-generating activities and achieve financial independence.

3.26.2. Group-Based Lending:

Microfinance often employs group-based lending approaches, where women form self-help groups or solidarity groups to access loans collectively. Group dynamics create a supportive environment, foster social cohesion, and enhance repayment rates.

3.26.3. Savings and Financial Inclusion:

Microfinance promotes financial inclusion by encouraging women to open savings accounts. Saving regularly helps women build financial resilience, plan for the future, and meet unexpected expenses.

3.26.4. Gender-Sensitive Services:

Microfinance institutions design services that are sensitive to the needs and constraints faced by women. These services may include flexible repayment options, gender-responsive training, and gender-specific products.

3.26.5. Capacity Building and Training:

Microfinance initiatives for women's empowerment often include training and capacity-building programs. These programs focus on financial literacy, entrepreneurship skills, and leadership development.

3.26.A. Benefits of Microfinance for Women's Empowerment:

3.26.A.1. Economic Empowerment: Microfinance enables women to gain economic independence by providing them with opportunities to generate income and build assets.

3.26.A.2. Poverty Reduction: Access to credit and financial services through microfinance helps lift women and their families out of poverty, contributing to improved living standards.

3.26.A.3. Gender Equality: Microfinance for women's empowerment promotes gender equality by breaking down barriers that hinder women's financial inclusion and access to economic opportunities.

3.26.A.4. Social Empowerment: As women become financially independent, they gain confidence, decision-making power, and greater control over their lives and future.

3.26.A.5. Community Development: Women's economic empowerment through microfinance has a positive impact on the entire community, fostering economic growth and social development.

Microfinance for women's empowerment plays a crucial role in advancing gender equality and promoting sustainable development. By addressing the financial needs of women and creating an enabling environment for their economic and social advancement, microfinance contributes to building more inclusive and equitable societies.

3.27. Microfinance for People with Disabilities:

Microfinance programs tailored for people with disabilities aim to provide them with access to credit and financial services, fostering economic independence and social inclusion.

Microfinance for people with disabilities is a specialized form of financial service that aims to promote financial inclusion and economic empowerment among individuals with disabilities. It provides access to credit, savings, insurance, and other financial products and services tailored to the specific needs and circumstances of people with disabilities. Here's how microfinance for people with disabilities works:

3.27.1. Inclusive Financial Products:

Microfinance institutions design financial products that are accessible and inclusive for people with disabilities. This may include customized loan terms, flexible repayment options, and special savings accounts.

3.27.2. Assistive Technology Financing:

Microfinance for people with disabilities may cover the financing of assistive devices and technologies that improve their mobility, communication, or ability to perform daily activities independently.

3.27.3. Income-Generating Activities:

Microfinance initiatives help people with disabilities engage in income-generating activities by providing loans to start or expand small businesses, thereby enhancing their economic independence.

3.27.4. Training and Capacity Building:

Microfinance for people with disabilities often includes training and capacity-building programs, focusing on financial literacy, entrepreneurship, and skills development.

3.27.5. Group-Based Approaches:

Group-based lending or self-help groups can be implemented to foster peer support, increase financial literacy, and improve repayment rates among people with disabilities.

3.27.A. Benefits of Microfinance for People with Disabilities:

3.27.A. 1. Economic Empowerment: Microfinance enables people with disabilities to participate in economic activities, generate income, and improve their financial well-being.

3.27.A.2. Financial Inclusion: Microfinance for people with disabilities ensures that they have access to formal financial services and are not excluded from the benefits of the financial system.

3.27.A.3. Increased Independence: Access to credit and financial resources allows individuals with disabilities to invest in assistive technologies and participate in income-generating activities, promoting greater independence and self-reliance.

3.27.A.4. Improved Quality of Life: Microfinance initiatives that support people with disabilities contribute to an improved quality of life by enhancing their social and economic participation.

3.27.A.5. Social Inclusion: By promoting the economic empowerment of people with disabilities, microfinance contributes to their social inclusion and challenges stereotypes and stigma.

Microfinance for people with disabilities plays a critical role in promoting social inclusion, economic empowerment, and the overall well-being of individuals with disabilities. It helps break down barriers and ensures that people with disabilities have equal opportunities to participate in economic activities and lead fulfilling lives.

3.28. Microfinance in Indigenous Communities:

Some microfinance models are customized to suit the needs and cultural context of indigenous communities. They focus on preserving traditional livelihoods and empowering these communities.

Microfinance in indigenous communities is a specialized approach that aims to promote financial inclusion and economic development among indigenous populations. Indigenous communities often face unique challenges, including limited access to formal financial services, cultural barriers, and socio-economic disparities. Microfinance initiatives tailored to their needs and cultural contexts can play a crucial role in empowering these communities. Here's how microfinance in indigenous communities works:

3.28.1. Culturally Sensitive Approach:

Microfinance programs in indigenous communities adopt a culturally sensitive approach, taking into account the customs, traditions, and values of the community. This helps build trust and ensure that financial services align with the community's cultural practices.

3.28.2. Inclusive Financial Products:

Microfinance institutions design inclusive financial products that cater to the specific needs of indigenous populations. This may include customized savings accounts, credit products, and insurance that reflect the community's livelihood patterns.

3.28.3. Community-Based Microfinance:

Microfinance initiatives often adopt community-based models where indigenous community members collectively participate in decision-making, loan management, and risk-sharing.

3.28.4. Capacity Building and Financial Education:

Microfinance programs provide capacity building and financial education to empower community members with the knowledge and skills needed to manage their finances effectively.

3.28.5. Income-Generating Activities:

Microfinance for indigenous communities may support income-generating activities that are culturally appropriate and sustainable, such as traditional crafts, agriculture, or eco-tourism ventures.

3.28.A. Benefits of Microfinance in Indigenous Communities:

3.28.A.1. Financial Inclusion: Microfinance ensures that indigenous communities have access to formal financial services, helping them overcome barriers to financial inclusion.

3.28.A.2. Poverty Alleviation: Access to credit and financial resources through microfinance can uplift indigenous communities, reducing poverty and enhancing livelihoods.

3.28.A.3. Cultural Preservation: Microfinance initiatives that respect and incorporate indigenous traditions contribute to the preservation of cultural heritage and traditional practices.

3.28.A.4. Community Empowerment: Microfinance empowers indigenous communities to take charge of their economic development and build financial resilience.

3.28.A.5. Social and Economic Development: Microfinance in indigenous communities promotes social and economic development, fostering self-reliance and sustainable growth.

3.28.B. Challenges in Microfinance in Indigenous Communities:

3.28.B.1. Language and Communication: Language barriers may pose challenges in delivering financial education and ensuring clear communication about financial products.

3.28.B.2. Land Tenure and Ownership: Land rights and ownership issues may impact the ability of indigenous communities to access credit and collateral-based loans.

3.28.B.3. External Pressures: External factors such as land exploitation, natural resource extraction, and climate change can influence the success of microfinance initiatives in indigenous communities.

By adopting an inclusive and culturally sensitive approach, microfinance in indigenous communities can make a positive impact, supporting economic development, preserving cultural heritage, and advancing social well-being.

3.29. Microfinance in Urban Slums:

Microfinance initiatives in urban slums address the unique financial challenges faced by residents, offering tailored solutions to promote economic growth and stability.

Microfinance in urban slums is a specialized approach aimed at promoting financial inclusion and empowering marginalized populations living in these areas. Similar to microfinance in indigenous communities, microfinance in urban slums faces unique challenges that require tailored solutions to address the specific needs of the population. Here's how microfinance in urban slums typically works:

3.29.1. Targeted Financial Services:

Microfinance institutions design financial products and services that cater to the needs of residents in urban slums. These services may include small loans, savings accounts, insurance, and other financial tools that help them manage their finances effectively.

3.29.2. Flexible Repayment Options:

Recognizing the irregular income streams of residents in urban slums, microfinance programs often provide flexible repayment options, allowing borrowers to make small and frequent payments.

3.29.3. Social Collateral:

In situations where traditional collateral is difficult to obtain, microfinance initiatives in urban slums may rely on social collateral, where borrowers come together to vouch for each other, fostering a sense of community responsibility.

3.29.4. Skill Development and Training:

Microfinance programs often complement financial services with skill development and training programs, equipping individuals with the necessary skills to generate income and become economically self-sufficient.

3.29.5. Entrepreneurship Support:

Microfinance in urban slums may also provide support for starting small businesses or income-generating activities, helping individuals escape poverty and improve their living conditions.

3.29.A. Benefits of Microfinance in Urban Slums:

3.29.A.1. Economic Empowerment: Microfinance helps residents in urban slums gain access to financial resources, enabling them to start businesses, invest in education, and improve their livelihoods.

3.29.A.2. Poverty Reduction: By providing financial tools and opportunities, microfinance contributes to poverty reduction in urban slums, breaking the cycle of poverty and improving overall living standards.

3.29.A.3. Community Development: Microfinance initiatives foster community development, as they often encourage cooperation and social cohesion among residents.

3.29.A.4. Women's Empowerment: Microfinance has shown to be particularly empowering for women in urban slums, offering them opportunities for entrepreneurship and financial independence.

3.29.A.5. Investment in Human Capital: With skill development and training, microfinance programs invest in the human capital of individuals, enhancing their employability and income prospects.

3.29.B. Challenges in Microfinance in Urban Slums:

3.29.B.1. High Risk: Urban slums often face higher economic and social risks, which can pose challenges in loan recovery and program sustainability.

3.29.B.2. Limited Access to Formal Institutions: Residents of urban slums may have limited access to formal financial institutions, making it crucial to establish trust and awareness about microfinance options.

3.29.B.3. Informal Financial Practices: Informal financial practices prevalent in urban slums may compete with formal microfinance programs, requiring efforts to integrate and promote the benefits of formal financial services.

3.29.B.4. Urbanization and Mobility: The transient nature of urban slum populations due to urbanization and mobility can impact the continuity of microfinance relationships and operations.

By addressing these challenges and adopting a community-driven approach, microfinance can create a positive impact in urban slums, contributing to economic empowerment, poverty reduction, and overall community development.

3.30. Bank Rakyat Indonesia (BRI):

Bank Rakyat Indonesia (BRI) is one of the largest banks in Indonesia. It provides a wide range of banking services, including savings accounts, loans, credit cards, and various financial products.

Bank Rakyat Indonesia (BRI) is also involved in microfinance, which is the provision of financial services to low-income individuals or microenterprises. BRI has been actively supporting microfinance initiatives in Indonesia, offering microloans, savings accounts, and other financial services tailored to the needs of small-scale entrepreneurs and those with limited access to traditional banking services. Microfinance plays a crucial role in promoting financial inclusion and empowering individuals in the informal sector to improve their livelihoods and businesses.

Bank Rakyat Indonesia (BRI) is a prominent Indonesian bank that has been actively involved in microfinance initiatives. BRI is known for its commitment to financial inclusion and has played a crucial role in providing microfinance services to underserved and marginalized communities in Indonesia, particularly in rural areas.

3.30.A. Microfinance at BRI typically involves the following key features:

3.30.A.1. Focus on Small Borrowers: BRI's microfinance programs primarily target small borrowers, including micro-entrepreneurs, farmers, and individuals with limited access to formal financial services.

3.30.A.2. Microcredit Services: BRI offers microcredit services, providing small loans to borrowers to support their income-generating activities and small businesses.

3.30.A.3. Group Lending Approach: BRI often employs a group lending approach, where borrowers are organized into small groups. The group members act as mutual guarantors, encouraging collective responsibility for loan repayments.

3.30.A.4. Rural Outreach: BRI has a strong rural outreach, establishing branches and microfinance units in remote areas, making financial services accessible to rural communities.

3.30.A.5. Financial Education and Capacity Building: BRI's microfinance initiatives emphasize financial education and capacity building, empowering borrowers with the knowledge and skills to manage their finances effectively.

3.30.B. Benefits of BRI's Microfinance:

3.30.B.1. Financial Inclusion: BRI's microfinance initiatives have significantly contributed to increasing financial inclusion in Indonesia by reaching out to underserved populations.

3.30.B.2. Poverty Alleviation: By providing access to credit and financial resources, BRI's microfinance has helped lift people out of poverty and improve their economic prospects.

3.30.B.3. Employment Generation: Microcredit from BRI has supported the establishment and expansion of small businesses, leading to employment generation and economic growth.

3.30.B.4. Empowerment of Women: BRI's microfinance programs have been instrumental in empowering women in rural areas by offering them financial independence and opportunities for entrepreneurship.

3.30.B.5. Community Development: BRI's focus on rural outreach and community-based lending has fostered community development, encouraging cooperation and economic growth in rural areas.

BRI's commitment to microfinance aligns with Indonesia's national goal of promoting financial inclusion and economic development, particularly in rural and underserved areas. Through its microfinance initiatives, BRI continues to play a significant role in improving the livelihoods of marginalized communities and contributing to the country's overall socio-economic progress.

3.30.C. Individual landing model of Indonesia in microfinance:

There was no widely recognized or commonly known microfinance model specifically referred to as the "Individual Landing Model" in Indonesia or elsewhere.

However, it's possible that there might be a specific microfinance program or initiative in Indonesia that follows a model emphasizing individual lending. In general microfinance practices, individual lending refers to the provision of financial services directly to individual borrowers rather than through group-based lending models like the Grameen Bank model.

In an individual lending model, borrowers are assessed and granted loans based on their individual creditworthiness and capacity to repay. This approach allows for more personalized financial services and may be suitable for borrowers who do not wish to be part of a group-based lending program.

3.30.D. The Group Model of Microfinance in Kenya and Indonesia:

The Group Model of Microfinance is a widely utilized approach in both Kenya and Indonesia, and it is commonly associated with the Grameen Bank's model of microfinance. Here's an overview of how the Group Model works in each country:

3.30.D.A. Group Model of Microfinance in Kenya:

In Kenya, the Group Model of Microfinance is often referred to as the "Chama" system. A Chama is a self-help group where members come together to pool their savings, contribute regularly, and receive loans from the accumulated savings. Chamas is typically formed by individuals with common interests or from the same community and have similar socio-economic backgrounds.

3.30. D.B. Key features of the Group Model in Kenya include:

3.30.D.B.1. Group Formation: Members voluntarily form Chamas and contribute a fixed amount of money regularly, which creates a common fund.

3.30.D.B.2. Rotating Savings and Credit: Chamas operate on a rotating savings and credit basis. Each member receives a lump sum loan from the collective savings during a specific period, and this rotation continues until all members have received their share.

3.30.D.B.3. Social Support: The Chama system fosters a sense of community and mutual support among members, who often participate in decision-making and collectively address members' financial needs.

3.30.D.B.4. Financial Discipline: Chama members are encouraged to save regularly, enhancing financial discipline and promoting responsible financial behavior.

3.30.D.C. Group Model of Microfinance in Indonesia:

In Indonesia, the Group Model of Microfinance is implemented through a concept called "Arisan" or "Kelompok Usaha Bersama" (KUBE). Arisan is a traditional community-based savings and lending system, while KUBE is a more structured approach introduced by the Indonesian government to support micro and small-scale enterprises.

3.30.D.C.A. Key features of the Group Model in Indonesia include:

3.30.D.C.A.1. Group Formation: In Arisan, community members form groups and contribute regular savings, which are then given to one member at each meeting, usually through a lottery system. KUBE groups are organized by the government or non-governmental organizations (NGOs) to support entrepreneurship and income-generating activities.

3.30.D.C.A.2. Social Cohesion: Both Arisan and KUBE foster a sense of community, mutual trust, and cooperation among members.

3.30.D.C.A.3. Income-Generating Activities: KUBE groups often focus on promoting income-generating activities and small-scale businesses, providing financial support and capacity-building programs to their members.

Both the Group Model of Microfinance in Kenya and Indonesia emphasize the importance of social capital, community involvement, and collective responsibility. These models have been successful in enhancing financial inclusion, supporting small businesses, and improving the socio-economic conditions of their members.

3.31. Bank Pertanian Malaysia:

Bank Pertanian Malaysia, also known as Agrobank, is an agricultural development bank in Malaysia. The bank offers a range of financial products and services to the agricultural and agro-based sectors, including farming, livestock, aquaculture, and agro-businesses. Agrobank aims to support the growth and development of the agricultural and agro-industry to increase income and improve the livelihoods of farmers and business operators in this sector. Additionally, Agrobank is also involved in microfinance, providing financial services tailored to the needs of small-scale entrepreneurs and individuals with limited access to conventional banking services. Its microfinance initiatives help promote entrepreneurship in the agricultural, aquaculture, and agro-business sectors while supporting rural development and enhancing the living standards of communities.

There are many financial institutions in Malaysia, including commercial banks, government-linked banks, and microfinance institutions, have been involved in promoting financial inclusion and microfinance services in the country.

Various microfinance programs and initiatives have been implemented in Malaysia to provide financial services and support to underserved and low-income individuals, including small business owners, farmers, and entrepreneurs. These programs often include microcredit, microinsurance, and financial literacy training to empower individuals economically and improve their livelihoods.

3.32. The Bank for Agriculture and Agricultural Cooperatives (BAAC):

The Bank for Agriculture and Agricultural Cooperatives (BAAC) is a specialized financial institution in Thailand. It serves as the main bank providing financial services to farmers, agricultural cooperatives, and related agricultural businesses in the country. BAAC offers a range of banking services, including agricultural loans, savings accounts, insurance, and other financial products tailored to the needs of the agricultural sector.

Established in 1966, BAAC's primary objective is to support and promote the development of agriculture and rural communities in Thailand. It plays a crucial role in enhancing the livelihoods of farmers, facilitating agricultural activities, and contributing to the overall growth and stability of the agricultural sector in the country.

In microfinance, the Bank for Agriculture and Agricultural Cooperatives (BAAC) in Thailand plays a significant role. BAAC provides microfinance services to small-scale farmers, agricultural workers, and rural entrepreneurs. These microfinance services are tailored to meet the specific financial needs of individuals and groups in the agricultural sector.

Through microfinance initiatives, BAAC offers small loans, savings accounts, and other financial products to support agricultural activities and rural development. By providing access to financial resources, BAAC empowers farmers and rural communities, enabling them to improve their livelihoods and invest in their agricultural businesses.

BAAC's microfinance programs also promote financial inclusion, allowing individuals and communities with limited access to traditional banking services to participate in economic activities and contribute to the growth of the agricultural sector in Thailand. Overall, microfinance offered by

BAAC plays a crucial role in supporting sustainable agriculture and rural development in the country.

The Bank for Agriculture and Agricultural Cooperatives (BAAC) is a specialized financial institution in Thailand that plays a significant role in supporting agricultural development and rural communities. BAAC is known for its involvement in providing microfinance services to small-scale farmers, agricultural cooperatives, and rural entrepreneurs. The bank's microfinance initiatives aim to promote financial inclusion, improve livelihoods, and enhance economic activities in rural areas of Thailand.

3.32.A. Key features of BAAC's microfinance programs include:

3.32.A.1. Targeted Agricultural Focus: BAAC's microfinance programs primarily target individuals and groups involved in agriculture-related activities, such as farmers, fishers, and agricultural cooperatives.

3.32.A.2. Tailored Financial Products: The bank designs tailored financial products to meet the specific needs of its clients, including microcredit, agricultural loans, savings accounts, and other financial services.

3.32.A.3. Group Lending Approach: Similar to other successful microfinance models, BAAC often adopts a group lending approach. Borrowers are organized into small groups, and members provide mutual support and guarantee for loan repayments.

3.32.A.4. Technical Assistance and Training: BAAC provides technical assistance, training, and financial education to its clients. This helps improve their financial management skills and enhances their productivity and income-generation potential.

3.32.A.5. Focus on Rural Outreach: BAAC has a strong rural outreach, with branches and service points in remote areas. This ensures that financial services are accessible to farmers and rural communities.

3.32.B. Benefits of BAAC's Microfinance:

3.32.B. 1. Financial Inclusion: BAAC's microfinance programs have contributed to increased financial inclusion in rural areas of Thailand, where access to formal financial services can be limited.

3.32.B. 2. Agricultural Development: By providing financial resources and support to farmers and agricultural cooperatives, BAAC's microfinance initiatives play a crucial role in agricultural development and rural economy enhancement.

3.32.B. 3. Poverty Reduction: Access to microcredit and financial services helps rural communities improve their livelihoods and reduce poverty, as they can invest in their businesses and agricultural activities.

3.32.B. 4. Empowerment of Farmers and Entrepreneurs: BAAC's microfinance empowers small-scale farmers and rural entrepreneurs, giving them the means to control their economic destinies and build a more secure future.

3.32.B. 5. Social and Economic Development: BAAC's focus on rural areas and agricultural activities contributes to social and economic development in these regions, fostering sustainable growth and prosperity.

BAAC's microfinance initiatives have been instrumental in supporting Thailand's agricultural sector, promoting financial inclusion, and uplifting rural communities by providing them with access to essential financial services and resources.

3.33. Village Banking Model of Microfinance in Bolivia and Thailand:

The Village Banking Model of Microfinance, also known as Village Savings and Loan Associations (VSLAs), is a community-based approach to microfinance that has been implemented in various countries, including Bolivia and Thailand. Here's an overview of how the Village Banking Model works in each country:

3.33.A. Village Banking Model of Microfinance in Bolivia:

In Bolivia, the Village Banking Model operates through VSLAs, which are community-based savings and credit groups. VSLAs are formed by individuals within a community who come together to save money regularly and access loans from the accumulated savings. These groups are often facilitated and supported by local NGOs or microfinance institutions.

3.33.B. Key features of the Village Banking Model in Bolivia include:

3.33.B.1. Group Formation: Community members voluntarily form VSLAs, with each member contributing a fixed amount of money during regular meetings.

3.33.B.2. Savings and Loan Activities: VSLAs focus on mobilizing savings from their members, and these savings serve as the primary source for providing small loans to group members.

3.33.B.3. Rotating Funds: The accumulated savings are used to provide loans to individual members on a rotating basis. As members repay their loans, the funds are made available to other members.

3.33.B.4. Financial Inclusion: The Village Banking Model aims to reach unbanked or underbanked individuals who lack access to formal financial services.

3.33.C. Village Banking Model of Microfinance in Thailand:

In Thailand, the Village Banking Model is referred to as "Savings Groups" or "Community-Based Microfinance." Similar to VSLAs, Savings Groups are community-based financial groups where members contribute savings regularly and access small loans from the group's funds.

3.33.C.A. Key features of the Village Banking Model in Thailand include:

3.33.C.A.1. Group Formation: Savings Groups are formed by community members with similar socio-economic backgrounds and interests, often with the support of local NGOs or microfinance institutions.

3.33.C.A.2. Savings and Credit Services: Members contribute regular savings, and the accumulated funds are used to provide small loans to group members at affordable interest rates.

3.33.C.A.3. Capacity Building: Along with financial services, Savings Groups often receive training and capacity-building support to improve financial literacy and business skills.

3.33.C.A.4. Community Empowerment: The Village Banking Model in Thailand emphasizes community empowerment, social cohesion, and collective decision-making.

Both the Village Banking Models in Bolivia and Thailand have shown success in promoting financial inclusion, improving livelihoods, and empowering communities through community-driven financial services. These models have proved effective in reaching underserved populations and supporting income-generating activities at the grassroots level.

3.34. Amanah Ikhtiar malaysia (AIM) of Malaysia:

Amanah Ikhtiar Malaysia (AIM) is a microcredit organization in Malaysia that provides financial assistance and support to low-income individuals and small-scale entrepreneurs. AIM aims to uplift the socio-economic status of its beneficiaries by offering microloans, training, and capacity-building programs. It has played a significant role in promoting financial inclusion and empowering marginalized communities in Malaysia.

Amanah Ikhtiar Malaysia (AIM) is a prominent microfinance institution in Malaysia. Microfinance refers to the provision of financial services, such as small loans, savings accounts, insurance, and financial education, to low-income individuals and small businesses that lack access to traditional banking services.

AIM's main focus is on providing microcredit to empower low-income communities, especially women, by supporting their entrepreneurial ventures and income-generating activities. By offering financial resources and capacity-building programs, AIM helps these individuals and communities break the cycle of poverty, improve their livelihoods, and contribute to local economic development.

Microfinance institutions like AIM play a crucial role in promoting financial inclusion, supporting small-scale businesses, and fostering economic growth, particularly in underserved and marginalized areas. Their efforts have a positive impact on reducing poverty, increasing employment opportunities, and empowering individuals to build a better future for themselves and their families.

These additional microfinance models illustrate the versatility and adaptability of microfinance in addressing various social and economic challenges faced by different communities worldwide. The overarching goal remains to enhance financial inclusion, promote sustainable development, and empower individuals and communities to improve their lives.

3.35. Agriculture development bank of Nepal:

The Agriculture Development Bank of Nepal (ADBN) is a state-owned development bank that primarily focuses on providing financial services to support agricultural development in Nepal. It was established in 1968 with the objective of promoting and enhancing the agricultural sector by offering various financial products and services to farmers, agribusinesses, and rural communities.

ADBN plays a vital role in providing credit facilities to farmers and agriculturists, helping them with agricultural inputs, modern farming technologies, and machinery. The bank also offers loans for rural infrastructure development and other income-generating activities related to agriculture.

Apart from credit facilities, the Agriculture Development Bank of Nepal also engages in capacity-building activities, technical assistance, and advisory services to support farmers and entrepreneurs in the agricultural sector. Its mission is to contribute to the overall development of Nepal by strengthening the agricultural base, improving rural livelihoods, and boosting the country's economy.

3.35.A. Agriculture development bank of Nepal and microfinance:

The Agriculture Development Bank of Nepal (ADBN) and microfinance institutions serve different but complementary roles in supporting agriculture and rural development in Nepal.

The Agriculture Development Bank of Nepal is a government-owned development bank that focuses on providing financial services and credit facilities to support the growth and development of the agricultural sector. It offers loans to farmers, agribusinesses, and rural communities for agricultural inputs, modern farming technologies, machinery, and other agricultural activities. The bank's mission is to promote and strengthen the agricultural base, improve rural livelihoods, and contribute to the overall economic development of the country.

On the other hand, microfinance institutions (MFIs) are specialized financial institutions that provide financial services to low-income individuals, especially those in rural areas, who lack access to traditional banking services. These services typically include small loans, savings accounts, insurance, and financial education. MFIs play a vital role in promoting financial inclusion, empowering the rural poor, and supporting small-scale businesses and income-generating activities in underserved communities.

While ADBN primarily focuses on larger-scale agricultural projects and initiatives, microfinance institutions target the grassroots level and cater to the financial needs of small farmers, rural entrepreneurs, and marginalized communities. Both institutions contribute to rural development, poverty reduction, and economic growth in Nepal, albeit with different approaches and target beneficiaries.

3.36. SHG model in South, East, and South Asia, including Indian Geographical Region, in Microfinance:

The Self-Help Group (SHG) model is a prominent microfinance approach that has been widely implemented in various regions, including South, East, and South Asia, with a particular focus on the Indian Geographical Region. The SHG model involves organizing groups of individuals, typically women, from similar socio-economic backgrounds into self-managed groups. These groups pool their savings and access microloans from their collective savings to meet their financial needs.

South Asia, especially India, has seen extensive implementation of the SHG model. The National Bank for Agriculture and Rural Development (NABARD) in India played a crucial role in promoting and supporting SHGs by providing financial assistance and capacity-building initiatives. SHGs have been successful in empowering women, enhancing their decision-making abilities, and improving their economic conditions.

In East Asia, countries like Bangladesh have also adopted the SHG model to address poverty and promote rural development. The Grameen Bank, founded by Muhammad Yunus, is a famous example of a microfinance institution that utilizes the SHG approach to empower rural communities, especially women, through access to microcredit.

In South Asia, Nepal has also embraced the SHG model, utilizing it to promote financial inclusion and rural development. The model has been successful in fostering entrepreneurship, improving livelihoods, and building social capital within communities.

The SHG model has proven to be an effective and sustainable approach to microfinance, particularly in the South, East, and South Asian regions, where it has played a vital role in promoting financial inclusion, poverty reduction, and women's empowerment.

3.37. ROSCAs modal of microfinance in Philippines:

ROSCAs, which stands for Rotating Savings and Credit Associations, are informal microfinance models that have been utilized in various countries, including the Philippines. ROSCAs are community-based financial arrangements where a group of individuals come together and agree to save and contribute a fixed amount of money regularly. The accumulated savings are then given as a lump sum to one member of the group, on a rotational basis, until each member has received their share.

3.37.A. Key features of ROSCAs in the context of microfinance in the Philippines include:

3.37.A.1. Informal Structure: ROSCAs are typically informal and community-driven, with members trusting each other and operating without formal legal documentation.

3.37.A.2. Social Capital: These arrangements rely on strong social ties and trust among members, as there is no collateral or formal paperwork involved.

3.37.A.3. Limited Interest: ROSCAs do not charge interest on the savings contributed by members, making them different from formal lending institutions.

3.37.A.4. Regular Contributions: Members contribute a fixed amount regularly, usually weekly or monthly, which creates a pool of funds available for distribution.

3.37.A.5. Lump Sum Distribution: The lump sum of savings is given to a different member in each cycle, allowing them to use it for their needs, including starting or expanding businesses.

ROSCAs play a crucial role in providing access to finance for individuals who may not have access to formal banking services or microfinance institutions. They serve as a safety net for emergencies and help support small businesses and income-generating activities in the community.

While ROSCAs can be beneficial, there are also challenges such as limited scalability and a lack of formal financial services, which can be addressed through the integration of formal microfinance institutions or digital financial solutions in the future.

3.38. Credit Union and Co-operative Sri Lanka in microfinance:

3.38.A. Credit Unions in Microfinance, Sri Lanka:

In Sri Lanka, credit unions are known as "Thrift and Credit Cooperative Societies" (TCCS). These credit unions are member-owned financial cooperatives that aim to promote thrift, savings, and provide credit facilities to their members. Credit unions in Sri Lanka are often community-based and focus on providing financial services to individuals in rural and underserved areas.

Key characteristics of credit unions in microfinance in Sri Lanka include:

3.38.A.1. Member Ownership: Credit unions are owned and governed by their members, who have equal voting rights in the decision-making process.

3.38.A.2. Savings and Credit Services: Members pool their savings, and these funds are used to provide loans to other members at competitive interest rates.

3.38.A.3. Financial Inclusion: Credit unions play a crucial role in extending financial services to individuals who may not have access to formal banking institutions.

3.38.A.4. Cooperative Principles: Credit unions operate based on cooperative principles such as voluntary membership, democratic control, and member participation.

3.38.B. Cooperatives in Microfinance, Sri Lanka:

Apart from credit unions, cooperatives in Sri Lanka also contribute to microfinance efforts. Cooperatives are member-owned and member-governed organizations that aim to provide various services, including savings, credit, insurance, and marketing support to their members.

3.38.C. Key characteristics of cooperatives in microfinance in Sri Lanka include:

3.38.C.1. Diverse Services: Cooperatives offer a range of services beyond credit, including agricultural support, marketing assistance, and other community-based initiatives.

3.38.C.2. Cooperative Principles: Cooperatives adhere to cooperative principles, fostering a sense of community, mutual support, and equitable benefits among members.

3.38.C.3. Sector-Specific Focus: Some cooperatives in Sri Lanka cater to specific sectors such as agriculture, helping farmers with credit and agricultural support.

3.38.C.4. Sustainable Development: Cooperatives aim for sustainable development, focusing on the long-term well-being of their members and communities.

Credit unions and cooperatives in Sri Lanka play pivotal roles in promoting financial inclusion, supporting small-scale businesses, and empowering rural communities. Their community-driven and member-focused approach contributes to poverty reduction and socio-economic development in the country.

All these additional models reflect the diverse approaches used to address financial inclusion challenges across the world. Each model brings unique benefits and opportunities for empowering marginalized populations and fostering economic development at the grassroots level.

Chapter - 4

Delivery Methodologies of Microfinance

4.1. Finance delivery methodologies refer to the processes and approaches used to manage financial operations and provide financial services within an organization. Some common finance delivery methodologies include:

1. Traditional Financial Management: This involves manual processes for accounting, budgeting, and financial reporting.

2. Enterprise Resource Planning (ERP) Systems: Utilizing integrated software solutions to streamline financial processes and data management.

3. Cloud-Based Finance Solutions: Leveraging cloud technology to access financial data and tools remotely, enhancing flexibility and scalability.

4. Agile Finance: Applying agile principles to financial operations, allowing for faster decision-making and adaptation to changing market conditions.

5. Lean Finance: Focusing on eliminating waste and improving efficiency in financial processes.

6. Robotic Process Automation (RPA): Using software robots to automate repetitive finance tasks, reducing human effort and potential errors.

7. Blockchain in Finance: Exploring blockchain technology for secure and transparent financial transactions.

Each methodology has its advantages and is suitable for different organizations based on their size, complexity, and goals. It's essential to choose the right approach to ensure effective financial management.

4.2. Objective of microfinance delivery methodologies:

The objective of microfinance delivery methodologies is to provide financial services and support to low-income individuals and small businesses who lack access to traditional banking services. Microfinance aims to empower the underserved population by offering them access to small loans, savings accounts, insurance, and other financial products.

The key objectives of microfinance delivery methodologies include:

1. **Poverty Alleviation:** By providing financial resources, microfinance helps the poor and unbanked individuals to generate income, improve their livelihoods, and escape the cycle of poverty.

2. **Financial Inclusion:** Microfinance seeks to include marginalized and financially excluded individuals into the formal financial system, allowing them to save, borrow, and invest for their future needs.

3. **Empowerment:** Microfinance empowers borrowers, especially women, by giving them control over their financial resources and decision-making power within their households and communities.

4. **Small Business Growth:** Microfinance supports small businesses and entrepreneurs by providing them with the necessary capital to start or expand their ventures.

5. **Social Impact:** The ultimate goal of microfinance delivery methodologies is to create positive social impact by fostering economic development and reducing income inequality.

6. **Sustainability:** Microfinance institutions strive to maintain financial sustainability while delivering services to ensure their long-term viability and ability to support more clients over time.

Microfinance aims to create a positive social and economic impact by extending financial services to those who are excluded from the traditional banking system, enabling them to build a better future for themselves and their families.

4.3. Introduction of Microfinance Delivery Methodology:

Microfinance delivery methodology refers to the strategies and approaches used by financial institutions and organizations to provide microfinance services to low-income individuals, often referred to as "the unbanked" or "the underbanked." These individuals typically lack access to traditional banking services due to their limited financial resources and absence of collateral.

The introduction of microfinance delivery methodology can be traced back to the 1970s when pioneers like Muhammad Yunus and the Grameen Bank in Bangladesh began offering small loans to impoverished individuals to support their entrepreneurial activities and help them break free from the cycle of poverty.

4.4. The core elements of microfinance delivery methodologies include:

1. Client-Cantered Approach: Microfinance institutions focus on understanding the specific needs and financial circumstances of their clients to tailor services accordingly. This approach fosters trust and ensures that the offered products are relevant and accessible.

2. Group Lending: Microfinance often employs the concept of group lending, where individuals within a community form borrowing groups. These groups provide mutual support and shared responsibility for loan repayments, encouraging a higher repayment rate.

3. Small Loan Sizes: Microfinance loans are typically small in size to meet the modest financial requirements of the target beneficiaries. These loans are often used for income-generating activities or to finance basic needs.

4. Minimal Collateral Requirements: Microfinance institutions usually have flexible collateral requirements or no collateral at all. Instead, they rely on social collateral, group guarantees, and trust to ensure loan repayments.

5. Financial Education and Capacity Building: Microfinance institutions often provide financial literacy training and capacity-building programs to help clients manage their finances more effectively and improve their businesses' success.

6. Technology Integration: Many modern microfinance institutions use technology to streamline operations, reach a broader client base, and provide services through digital platforms and mobile banking.

Microfinance delivery methodologies have proven to be effective tools for poverty alleviation, financial inclusion, and empowerment, making a significant impact on the lives of millions of low-income individuals around the world. Over time, the microfinance sector has evolved, incorporating innovative practices and expanding its range of financial services to address the diverse needs of its clients.

4.5. Microfinance Delivery Methodologies:

Microfinance delivery methodologies encompass various strategies and models used by financial institutions and organizations to provide microfinance services to low-income individuals and small businesses. These methodologies are designed to address the unique challenges faced by the unbanked and underbanked population and to promote financial inclusion. Some common microfinance delivery methodologies include:

1. Group Lending Model: This model involves forming small borrower groups where members mutually guarantee each other's loans. The group's collective responsibility encourages timely repayments and provides social support.

2. Individual Lending Model: In this approach, microfinance institutions extend loans to individuals without the need for group formation. Each borrower is independently responsible for loan repayment.

3. **Self-Help Group (SHG) Model:** SHGs are community-based organizations where members save regularly, and the group can collectively access loans from the microfinance institution. This model emphasizes empowerment through community participation.

4. **Village Banking Model:** Village banking, also known as community banking, involves providing financial services to remote areas through a mobile banking agent or community-based center.

5. **Microfinance through Cooperatives:** Cooperatives act as intermediaries between the microfinance institution and the beneficiaries, pooling resources to offer financial services and other support to their members.

6. **Digital Microfinance:** Leveraging digital technology, such as mobile banking and online platforms, to reach underserved populations efficiently and cost-effectively.

7. **Microinsurance:** Providing insurance products tailored to the needs of low-income individuals and small businesses, protecting them from financial shocks.

8. **Micro savings:** Encouraging small savings deposits among low-income individuals to build financial resilience and access credit in the future.

9. **Micro leasing:** Offering microfinance in the form of leasing arrangements, enabling small businesses to acquire assets or equipment without a large upfront cost.

10. **Green Microfinance:** Focusing on financing environmentally sustainable projects and promoting eco-friendly practices among clients.

These microfinance delivery methodologies vary in their structure, target audience, and geographic reach. The success of microfinance lies in its ability to adapt to local contexts, promote financial literacy, and provide essential financial services that empower individuals and communities to improve their economic well-being.

4.6. Methodologies of Group Lending Model of Microfinance:

The Group Lending Model of microfinance is a widely used approach that involves forming small borrower groups, where members collectively guarantee each other's loans. This methodology fosters social cohesion and shared responsibility among the borrowers, promoting higher loan repayment rates and reducing the risk for the microfinance institution. Here are the key methodologies associated with the Group Lending Model:

1. Formation of Borrower Groups: The microfinance institution facilitates the formation of small borrower groups, typically consisting of 5 to 25 members. The group members often have some social ties within their community, such as living in the same locality or belonging to similar economic backgrounds.

2. Group Selection and Training: The microfinance institution selects the potential group members based on certain criteria, such as their creditworthiness and willingness to participate actively in the group. The selected members undergo training on financial literacy, loan terms, and group dynamics to ensure they understand their responsibilities and obligations.

3. Joint Liability: One of the essential features of the Group Lending Model is joint liability. Each group member is jointly liable for the entire group's loan. If one member defaults on their repayment, the other members are responsible for covering the shortfall to ensure full loan repayment.

4. Regular Meetings: The borrower group meets regularly, usually weekly or biweekly, to discuss loan utilization, savings, and upcoming repayments. These meetings create a sense of accountability and support among the group members.

5. Loan Disbursement: After forming the borrower group and conducting the necessary training, the microfinance institution disburses the loans to each member based on their individual needs and business plans. The loan amount is often small to meet their modest financial requirements.

6. Loan Utilization: Group members use their loans for various income-generating activities, such as starting or expanding small businesses, agriculture, or artisanal work.

7. Repayment Collection: Loan repayments are collected during the group meetings, which further strengthens the group's cohesion and ensures timely repayments.

8. Graduation Model: Some Group Lending programs include a graduation model, where successful borrowers who have demonstrated creditworthiness and financial discipline may become eligible for individual loans, offering them greater financial independence and flexibility.

Group Lending Model of microfinance emphasizes community-based support and accountability, making it an effective tool for financial inclusion and poverty alleviation among the unbanked and underbanked population.

4.7. Methodology of Individual Landing Model of Microfinance:

The Individual Lending Model of microfinance is an approach where microfinance institutions provide loans directly to individual borrowers without the need for forming borrower groups. In this methodology, each borrower is independently responsible for the loan repayment, and there is no joint liability as seen in the Group Lending Model. Here are the key methodologies associated with the Individual Lending Model:

1. Client Assessment: Microfinance institutions conduct a thorough assessment of each individual borrower's creditworthiness, repayment capacity, and business plans before approving the loan. This assessment helps in determining the loan amount and terms tailored to the specific needs of the borrower.

2. Collateral or Guarantees: In the Individual Lending Model, borrowers may be required to provide collateral or personal guarantees to secure the loan. Collateral could be in the form of assets or property, while guarantees involve a third party vouching for the borrower's repayment ability.

3. Loan Disbursement: Once the loan is approved, the microfinance institution disburses the loan amount directly to the borrower. The borrower can use the funds for various purposes, such as starting or expanding a business, investing in agriculture, or meeting personal needs.

4. Loan Repayment: Individual borrowers are responsible for making timely loan repayments according to the agreed-upon schedule. The repayment frequency could be weekly, bi-weekly, or monthly, depending on the borrower's cash flow and income sources.

5. Interest Rates and Fees: Microfinance institutions determine interest rates and any applicable fees based on the borrower's risk profile, prevailing market conditions, and the institution's financial sustainability.

6. Monitoring and Support: Microfinance institutions often provide ongoing support and monitoring to individual borrowers, assisting them with financial education, business development, and other services to improve their financial well-being.

7. Graduation Model: Similar to the Group Lending Model, some Individual Lending programs may include a graduation model, where successful borrowers who demonstrate creditworthiness and financial discipline may become eligible for larger loans or more favourable terms in the future.

The Individual Lending Model allows microfinance institutions to reach a diverse range of borrowers with unique financial needs and offers more flexibility compared to the Group Lending Model. However, it requires a robust credit assessment process to manage individual risk effectively and ensure sustainable loan performance.

4.8. Methodologies of SHG Self-Help Group Model of Microfinance:

The Self-Help Group (SHG) Model of microfinance is a community-based approach that empowers women and marginalized individuals by forming self-managed groups. These groups collectively save money and access loans from their savings, and in some cases, they receive support from external microfinance institutions. Here are the key methodologies associated with the SHG Self-Help Group Model:

1. **Formation of Self-Help Groups:** The SHG model starts with the formation of self-help groups, typically comprising 10 to 20 members from the same community or village. These groups are often homogenous in terms of socio-economic background and share common interests.

2. **Regular Savings:** SHG members contribute to regular savings during group meetings. These savings accumulate over time and form the collective savings pool of the group.

3. **Group Meetings and Decision-Making:** SHGs hold regular meetings, usually weekly or monthly, where members discuss financial matters, share their experiences, and collectively make decisions regarding savings, loans, and other group activities.

4. **Group Fund Management:** The accumulated savings in the SHG's common fund are managed by the group itself. The SHG may elect a committee to handle financial transactions and maintain records.

5. **Internal Lending:** SHGs provide internal loans to their members from the common fund based on their financial needs. Members can access these loans for various purposes, such as starting or expanding a business, meeting emergency expenses, or investing in education.

6. **Interest on Loans:** SHGs charge interest on the internal loans provided to their members. The interest rates are typically lower than those of traditional lenders, making borrowing more affordable for the group members.

7. Loan Repayment: Borrowers repay the internal loans to the SHG over a predetermined period. The group enforces peer pressure and social sanctions to ensure timely repayments.

8. External Support: In some cases, SHGs receive external support from microfinance institutions or non-governmental organizations (NGOs). This support may include capacity-building training, access to additional loans, or linkage to formal financial institutions.

9. Graduation Model: Successful SHGs that demonstrate strong financial management and discipline may eventually graduate to accessing formal financial services, including loans from banks or microfinance institutions.

The SHG Self-Help Group Model emphasizes women's empowerment and community-based financial inclusion. It provides a platform for women to pool their resources, support each other's economic activities, and collectively build their financial resilience and social capital. As SHGs become more self-reliant, they contribute to poverty reduction and social development in their communities.

4.9. Methodologies of Village Banking Model of Microfinance:

The Village Banking Model of microfinance, also known as the Community Banking Model, is an approach that aims to provide financial services to rural and remote areas through community-based centers or village banking agents. This model focuses on delivering microfinance services in areas where traditional banking institutions may not be accessible. Here are the key methodologies associated with the Village Banking Model:

1. Community-Based Centers: Microfinance institutions set up community-based centers or branches in villages or remote areas. These centers act as points of service delivery, providing financial services to the local population.

2. Village Banking Agents: In areas where establishing permanent centers may not be feasible, microfinance institutions appoint village banking agents who act as representatives and conduct financial transactions on behalf of the institution within the community.

3. Doorstep Services: The Village Banking Model emphasizes bringing financial services directly to the doorsteps of the clients. This convenience ensures that individuals, especially those with limited mobility, can easily access services like savings, loans, and insurance.

4. Savings Mobilization: Village banking centers and agents encourage community members to save regularly. Clients can deposit their savings at the centers or through the agents, promoting financial inclusion and building a savings culture within the community.

5. Credit Delivery: The Village Banking Model offers small loans to individuals and small businesses within the community. These loans are typically used for income-generating activities and are tailored to meet the specific needs of the borrowers.

6. Flexible Loan Terms: The model often offers flexible loan terms, such as affordable interest rates and customized repayment schedules, to accommodate the irregular income patterns of rural borrowers.

7. Financial Literacy: The Village Banking Model emphasizes financial education and literacy programs to improve the financial knowledge and capabilities of the community members.

8. Group Dynamics: In some variations of the model, the concept of peer support and group dynamics is incorporated, similar to the Group Lending Model. This fosters accountability and helps in ensuring timely loan repayments.

9. Leveraging Technology: In recent years, the Village Banking Model has been enhanced through the integration of digital technology. Mobile banking and agent networks enable easier and more efficient delivery of financial services in remote areas.

The Village Banking Model plays a crucial role in extending financial services to underserved rural communities, contributing to poverty reduction, economic development, and improved livelihoods in remote regions.

4.10. Methodology of microfinance through co-operatives:

Microfinance through cooperatives is an approach that involves providing financial services and support to individuals and small businesses through cooperative societies. In this model, cooperatives act as intermediaries between the microfinance institution and the beneficiaries, pooling resources to offer financial products and services. Here are the key methodologies associated with microfinance through cooperatives:

1. **Formation of Cooperatives:** The process begins with the formation of cooperative societies, where individuals or businesses voluntarily come together to pool their financial resources and support each other's economic activities.

2. **Membership and Governance:** Cooperatives have members who actively participate in decision-making and governance. Each member typically has equal voting rights, promoting democratic and inclusive decision-making processes.

3. **Savings Mobilization:** Cooperatives encourage their members to save regularly. These savings form the collective pool of funds that the cooperative can use to offer loans and other financial services to its members.

4. **Loan Provision:** Microfinance institutions collaborate with cooperatives to provide loans to individual members or small businesses within the cooperative. The cooperative acts as an intermediary in the loan disbursal process.

5. **Collateral and Guarantees:** Cooperatives may provide collateral or guarantees on behalf of their members, reducing the risk for the microfinance institution and making loans more accessible to individuals without significant assets.

6. Loan Repayment: Members repay the loans to the cooperative, which, in turn, ensures timely repayments to the microfinance institution. The cooperative enforces peer pressure and social norms to promote loan repayment discipline.

7. Interest Rates and Fees: Cooperatives determine interest rates and fees for their members' loans based on the prevailing market conditions and the financial sustainability of the cooperative.

8. Financial Inclusion and Social Impact: Microfinance through cooperatives contributes to financial inclusion by reaching marginalized and underserved communities. It also fosters social impact by promoting cooperation, community development, and mutual support.

9. Capacity Building: Cooperatives may offer capacity-building programs and training to their members, enhancing financial literacy, business skills, and entrepreneurial capabilities.

10. Profit-Sharing and Surplus Distribution: Cooperatives often operate on a not-for-profit basis, and any surplus generated from interest income or other sources is distributed back to the members in the form of dividends or reinvested in the cooperative's activities.

Microfinance through cooperatives leverages the strengths of cooperative societies to deliver financial services and promote socio-economic development within communities. This approach allows for more personalized and community-focused financial solutions, fostering a sense of ownership and empowerment among the members.

4.11. Methodologies of Digital Microfinance:

Digital Microfinance is a modern approach that utilizes digital technology to deliver financial services and products to the unbanked and underbanked population. It leverages mobile banking, online platforms, and other digital tools to extend financial inclusion and reach a broader client base efficiently. Here are the key methodologies associated with Digital Microfinance:

1. **Mobile Banking:** Digital Microfinance enables individuals to access financial services through their mobile phones. Mobile banking apps or USSD (Unstructured Supplementary Service Data) codes allow users to perform various financial transactions, such as deposits, withdrawals, transfers, and loan repayments.

2. **Agent Banking:** Digital Microfinance often employs a network of banking agents who act as intermediaries to facilitate financial transactions in remote or underserved areas. These agents use mobile devices to provide financial services to customers who may not have direct access to brick-and-mortar bank branches.

3. **Online Platforms:** Digital Microfinance institutions offer online platforms where individuals can apply for loans, open savings accounts, and access other financial products without the need for physical visits to a branch.

4. **Digital Identification:** To overcome traditional Know Your Customer (KYC) challenges, digital microfinance may utilize biometric identification and other digital authentication methods to verify the identity of customers, allowing for faster and more secure onboarding.

5. **Big Data and Credit Scoring:** Digital Microfinance institutions often leverage big data and alternative credit scoring methods to assess creditworthiness, especially for individuals with limited or no formal credit history.

6. **E-Wallets:** Digital Microfinance facilitates the use of e-wallets, allowing customers to store and manage their funds digitally, make payments, and conduct transactions with ease.

7. **Instant Disbursement:** With digital channels, loans can be disbursed instantly to eligible customers, reducing processing time and enhancing customer convenience.

8. **Financial Education:** Digital Microfinance institutions may offer financial literacy training and educational content through digital platforms to empower customers with better financial management skills.

9. Remote Customer Support: Digital Microfinance provides remote customer support through online chat, email, or helplines, assisting customers with their queries and concerns.

10. Integration with Digital Ecosystem: Some Digital Microfinance providers integrate with other digital ecosystems, such as e-commerce platforms and utility bill payment systems, to offer a seamless and comprehensive financial experience for their customers.

Digital Microfinance has significantly transformed the microfinance landscape, increasing accessibility, efficiency, and convenience for clients, while also reducing operational costs for the microfinance institutions. This innovative approach continues to play a crucial role in advancing financial inclusion and economic development worldwide.

4.12. Methodologies of Microinsurance:

Microinsurance is a specialized form of insurance designed to cater to the needs of low-income individuals and vulnerable communities. It provides affordable insurance coverage against specific risks, offering financial protection and security. The methodologies of microinsurance include:

1. Product Customization: Microinsurance products are tailored to the specific needs and risks faced by low-income individuals and communities. The coverage may include life insurance, health insurance, crop insurance, property insurance, and other relevant coverage options.

2. Simplified Products: Microinsurance policies are designed to be simple and easy to understand, as many potential policyholders may have limited financial literacy. This ensures that beneficiaries comprehend the terms and conditions of the insurance coverage.

3. Low Premiums: Microinsurance policies have affordable premiums to make them accessible to low-income clients. The premiums are usually smaller than traditional insurance policies, reflecting the limited financial capacity of the target market.

4. Group Policies: Microinsurance often adopts a group-based approach, where a group of individuals or families collectively purchases insurance coverage. This approach helps spread the risk and lower the cost per individual.

5. Distribution Channels: Microinsurance utilizes various distribution channels to reach the target market effectively. These channels may include microfinance institutions, community-based organizations, mobile network operators, and agent networks.

6. Use of Technology: Digital technology, such as mobile phones and mobile money platforms, is leveraged for premium collection, claims processing, and policy administration. This enhances efficiency and reduces administrative costs.

7. **Low-Value Claims Processing:** Microinsurance focuses on efficiently processing low-value claims, ensuring quick payouts to policyholders in times of need.

8. Capacity Building: Microinsurance providers offer capacity-building initiatives and financial education to policyholders to help them understand the benefits and proper usage of insurance.

9. Partnerships and Reinsurance: Microinsurance providers often collaborate with larger insurance companies and reinsurers to manage risk effectively and ensure financial stability.

10. Social and Impact Measurement: Microinsurance providers may assess the social impact of their policies, evaluating the extent to which the insurance coverage contributes to the well-being and resilience of the insured population.

Microinsurance plays a crucial role in safeguarding the economic and social welfare of vulnerable communities, protecting them from unforeseen risks and reducing the financial burden during difficult times. The methodologies of microinsurance are continuously evolving to better serve the needs of low-income individuals and promote financial inclusion.

4.13. Methodology of Micro savings:

Micro savings is a financial service designed to encourage small-scale savings among low-income individuals, enabling them to build financial resilience and improve their economic well-being. The methodology of micro savings includes the following key elements:

1. **Low Minimum Deposit:** Micro savings accounts have low or no minimum deposit requirements, making it accessible to individuals with limited financial resources. This allows even those with modest incomes to open and maintain an account.

2. **No or Low Account Maintenance Fees:** Micro savings accounts typically have minimal or no account maintenance fees, ensuring affordability for the target clientele.

3. **Flexible Deposit Frequency:** Micro savings accounts offer flexibility in deposit frequency. Clients can make regular contributions to their accounts based on their cash flow and financial capacity.

4. **Passbook or Mobile-Based Accounts:** Micro savings accounts may be managed using a physical passbook or through mobile-based platforms. Mobile-based accounts provide convenience and accessibility, especially for individuals without easy access to physical bank branches.

5. **Group-Based Savings:** Some micro savings programs adopt group-based savings approaches, where individuals join savings groups and contribute regularly. These groups provide social support and encourage consistent savings behaviour.

6. **Financial Education:** Micro savings initiatives often incorporate financial literacy training to educate clients on the benefits of saving, budgeting, and building financial goals.

7. **Encouraging Goal-Based Savings:** Micro savings programs may promote goal-based savings, encouraging clients to save for specific purposes, such as education, healthcare, or business expansion.

8. Cash Collection Points: To enhance accessibility, micro savings programs may establish cash collection points in communities or partner with local agents to facilitate deposits and withdrawals.

9. Safe and Secure Deposits: micro savings institutions prioritize safety and security, ensuring that clients' deposits are protected and insured, if possible.

10. Incentives and Rewards: Some micro savings programs offer incentives and rewards to encourage regular savings behaviour. These may include matching contributions, interest bonuses, or loyalty programs.

micro savings play a vital role in promoting financial inclusion and empowering low-income individuals by providing them with a safe and accessible means to save and accumulate assets. This financial service contributes to poverty reduction and helps individuals achieve their financial goals and aspirations.

4.14. The Methodology of Micro leasing:

The methodology of Micro leasing, also known as microfinance leasing or asset-based microfinance, involves providing microfinance in the form of leasing arrangements to small businesses and individuals with limited access to traditional credit. Micro leasing allows clients to acquire essential assets and equipment needed for their businesses without the need for significant upfront capital. The key elements of the micro leasing methodology include:

1. Asset Identification: Microleasing providers identify income-generating assets and equipment that are essential for the target clients' businesses. These assets may include machinery, vehicles, agricultural equipment, computers, and other productive assets.

2. Credit Assessment: Micro leasing institutions evaluate the creditworthiness of potential clients based on their business plans, cash flow, and ability to generate income from the leased assets. Collateral requirements may be less stringent compared to traditional lending.

3. Lease Agreement: Upon approval, the micro leasing institution enters into a lease agreement with the client. The agreement outlines the terms of the lease, including the duration, lease payments, and the transfer of ownership at the end of the lease term.

4. Affordable Payments: Micro leasing payments are structured to be affordable for the clients, taking into consideration their cash flow and income patterns. Lease payments are typically made on a regular basis, such as monthly or quarterly.

5. Ownership Transfer: Micro leasing arrangements often provide the option for the client to purchase the asset at the end of the lease term. This transfer of ownership is usually done at a nominal price or a pre-agreed residual value.

6. Maintenance and Insurance: Micro leasing institutions may require clients to maintain and insure the leased assets to protect their value and ensure their proper functioning during the lease term.

7. End-of-Lease Options: At the end of the lease term, clients may have the flexibility to renew the lease, upgrade to newer assets, or return the asset without further obligations.

8. Monitoring and Support: Micro leasing providers may offer monitoring and support to clients throughout the lease term, ensuring that the assets are being used effectively and generating the intended income.

Micro leasing plays a crucial role in supporting small businesses and entrepreneurs by enabling them to access the necessary assets without facing the financial burden of an outright purchase. It fosters economic growth and empowers individuals to expand their businesses, create employment opportunities, and improve their livelihoods.

4.15. Methodologies of Green Microfinance:

Green Microfinance, also known as Environmental Microfinance or Eco Microfinance, is a specialized approach within the microfinance sector that aims to promote environmentally sustainable projects and initiatives. The methodologies of Green Microfinance focus on supporting businesses and projects that have positive environmental impacts. Here are some key methodologies associated with Green Microfinance:

1. **Project Selection:** Green Microfinance providers prioritize projects and businesses that align with environmental sustainability goals. These projects could include renewable energy, sustainable agriculture, clean technologies, waste management, reforestation, and other eco-friendly initiatives.

2. **Environmental Impact Assessment:** Before providing financing, Green Microfinance institutions assess the potential environmental impact of the proposed projects. This evaluation helps ensure that the projects adhere to sustainable practices and do not harm the environment.

3. **Technical Assistance:** Green Microfinance providers offer technical assistance to borrowers engaged in green projects. This support may include guidance on eco-friendly practices, renewable energy technologies, sustainable farming methods, and waste reduction strategies.

4. **Sustainable Finance Products:** Green Microfinance institutions design financial products tailored to the specific needs of environmentally sustainable projects. These products may include green loans, green working capital financing, and green energy financing.

5. **Environmental Risk Management:** Green Microfinance providers incorporate environmental risk management practices into their lending processes. This involves identifying and managing potential environmental risks associated with funded projects.

6. **Monitoring and Impact Assessment:** Green Microfinance institutions track the environmental impact of their funded projects and conduct regular impact assessments. This monitoring helps measure the positive contributions of the projects to environmental sustainability.

7. **Partnerships:** Green Microfinance providers often collaborate with environmental organizations, NGOs, and sustainability-focused initiatives

to leverage expertise, share knowledge, and extend the reach of their green initiatives.

8. Green Financial Literacy: Green Microfinance institutions may offer financial literacy programs that focus on environmental sustainability, helping borrowers understand the benefits of green practices and responsible resource management.

9. Green Certification: Some Green Microfinance institutions use green certification standards to identify eligible projects and businesses that meet specific environmental criteria.

10. Social and Environmental Reporting: Green Microfinance providers transparently report on their social and environmental impact, demonstrating their commitment to promoting environmental sustainability.

The methodologies of Green Microfinance aim to combine financial inclusion with environmental responsibility, creating a positive impact on both society and the planet. By supporting environmentally sustainable projects, Green Microfinance contributes to mitigating climate change, conserving natural resources, and fostering a greener and more resilient future.

4.16. Methodology of Federated Self-Help Group Model:

The Federated Self-Help Group Model in microfinance is an extension of the traditional Self-Help Group (SHG) model, where individual SHGs come together to form higher-level federations or associations. These federations provide a platform for SHGs to collaborate, share resources, and address common issues collectively. The methodology of the Federated Self-Help Group Model includes the following key elements:

1. Formation of Individual SHGs: The process starts with the formation of individual SHGs at the grassroots level. Each SHG typically comprises 10 to 20 members from the same community or locality.

2. SHG Capacity Building: Each individual SHG undergoes capacity-building training, including financial literacy, group dynamics, and leadership skills. This training empowers SHG members to manage their groups effectively.

3. Formation of Federations: After establishing several individual SHGs in a specific geographic area, these groups come together to form a higher-level federation or association. The formation of federations may occur at the village, cluster, or district level.

4. Governance Structure: The federation establishes a governance structure, including a board or committee, to manage its operations and represent the member SHGs.

5. Resource Sharing: The federated model allows for resource sharing among the member SHGs. This includes sharing experiences, knowledge, best practices, and even financial resources, if needed.

6. Advocacy and Representation: Federations act as the voice of their member SHGs, advocating for their interests, raising common issues, and representing their concerns to relevant stakeholders, including government authorities and financial institutions.

7. Skill Development and Training: Federations offer additional skill development and training programs to SHG members, enabling them to enhance their livelihood activities and entrepreneurial ventures.

8. Financial Linkages: Federations facilitate financial linkages with banks and other financial institutions, helping SHGs access formal credit and financial services.

9. Collaborative Initiatives: Federations may undertake joint initiatives, such as community development projects, income-generating activities, and social programs that benefit the member SHGs and their communities.

10. Impact Assessment: Federations may conduct impact assessments to measure the social and economic progress of the member SHGs and evaluate the effectiveness of their programs and interventions.

The Federated Self-Help Group Model fosters collaboration and collective action among individual SHGs, enhancing their capacity to address challenges, access resources, and drive community development. This model has proven effective in promoting financial inclusion, empowering women, and generating positive socio-economic impacts in the communities they serve.

4.17. Why Federation in SHG Model of Microfinance?

The formation of federations in the Self-Help Group (SHG) model of microfinance serves several important purposes and brings several benefits to the individual SHGs and their members. Here are some reasons why federations are essential in the SHG model of microfinance:

1. **Collective Representation:** Federations act as a collective voice for individual SHGs, representing their interests and concerns to external stakeholders, such as government authorities, financial institutions, and development agencies. By coming together, SHGs gain more visibility and influence in decision-making processes.

2. **Resource Pooling and Sharing:** Federations facilitate resource pooling and sharing among individual SHGs. This includes sharing best practices, knowledge, experiences, and lessons learned. It also enables SHGs to access a broader network of resources, such as training programs and technical assistance.

3. **Capacity Building:** Federations provide additional capacity-building support to SHGs, offering specialized training and skill development programs that individual SHGs might not be able to provide on their own. This enhances the knowledge and skills of SHG members, contributing to their personal and economic development.

4. **Advocacy and Policy Influence:** Federations play a vital role in advocating for the interests and needs of SHGs at higher levels of governance. They can influence policies and programs that directly affect SHGs and their

communities, promoting an enabling environment for microfinance and poverty alleviation initiatives.

5. Financial Linkages: Federations help individual SHGs access formal financial services, such as bank loans and other financial products. The collective strength of the federation can improve the SHGs' credibility and creditworthiness in the eyes of financial institutions.

6. Scale and Impact: By working together as a federation, SHGs can undertake larger and more impactful projects that benefit their communities. This allows SHGs to address bigger challenges and have a broader reach in terms of social and economic development.

7. Risk Management: Federations can support SHGs in managing risks associated with microfinance activities. They can provide guidance on financial management, risk assessment, and crisis response, enhancing the overall resilience of SHGs.

8. Collaboration and Networking: Federations foster collaboration and networking among SHGs, allowing them to learn from each other's experiences and strengthen their ties within the microfinance community.

The formation of federations in the SHG model of microfinance empowers individual SHGs by giving them a unified platform to share resources, build capacity, advocate for their interests, and achieve greater impact in their efforts to uplift their members and communities out of poverty.

4.17. Activities of SHG Federation:

The activities of a Self-Help Group (SHG) Federation revolve around supporting and empowering individual SHGs and their members. SHG Federations play a crucial role in strengthening the collective capacity of SHGs and enhancing their impact on socio-economic development. Here are some key activities of SHG Federations:

1. Capacity Building: SHG Federations provide capacity-building support to individual SHGs and their members. This includes training programs on financial literacy, entrepreneurship, leadership, and other relevant skills to enhance the capabilities of SHG members.

2. Resource Mobilization and Sharing: Federations facilitate resource mobilization among SHGs, pooling funds and sharing resources to meet common needs. This may include setting up a common fund, revolving loan fund, or collective savings initiatives.

3. Advocacy and Representation: SHG Federations represent the interests of individual SHGs and their members at higher levels of governance. They advocate for favourable policies and programs that support the growth and sustainability of microfinance and poverty alleviation initiatives.

4. Financial Linkages: Federations help SHGs access formal financial services and establish linkages with banks and other financial institutions. They can negotiate better terms and conditions for loans and financial products, leveraging the collective strength of SHGs.

5. Networking and Knowledge Exchange: SHG Federations foster networking and knowledge exchange among individual SHGs. They organize workshops, seminars, and learning sessions, allowing SHGs to share best practices and experiences.

6. Monitoring and Evaluation: Federations conduct monitoring and evaluation of SHG activities to assess their impact and performance. This helps identify areas for improvement and ensures transparency and accountability among SHGs.

7. Social and Community Development Projects: SHG Federations undertake collective social and community development projects that benefit their members and the broader community. These projects may include healthcare initiatives, education support, women empowerment programs, and environmental sustainability efforts.

8. Linkages with Government Programs: Federations collaborate with government agencies and development organizations to link SHGs with various government programs and schemes. This helps SHGs access additional resources and support.

9. Crisis Response and Risk Management: Federations assist SHGs in managing risks associated with microfinance activities and provide support during times of crisis, such as natural disasters or economic challenges.

10. Impact Assessment and Reporting: SHG Federations regularly assess the social and economic impact of SHG activities and report on their progress and achievements. This helps showcase the collective contributions of SHGs to development outcomes.

Through these activities, SHG Federations strengthen the self-reliance and collective empowerment of SHGs, creating a supportive and sustainable ecosystem for microfinance initiatives and community development.

4.18. Methodologies of Grameen Bank Model:

The Grameen Bank Model, developed by Muhammad Yunus in Bangladesh, is a microfinance institution that provides small loans to poor individuals, especially women, to help them start or expand small businesses. The methodologies of the Grameen Bank Model include:

1. Group lending: Borrowers are organized into small groups, typically comprising five members, who mutually support and encourage each other. The group members are collectively responsible for loan repayments, fostering a strong sense of accountability.

2. Peer pressure and social collateral: The model relies on social ties and peer pressure to ensure timely loan repayments. If one member defaults, it may affect the entire group's access to future loans.

3. No collateral requirement: Unlike traditional banks, Grameen Bank does not require borrowers to provide collateral for their loans. This approach increases access to credit for those who lack valuable assets.

4. **Gradual loan disbursement:** Borrowers receive loans in small instalments, encouraging responsible use and gradual growth of their businesses.

5. **Focus on women empowerment:** The Grameen Bank places a strong emphasis on empowering women by providing them with financial resources and a platform to build their businesses, contributing to gender equality and poverty reduction.

6. **Diversification of loan usage:** Loans are not limited to specific sectors; borrowers can utilize the funds for various income-generating activities.

7. **Frequent loan repayments:** Borrowers are required to make frequent and small repayments (often weekly) to improve repayment discipline and reduce the risk of default.

8. **Financial literacy and social development:** Grameen Bank provides financial literacy training to borrowers, enabling them to manage their finances effectively and make informed decisions.

9. **Replication and expansion:** The Grameen Bank Model has been replicated in various countries worldwide, adapting to different local contexts and helping to alleviate poverty in numerous communities.

Grameen Bank Model is renowned for its innovative approach to microfinance and its significant impact on poverty alleviation and socio-economic development.

4.19. Comparative Strength and Weakness of Grameen Model and SHG Model:

The Grameen Bank Model and the Self-Help Group (SHG) Model are both successful microfinance approaches aimed at empowering impoverished communities. Each model has its strengths and weaknesses:

Grameen Bank Model:

Strengths:

1. **Group lending and peer pressure:** The Grameen Bank's group lending approach fosters a strong sense of accountability and mutual support among borrowers, increasing the likelihood of timely repayments.

2. **No collateral requirement:** The absence of collateral allows even those without valuable assets to access credit, promoting financial inclusion.

3. **Women empowerment:** The model places a specific emphasis on empowering women, leading to increased gender equality and social development.

4. **Financial literacy:** Grameen Bank provides borrowers with financial literacy training, equipping them with the knowledge to manage their finances effectively.

5. **Proven success:** The Grameen Bank Model has been replicated and adapted in various countries, demonstrating its scalability and effectiveness.

Weaknesses:

1. Frequent repayments: The requirement for borrowers to make frequent and small repayments can be burdensome for some, leading to potential difficulties in meeting repayment obligations.

2. High interest rates: The interest rates charged by microfinance institutions like Grameen Bank can be relatively high compared to traditional banks, affecting borrowers' overall financial burden.

4.20. SHG Model:

Strengths:

1. **Social cohesion:** SHGs are community-based groups, fostering strong social ties and support systems among members.

2. Flexibility: SHGs often focus on the specific needs of the community and can provide financial services beyond credit, such as savings and insurance.

3. Lower interest rates: SHGs typically charge lower interest rates compared to formal financial institutions, reducing the financial burden on borrowers.

4. Empowerment at the grassroots level: The SHG approach empowers local communities to take charge of their own development, leading to sustainable change.

Weaknesses:

1. Limited access to formal financial institutions: SHGs may face challenges in accessing funds from formal financial institutions due to their informal structure.

2. Capacity and scalability: Scaling up SHG initiatives can be challenging due to the need for continuous capacity-building and training of group members.

3. Repayment discipline: As SHGs are self-regulated, maintaining repayment discipline may be less structured than in the Grameen Bank Model, leading to potential defaults.

Both the Grameen Bank Model and the SHG Model have proven to be effective in promoting financial inclusion and poverty reduction, each with its unique strengths and weaknesses. The choice between the two models depends on the specific needs and context of the target community.

4.21. The methodology of the cooperative/mutually aided cooperative models:

The cooperative and mutually aided cooperative models are community-based financial institutions that operate on the principles of self-help and mutual cooperation. These models aim to provide financial services and support to their members while promoting democratic decision-making and community ownership. The methodologies of these models include:

1. **Membership and Ownership:** The cooperative model operates on the principle of open membership, allowing individuals with a common interest or need to join as members. Each member has an equal say in the decision-making process, regardless of their financial contribution.

2. **Democratic Governance:** Members participate in the decision-making process through regular meetings, where they collectively elect a board of directors or management committee. Decisions are made on a one-member, one-vote basis, ensuring democratic control.

3. **Mutual Aid and Support:** Cooperative members pool their resources, often through savings or share contributions, to create a common fund. This fund is used to provide financial services to members, such as loans, savings facilities, and insurance, based on their needs.

4. **Financial Inclusion:** Cooperatives aim to serve individuals and communities that may have limited access to formal financial institutions, promoting financial inclusion and economic empowerment.

5. **Interest Rate Policy:** The cooperative model typically offers financial services at lower interest rates compared to traditional banks and microfinance institutions, aiming to benefit members rather than maximize profits.

6. **Social Objectives:** Cooperative and mutually aided cooperative models prioritize social objectives over profit-making. They seek to address community needs and promote sustainable development.

7. **Education and Training:** These models often provide financial literacy and capacity-building training to their members, enabling them to make informed financial decisions and manage their resources effectively.

8. **Community Development:** Cooperatives may engage in community development initiatives, such as supporting education, health, and

infrastructure projects, to improve the overall well-being of their members and the community.

9. Risk Sharing: In times of economic hardship, cooperative members share the risks collectively, providing a safety net for those facing financial difficulties.

The cooperative and mutually aided cooperative models are based on the principles of cooperation, mutual aid, and democratic governance. These models have proven to be successful in promoting financial inclusion, community development, and sustainable economic growth, particularly in rural and marginalized areas where formal financial institutions may be limited.

4.22. The methodology of MFI- Bank Linkage Programming:

The non-banking finance company (NBFC) model is a financial institution that provides a range of financial services similar to traditional banks but does not hold a banking license. NBFCs play a crucial role in providing credit and financial services to various segments of the population, especially those underserved by formal banking institutions. The methodology of the NBFC model includes the following key aspects:

1. Registration and Regulation: NBFCs are required to register with the relevant financial regulatory authority in their country, such as the Reserve Bank of India (RBI) in India or the Securities and Exchange Commission (SEC) in the United States. They must comply with the regulatory framework specific to NBFCs, which includes capital adequacy norms, risk management guidelines, and reporting requirements.

2. Financial Services: NBFCs offer a variety of financial services, such as lending (including personal loans, business loans, and consumer loans), leasing, hire-purchase, investment and wealth management, insurance, and microfinance.

3. Source of Funds: NBFCs raise funds through different sources, including deposits, commercial paper, debentures, term loans from banks, and equity capital. They do not accept demand deposits like traditional banks but may accept fixed deposits from the public with specific maturities.

4. Credit Assessment: NBFCs employ credit assessment and risk management practices to evaluate the creditworthiness of borrowers. They use various parameters, including credit history, income levels, and collateral, to determine loan eligibility and interest rates.

5. Focus on Specific Segments: Some NBFCs specialize in catering to specific customer segments, such as small and medium-sized enterprises (SMEs), rural populations, or low-income individuals, addressing their unique financial needs.

6. Technology Adoption: Many NBFCs leverage technology to streamline operations, enhance customer experience, and expand their reach. This may include mobile apps, online lending platforms, and digital payment solutions.

7. Non-Banking Nature: While NBFCs offer various financial services, they cannot issue checks or demand drafts in their own name. They also cannot engage in the activities of receiving demand deposits like traditional banks.

8. Financial Inclusion: NBFCs contribute significantly to financial inclusion by reaching out to underserved and unbanked populations, enabling them to access credit and other financial services.

9. Risk Management: NBFCs implement robust risk management practices to mitigate credit risk, market risk, and liquidity risk. This is vital to maintain stability and sustainability in their operations.

NBFC model provides a valuable alternative to traditional banking institutions, offering diverse financial services and playing a crucial role in expanding access to credit and financial inclusion. As with any financial institution, regulatory compliance and prudent risk management are essential to ensure the stability and effectiveness of the NBFC model.

4.23. Structures of Intermediation for Microfinance in India:

In India, microfinance is facilitated through various structures of intermediation that connect the financial needs of low-income individuals and micro-entrepreneurs with sources of funding. Some of the common structures of intermediation for microfinance in India include:

1. **Microfinance Institutions (MFIs):** MFIs are specialized financial institutions that focus on providing microloans and other financial services to low-income individuals, especially those in rural areas. They operate as Non-Banking Financial Companies (NBFCs) or Section 8 Companies under the Companies Act.

2. **Self-Help Groups (SHGs):** SHGs are informal community-based groups formed by a small number of women with a shared objective of savings and credit. They are often facilitated and supported by NGOs, banks, or government agencies. SHGs pool their savings and can access loans from banks through a group-banking linkage model.

3. **Non-Governmental Organizations (NGOs):** Many NGOs in India play a vital role in microfinance by promoting and supporting SHGs and other community-based initiatives. They provide capacity-building, training, and support to micro-entrepreneurs and often act as intermediaries between beneficiaries and financial institutions.

4. **Cooperative Societies:** Cooperative societies in rural areas also contribute to microfinance by mobilizing savings from their members and providing credit to small-scale entrepreneurs and farmers. They operate on cooperative principles and are regulated by state governments.

5. **Regional Rural Banks (RRBs):** RRBs are financial institutions established to promote rural credit and financial inclusion. They provide

banking services, including microloans, to rural communities and low-income individuals.

6. Commercial Banks: Commercial banks in India also participate in microfinance by providing microloans through priority sector lending requirements. They may directly lend to micro-entrepreneurs or partner with MFIs and NGOs to extend credit to underserved communities.

7. Small Finance Banks (SFBs): SFBs are specialized banks focused on providing financial services to unserved and underserved segments, including micro-entrepreneurs and small businesses. They often have a strong microfinance focus in their portfolio.

8. Microfinance Development and Equity Funds: These are specialized funds that invest in MFIs and microfinance-related enterprises. They provide financial support and equity capital to MFIs, enabling them to expand their operations and reach more beneficiaries.

These structures of intermediation for microfinance in India work together to promote financial inclusion and provide access to credit and financial services to vulnerable and marginalized communities. The diverse network of institutions ensures a multi-faceted approach to address the specific needs of various segments of the population and promote sustainable socio-economic development.

4.24. Microfinance products under both SHG and MFI model:

Under both the Self-Help Group (SHG) and Microfinance Institution (MFI) models, various microfinance products are offered to cater to the financial needs of low-income individuals and micro-entrepreneurs. Some common microfinance products under both models include:

1. Group Loans: Both SHGs and MFIs offer group loans to their members. In SHGs, members pool their savings and access loans from their collective fund. In MFIs, group loans are provided to small groups of borrowers who act as guarantors for each other.

2. Individual Loans: Both SHGs and MFIs may offer individual loans to clients based on their specific needs and repayment capacity. Individual loans are usually provided for income-generating activities or personal emergencies.

3. Income-Generating Loans: These loans are designed to support micro-entrepreneurs and small businesses in starting or expanding income-generating activities. They can be used for purchasing inventory, equipment, or raw materials.

4. Livelihood Improvement Loans: SHGs and MFIs may offer loans for improving livelihoods, such as agricultural loans for purchasing seeds, fertilizers, or livestock.

5. Microenterprise Loans: Microenterprise loans are targeted at small businesses and micro-entrepreneurs to help them grow their businesses and generate more income.

6. Emergency Loans: These loans are provided to clients to cope with unforeseen emergencies or unexpected expenses, such as medical emergencies or natural disasters.

7. Housing Loans: Some SHGs and MFIs offer housing loans to help clients improve their living conditions or construct/upgrade their homes.

8. Education Loans: Education loans may be provided to support clients in financing education expenses for themselves or their children.

9. Health Loans: These loans are meant to cover medical expenses and support clients in accessing healthcare services.

10. Savings Products: Both SHGs and MFIs encourage their members/clients to save regularly. SHGs facilitate savings through group-based savings, while MFIs offer individual savings accounts.

11. Microinsurance: In some cases, SHGs and MFIs collaborate with insurance companies to offer microinsurance products, providing coverage for life, health, or other risks.

It's important to note that the specific range of microfinance products offered may vary based on the target clientele, regulatory requirements, and the operational focus of the SHG or MFI. The goal of these microfinance products is to promote financial inclusion, empower low-income individuals, and support sustainable socio-economic development in underserved communities.

4.25. Group loans under SHG and MFI:

Under both the Self-Help Group (SHG) and Microfinance Institution (MFI) models, group loans are an essential microfinance product that fosters collective responsibility and support among borrowers. However, the mechanisms for providing group loans differ slightly between the two models:

4.26. Group Loans under SHG Model:

1. **Savings-based Approach:** In the SHG model, group loans are often funded by the members' collective savings. The SHG members regularly contribute to a common fund through their savings, and these savings form the basis for lending within the group.

2. **Revolving Fund:** The accumulated savings in the SHG are managed as a revolving fund, from which loans are disbursed to individual members. Each member can access credit from this fund based on their needs and repayment capacity.

3. **Internal Lending:** SHG members may borrow from the group for various purposes, such as income-generating activities, emergencies, or other personal needs. The loans are repaid over a specific period, and the repaid amount goes back into the group's common fund.

4. **Joint Liability:** In the SHG model, the loans are typically granted with joint liability, which means all members of the group are jointly responsible for each other's loan repayment. This fosters a strong sense of collective responsibility and ensures timely repayments.

4.27. Group Loans under MFI Model:

1. Group Formation: Under the MFI model, small groups of borrowers are formed to act as a cohesive unit. These groups consist of 5 to 10 individuals, and members support and guarantee each other's loans.

2. Group Selection: MFIs often follow a rigorous process to select group members based on their creditworthiness and willingness to work together. The groups are usually homogeneous in terms of socio-economic characteristics.

3. Individual Loan Disbursement: While the loan is taken by the group collectively, individual borrowers are responsible for their share of the loan. Each member's creditworthiness is evaluated separately, and loans are disbursed to individual members.

4. Joint Liability: Similar to the SHG model, group loans under the MFI model often come with joint liability. This means if one member of the group defaults, it affects the other members' access to future loans, encouraging mutual support and timely repayments.

Both the SHG and MFI models leverage the concept of group loans to encourage collective responsibility, mutual support, and timely repayments. However, the SHG model primarily relies on internal savings for funding, while the MFI model involves individual loan disbursement to group members with joint liability. Both approaches have proven effective in promoting financial inclusion and empowering low-income individuals and communities.

4.28. Individual loan under MFI and SHG:

Apologies for the confusion in my previous responses. Let me clarify the individual loan offerings under both the Microfinance Institution (MFI) and Self-Help Group (SHG) models:

4.29. Individual Loan under MFI Model:

1. Borrower Assessment: Under the MFI model, individual loan applicants go through a thorough credit assessment to determine their eligibility for the loan. The assessment includes evaluating the borrower's credit history, repayment capacity, and other relevant factors.

2. Loan Disbursement: If the individual meets the MFI's credit criteria, the loan is disbursed directly to the borrower's account. The loan amount, interest rate, and repayment schedule are agreed upon between the borrower and the MFI.

3. Collateral and Guarantees: MFIs may require collateral or guarantees from individual borrowers as a form of security against the loan. However, not all MFIs require collateral, and some may offer unsecured loans based on the borrower's creditworthiness.

4. Interest Rates: MFIs typically charge interest rates that reflect the level of risk associated with the individual borrower. Interest rates can vary based on the borrower's risk profile, loan size, and tenure.

5. Repayment Schedule: Individual loans are repaid in fixed instalments over a specified period, such as weekly, bi-weekly, or monthly. The repayment schedule is agreed upon during the loan application process.

4.30. Individual Loan under SHG Model:

1. Savings and Internal Lending: In the SHG model, individual loans are facilitated by the collective savings of the group. SHG members pool their savings, and members can borrow from this common fund for various purposes, such as income-generating activities or personal needs.

2. Interest Rates: SHGs charge relatively lower interest rates compared to MFIs since the loans are funded by the collective savings of the group. The interest earned is shared among the members or reinvested in the SHG's common fund.

3. Flexible Repayment: SHGs usually provide more flexible repayment terms to their members compared to MFIs. The repayment schedule can be tailored to the individual borrower's cash flow and income-generating cycles.

4. Joint Liability: Under the SHG model, individual borrowers have joint liability for their loans within the group. If one member defaults, the other group members collectively take responsibility to ensure timely repayments.

Both the MFI and SHG models offer individual loans to serve the financial needs of low-income individuals. The MFI model involves formal credit assessment and potential collateral requirements, while the SHG model relies on internal lending from the group's collective savings with more flexible repayment terms and lower interest rates.

4.31. Income generation loan under microfinance and SHG:

Income generation loans are an essential microfinance product offered under both the Microfinance Institution (MFI) and Self-Help Group (SHG) models. These loans are designed to support individuals and micro-entrepreneurs in starting or expanding income-generating activities. Here's how income generation loans are provided under each model:

4.31.A. Income Generation Loan under MFI Model:

1. Borrower Assessment: Under the MFI model, potential borrowers seeking income generation loans undergo a credit assessment to determine their eligibility and creditworthiness. The assessment includes evaluating the borrower's income, cash flow, and the viability of their proposed income-generating activity.

2. Loan Disbursement: Once the borrower is approved for the income generation loan, the funds are disbursed directly to the borrower's account.

The loan amount, interest rate, and repayment schedule are agreed upon between the borrower and the MFI.

3. Purpose-Specific: Income generation loans under the MFI model are explicitly provided to finance income-generating activities such as small businesses, trading, farming, or other ventures that can generate regular income for the borrower.

4. Repayment Schedule: The borrower is provided with a structured repayment schedule based on the expected cash flows from the income-generating activity. The repayment period is usually aligned with the borrower's income cycle.

5. Collateral and Guarantees: MFIs may require collateral or guarantees from borrowers as security against the loan. However, some MFIs may offer unsecured income generation loans based on the borrower's creditworthiness and the viability of the proposed activity.

4.31.B. Income Generation Loan under SHG Model:

1. Internal Lending: In the SHG model, income generation loans are facilitated by the collective savings of the group. SHG members contribute to a common fund through their savings, and members can borrow from this fund for income-generating activities.

2. Interest Rates: SHGs charge relatively lower interest rates compared to MFIs since the loans are funded by the collective savings of the group. The interest earned is shared among the members or reinvested in the SHG's common fund.

3. Flexible Repayment: SHGs usually provide more flexible repayment terms to their members compared to MFIs. The repayment schedule can be tailored to the individual borrower's cash flow from the income-generating activity.

4. Joint Liability: Under the SHG model, individual borrowers have joint liability for their loans within the group. If one member defaults, the other group members collectively take responsibility to ensure timely repayments.

Both the MFI and SHG models offer income generation loans to support individuals and micro-entrepreneurs in starting or expanding income-generating activities. The MFI model involves formal credit assessment, potential collateral requirements, and individual loan disbursement, while the SHG model relies on internal lending from the group's collective savings with more flexible repayment terms and lower interest rates.

4.31.C. Livelihood Improvement Loans under SHG and MFI:

Livelihood Improvement Loans offered by Self Help Groups (SHGs) and Microfinance Institutions (MFIs) are designed to empower individuals and small entrepreneurs, particularly those in low-income and underserved communities, to enhance their livelihoods and income-generating activities.

1. Self Help Groups (SHGs): SHGs are community-based organizations formed by a group of individuals, mostly women, who come together to address their common financial and social needs. SHGs promote savings, pooling of resources, and offer small loans to their members for income-generating activities. These loans aim to create sustainable livelihoods, foster entrepreneurship, and improve the economic status of the members and their families.

2. Microfinance Institutions (MFIs): MFIs are specialized financial institutions that provide financial services, including small loans, to individuals who lack access to formal banking systems. MFIs focus on providing financial support to low-income individuals and micro-entrepreneurs, especially in rural and marginalized areas. Livelihood Improvement Loans from MFIs enable borrowers to start or expand small businesses, purchase assets, or invest in skills training, thereby helping them improve their economic prospects.

Both SHGs and MFIs play a vital role in promoting financial inclusion and socio-economic development by extending credit to individuals and communities often overlooked by traditional banks. These loans contribute to poverty reduction, job creation, and overall improvement in the quality of life for borrowers and their communities.

4.31.D. Microenterprises loans in MFI and SHG:

Microenterprise loans offered by Microfinance Institutions (MFIs) and Self Help Groups (SHGs) are targeted financial products designed to support small-scale entrepreneurs and microenterprises in their growth and development. These loans cater to individuals who have limited access to formal financial services but are engaged in income-generating activities or running small businesses.

4.31.E. Microfinance Institutions (MFIs) Microenterprise Loans:

MFIs provide microenterprise loans to individuals and small businesses, offering access to credit for working capital, business expansion, and investment in assets and equipment.

The loan amounts are generally small, tailored to the specific needs of the microenterprise, and can be used for various purposes, such as purchasing inventory, equipment, or raw materials.

MFIs often use a group lending model, where borrowers are organized into small groups, and each member serves as a guarantor for the others, fostering peer support and accountability in loan repayment.

4.31.F. Self Help Groups (SHGs) Microenterprise Loans:

SHGs also offer microenterprise loans to their members, particularly women, who pool their savings to create a fund that provides financial assistance to members for income-generating activities.

SHGs operate on the principles of collective responsibility, trust, and solidarity, allowing members to borrow based on their savings and group dynamics.

The loans provided by SHGs are generally small and short-term, with a focus on supporting local microenterprises and individual income-generating projects.

Both MFIs and SHGs play a crucial role in empowering microentrepreneurs and small-scale businesses, fostering economic growth, and promoting financial inclusion. These microenterprise loans enable individuals to access capital and resources that would otherwise be out of reach, contributing to poverty reduction and sustainable livelihoods in underserved communities.

4.31.G. Emergency Loan under MFI and SHG:

Emergency loans offered by Microfinance Institutions (MFIs) and Self Help Groups (SHGs) are financial products designed to provide immediate financial assistance to individuals and families facing unexpected crises or emergencies. These loans help borrowers overcome sudden financial hardships and meet urgent needs without resorting to high-interest borrowing options.

4.31.H. Emergency Loans from MFIs:

MFIs offer emergency loans to their clients, who may be facing unforeseen circumstances such as medical emergencies, natural disasters, or unexpected business setbacks.

These loans are typically disbursed quickly to address the urgent financial needs of the borrower.

The loan amounts may vary based on the borrower's repayment capacity and the policies of the specific MFI.

4.31.I. Emergency Loans from SHGs:

Self Help Groups also provide emergency loans to their members in times of crisis.

The group-based nature of SHGs often allows for faster decision-making and loan disbursement during emergencies.

SHGs may have established contingency funds from their collective savings to help members access emergency loans without delay.

Both MFIs and SHGs play a critical role in supporting vulnerable individuals and communities during difficult times. Emergency loans not only provide immediate financial relief but also help prevent individuals from falling deeper into debt due to high-interest loans or selling essential assets during emergencies. By offering these loans, MFIs and SHGs contribute to financial resilience and stability for their clients, fostering social and economic development in underserved areas.

4.31.J. Housing loan under MFI and SHG:

Housing loans offered by Microfinance Institutions (MFIs) and Self Help Groups (SHGs) are financial products designed to assist individuals and families in acquiring or improving their housing conditions. These loans aim to address the housing needs of low-income and underserved communities who might not have access to traditional mortgage options.

431.K. Housing Loans from MFIs:

MFIs provide housing loans to individuals or households to support the construction, repair, or renovation of residential properties.

These loans cater to low-income borrowers who may not meet the stringent eligibility criteria of conventional banks.

The loan terms and repayment schedules are designed to be flexible and affordable for the borrower's financial situation.

4.31.L. Housing Loans from SHGs:

Self Help Groups may also offer housing loans to their members to improve their living conditions.

SHGs utilize their collective savings and contributions from members to create a housing loan fund, which is then made available to eligible members.

The loan amounts and repayment terms are determined based on the group's internal guidelines and the borrower's ability to repay.

Housing loans from MFIs and SHGs can make a significant difference in the lives of low-income families by providing them with access to safe and decent housing. These loans contribute to poverty alleviation and sustainable development, as improved housing conditions positively impact health, education, and overall quality of life for individuals and communities. It's essential to check with specific MFIs or SHGs to understand their exact loan offerings, eligibility criteria, and terms before applying for a housing loan.

4.31.M. Education loan under MFI and SHG:

Education loans offered by Microfinance Institutions (MFIs) and Self Help Groups (SHGs) are financial products designed to support individuals and students in pursuing higher education and skill development. These loans aim to make education more accessible to those who may face financial constraints in paying for educational expenses.

4.31.N. Education Loans from MFIs:

MFIs provide education loans to individuals who wish to pursue vocational training, professional courses, or higher education.

These loans can cover tuition fees, study materials, examination fees, and other related expenses.

The loan terms and interest rates are typically designed to be affordable for the borrower, taking into account their financial situation and repayment capacity.

4.31.O. Education Loans from SHGs:

Self Help Groups may also offer education loans to their members or eligible students in their communities.

SHGs use their collective savings and contributions from members to create an education loan fund to support education-related expenses.

The loan amounts and repayment terms are determined based on the group's guidelines and the borrower's ability to repay.

Education loans from MFIs and SHGs play a crucial role in promoting education and skill development, particularly for individuals who lack access to formal banking channels. By providing financial support for education, these loans contribute to enhancing the employability and income-generating potential of students and individuals, thus helping in poverty reduction and socio-economic development. If you are interested in an education loan from an MFI or SHG, it's essential to inquire about their specific loan offerings, eligibility criteria, and terms to ensure a smooth application process.

4.31.P. Health Loan under MFI and SHG:

Health loans offered by Microfinance Institutions (MFIs) and Self Help Groups (SHGs) are financial products designed to provide individuals and families with access to funds for medical expenses and healthcare needs. These loans aim to support individuals who may not have adequate health insurance coverage or face financial constraints in meeting healthcare costs.

4.31.Q. Health Loans from MFIs:

MFIs offer health loans to individuals who require funds for medical treatments, surgeries, hospitalization, or purchasing medications and medical equipment.

These loans can be used to cover various health-related expenses, including diagnostic tests, doctor consultations, and specialized treatments.

The loan terms and interest rates are usually tailored to be affordable for the borrower's financial situation.

4.31.R. Health Loans from SHGs:

Self Help Groups may also provide health loans to their members to meet medical expenses for themselves or their family members.

SHGs utilize their collective savings to create a health loan fund, allowing members to access financial support during medical emergencies or for planned healthcare needs.

The loan amounts and repayment terms are determined based on the SHG's internal guidelines and the borrower's repayment capacity.

Health loans from MFIs and SHGs can make a significant difference in enabling individuals to access quality healthcare services and timely medical interventions. These loans play a crucial role in improving health outcomes and reducing the financial burden on families during medical emergencies or treatment requirements. It's essential to inquire with specific MFIs or SHGs about their health loan offerings, eligibility criteria, and terms before applying for a health loan.

4.31.S. Saving products under microfinance and SHG:

Microfinance Institutions (MFIs) and Self-Help Groups (SHGs) offer various saving products to their members, promoting a culture of savings and financial inclusion. These saving products are designed to encourage individuals, particularly those with limited access to formal banking services, to save and build financial security for the future. Here are some common saving products offered by MFIs and SHGs:

1. Savings Accounts:

MFIs and SHGs provide basic savings accounts to their members, allowing them to deposit and withdraw money as needed.

These accounts often have lower minimum balance requirements and simplified documentation compared to traditional bank accounts.

2. Recurring Deposit (RD) Accounts:

RD accounts enable members to save a fixed amount of money regularly, usually on a monthly basis.

Over time, these deposits accumulate interest and help individuals build savings for specific goals or emergencies.

3. Fixed Deposit (FD) Accounts:

FD accounts allow members to deposit a lump sum amount for a specified period at a fixed interest rate.

These accounts provide higher interest rates compared to regular savings accounts, making them attractive for long-term savings.

4. Group Savings:

SHGs encourage members to participate in group savings, where each member contributes a fixed amount regularly.

These collective savings are then used to provide loans to members or invest in income-generating activities.

5. Emergency Funds:

Some MFIs and SHGs may offer specialized savings accounts for emergency funds, helping members build financial resilience for unexpected expenses.

6. Education and Health Savings:

Certain MFIs and SHGs provide dedicated savings accounts for education and health-related expenses, encouraging members to save for specific purposes.

Promoting savings through these various products is essential for individuals and communities to build assets, access credit, and improve their economic well-being over time. These saving products offered by MFIs and SHGs contribute to poverty reduction and financial empowerment in underserved areas.

4.31.T. Micro-insurance with MFI and SHG:

Micro-insurance is a type of insurance product designed to provide affordable and accessible coverage to low-income individuals, micro-entrepreneurs, and members of Self Help Groups (SHGs) who may not have access to traditional insurance options. Microfinance Institutions (MFIs) and SHGs often collaborate with insurance providers to offer micro-insurance products to their clients, providing them with a safety net against various risks and uncertainties. Here are some common micro-insurance products offered by MFIs and SHGs:

1. Life Micro-Insurance:

Life micro-insurance provides a payout to the insured person's beneficiaries in case of the policyholder's death.

It offers financial protection to the family and dependents of the insured, helping them cope with the loss of income.

2. Health Micro-Insurance:

Health micro-insurance covers medical expenses, hospitalization costs, and sometimes outpatient treatments for the insured and their family members.

It helps individuals access healthcare services without incurring substantial financial burdens during medical emergencies.

3. Asset Micro-Insurance:

Asset micro-insurance covers losses or damages to specific assets, such as agricultural crops, livestock, or small businesses.

It helps protect against unexpected events that could have a significant impact on the livelihoods of individuals and microenterprises.

4. Weather Index Micro-Insurance:

Weather index micro-insurance provides coverage against weather-related risks, such as droughts or floods, that may adversely affect farmers and rural communities.

Payouts are triggered based on predetermined weather conditions, simplifying claim processes.

Micro-insurance through MFIs and SHGs enables vulnerable communities to access risk mitigation tools and financial protection, thereby promoting financial resilience. These products are designed to have lower premiums, simplified documentation, and convenient claim processes, making them more suitable for individuals with limited resources and financial literacy. By offering micro-insurance, MFIs and SHGs contribute to poverty reduction and empower their members to better manage risks and improve their overall financial well-being.

4.31.U. Definition of Self-Help Group:

A Self-Help Group (SHG) is a community-based organization formed by a group of individuals, usually from similar socio-economic backgrounds, who come together voluntarily to address their common financial, social, and developmental needs. SHGs are prevalent in various countries and play a significant role in promoting financial inclusion, empowering women, and fostering socio-economic development in underserved communities.

4.31.V. Key characteristics of a Self-Help Group include:

1. **Voluntary Membership** SHGs are formed on a voluntary basis, where individuals with similar objectives and interests join together to support one another.

2. **Collective Savings and Credit:** Members contribute regular savings to a common fund, which is then used to provide internal loans to the members based on their needs. This collective saving and lending model promote financial discipline and community solidarity.

3. **Peer Support and Accountability:** SHGs often function on the principle of collective responsibility, where each member becomes a guarantor for the others. This fosters peer support and ensures timely repayment of loans.

4. Regular Meetings and Discussions: SHG members hold regular meetings to discuss financial matters, share experiences, and collectively decide on the group's activities and future plans.

5. Skill Development and Capacity Building: SHGs often provide training and capacity-building programs to enhance the members' knowledge and skills in various areas, including financial management, entrepreneurship, and health.

6. Focus on Women Empowerment: Many SHGs prioritize women's participation and leadership, aiming to empower women by providing them with a platform to improve their economic and social status.

SHGs have proven to be effective in promoting savings, providing access to credit, and creating a supportive environment for their members to address various challenges they face. These groups contribute to poverty reduction, women's empowerment, and community development, making them an essential component of many poverty alleviation and social development initiatives worldwide.

4.31.W. Definition of SHG Federation:

A Self Help Group (SHG) Federation is an umbrella organization that brings together multiple individual SHGs under one cohesive structure. It acts as a higher-level entity that coordinates and supports the activities of its member SHGs. The main objective of an SHG Federation is to strengthen the capacity and collective power of SHGs to address larger-scale challenges and opportunities.

4.31.X. Key characteristics of an SHG Federation include:

1. Coordination and Networking: The SHG Federation facilitates communication and collaboration among its member SHGs, promoting information exchange and sharing of experiences and best practices.

2. **Resource Mobilization:** The Federation may work towards securing additional resources, such as funding, training opportunities, and technical support, to strengthen the capacity of its member SHGs.

3. **Advocacy and Representation:** The SHG Federation represents the collective interests and concerns of its member SHGs to relevant authorities, policymakers, and other stakeholders.

4. **Capacity Building:** The Federation provides capacity-building support to individual SHGs, helping them improve their financial management, governance, and overall effectiveness.

5. **Scaling up Impact:** By uniting multiple SHGs, an SHG Federation enables the collective impact of the groups to extend beyond their individual capacities, making a broader and more significant difference in their communities.

6. **Policy Engagement:** The SHG Federation may engage in policy dialogue and advocacy to influence favourable policies and regulations that support the growth and sustainability of SHGs and their socio-economic development initiatives.

SHG Federations play a crucial role in empowering SHGs, promoting financial inclusion, and fostering socio-economic development at the grassroots level. Through their collaborative approach, these Federations contribute to poverty reduction and the overall empowerment of their member SHGs and their members.

4.32. Definition of non-banking financial institution:

A non-banking financial institution (NBFI) is a financial institution that provides various financial services similar to traditional banks but does not hold a full banking license. NBFI operates outside the purview of central banking regulations and may offer a diverse range of financial products and services to individuals, businesses, and other organizations.

Key characteristics of non-banking financial institutions include:

1. **No Banking License:** Unlike traditional banks, NBFI does not have a banking license and is not authorized to accept deposits from the public.

2. **Financial Services:** NBFI provides various financial services such as lending, investment management, insurance, leasing, factoring, and other activities related to finance and investments.

3. **Regulation:** While NBFI does not operate as a full-fledged bank, it is still subject to financial regulations and oversight from relevant regulatory authorities, depending on the country's legal framework.

4. **Complementary to Banks:** NBFIs often complement the services offered by traditional banks, filling gaps in financial markets and catering to specific customer needs.

5. **Specialization:** Some NBFIs specialize in specific areas such as housing finance, mutual funds, insurance, or leasing, allowing them to focus on niche markets.

Examples of non-banking financial institutions include investment banks, insurance companies, credit unions, leasing companies, asset management firms, and microfinance institutions. These institutions play a crucial role in the financial ecosystem, providing diverse financial products and services to individuals and businesses, contributing to financial inclusion, and fostering economic growth.

Chapter - 5

Evolutionary Path and Notable Characteristics of Indian Microfinance

5.1. Microfinance Evolution and Characteristics in India:

Microfinance in India has undergone significant evolution over the years. Initially established as a means to provide financial services to the unbanked and economically vulnerable populations, it has expanded to encompass various services beyond credit.

5.2. Key characteristics of microfinance in India include:

1. **Inclusivity:** Microfinance institutions (MFIs) aim to include those who lack access to traditional banking services, especially in rural areas.

2. **Group lending:** MFIs often follow a group-based lending model, where members of a self-help group jointly take loans and are collectively responsible for repayment.

3. **Small-ticket loans:** Microfinance typically provides small loan amounts to cater to the needs of low-income borrowers.

4. **Interest rates:** Interest rates can be higher compared to traditional banks due to the higher cost of reaching remote areas and serving small-sized loans.

5. Technology integration: With the growth of digital infrastructure, many MFIs have adopted technology to enhance efficiency and outreach.

6. Diversification of services: Besides credit, MFIs have expanded their offerings to include savings, insurance, and other financial products.

7. Social impact: Microfinance aims to alleviate poverty, empower women, and promote financial inclusion.

Over the time, the microfinance sector in India has become more regulated to ensure consumer protection and prevent over-indebtedness. The Reserve Bank of India (RBI) plays a crucial role in supervising and guiding the industry's development.

5.3. SEWA:

The Self-Employed Women's Association, is a prominent trade union and self-help organization based in the state of Gujarat, India. It was founded in 1972 by the pioneering labour and women's rights activist, Ela Bhatt. SEWA's main objective is to uplift and empower women in the informal sector, particularly those engaged in self-employment and daily wage labour.

Key features and initiatives of SEWA include:

1. Advocacy: SEWA advocates for the rights of informal women workers, striving to improve their working conditions, wages, and social security benefits.

2. Financial Services: SEWA provides financial services to its members, including access to microcredit and savings facilities.

3. Social Security: The organization promotes social security schemes such as health insurance, maternity benefits, and accident coverage for its members.

4. Skill Development: SEWA offers skill development and training programs to enhance the economic capabilities of women workers.

5. Cooperatives: SEWA helps establish and run various cooperatives to promote collective entrepreneurship among women in the informal sector.

6. Political Participation: SEWA encourages women to participate in local governance and political processes, empowering them to have a voice in decision-making.

7. SEWA Bank: SEWA also founded a separate cooperative bank called the SEWA Bank, which caters to the financial needs of its members.

SEWA has been recognized globally for its significant contributions to women's empowerment, poverty alleviation, and social justice. It has served as a model for similar initiatives worldwide and has been instrumental in uplifting the status of millions of women workers in India.

5.4. Syndicate Mahila Sahakari Bank:

The first microfinance organization in India after the country gained independence was the "Syndicate Mahila Sahakari Bank" (Syndicate Women's Cooperative Bank), which was established in 1976 in the state of Kerala. This cooperative bank primarily focused on providing financial services to women, especially in rural areas, and played a significant role in promoting financial inclusion and empowering women through microcredit. The success of Syndicate Mahila Sahakari Bank inspired the growth of many other microfinance institutions across India in the subsequent years.

5.5. The microfinance industry in India has been experiencing both challenges and growth opportunities:

Challenges:

1. Regulatory Changes: The industry has faced periodic changes in regulations by the Reserve Bank of India (RBI) to prevent over-indebtedness and ensure consumer protection. These changes sometimes lead to uncertainties and adjustments for microfinance institutions (MFIs).

2. COVID-19 Pandemic: The COVID-19 pandemic posed significant challenges for the microfinance sector, especially in terms of loan repayment and liquidity issues, particularly in the early months of the pandemic.

3. Credit Risk: Serving low-income and underserved populations comes with inherent credit risk, as these borrowers might have limited credit histories and collateral.

Growth Opportunities:

1. Digital Transformation: Many MFIs have embraced digital technologies to expand their reach and improve operational efficiency, enabling them to reach remote areas and serve more clients.

2. Financial Inclusion: The push for financial inclusion by the government and financial institutions has created opportunities for MFIs to play a crucial role in reaching the unbanked and underbanked segments of the population.

3. Diversification of Services: MFIs are increasingly diversifying their offerings to include various financial products and services beyond credit, such as savings, insurance, and remittance services.

5.6. The Small Industries Development Bank of India (SIDBI):

Is a specialized financial institution that operates under the Department of Financial Services, Ministry of Finance, Government of India. Established in April 1990, SIDBI's primary focus is to promote, finance, and develop the Micro, Small, and Medium Enterprises (MSMEs) sector in India.

Key functions and roles of SIDBI include:

1. Financial Support: SIDBI provides financial assistance to MSMEs through various credit schemes, including term loans, working capital loans, and project finance.

2. Refinancing: SIDBI refinances loans extended by commercial banks, state financial corporations, and other financial institutions to MSMEs.

3. Developmental Initiatives: The bank undertakes various developmental initiatives to enhance the competitiveness and productivity of MSMEs through capacity-building programs, skill development, and technology upgradation.

4. Venture Capital: SIDBI offers venture capital assistance to startups and innovative MSMEs through its subsidiary, SIDBI Venture Capital Limited (SVCL).

5. Credit Guarantee: SIDBI operates the Credit Guarantee Fund Trust for Micro and Small Enterprises (CGTMSE) to provide collateral-free credit to MSMEs.

6. Sustainable Finance: SIDBI promotes environmentally sustainable practices in MSMEs by providing assistance for projects focusing on renewable energy and clean technologies.

7. Direct Lending: SIDBI also directly lends to MSMEs through its various branches and financial assistance programs.

SIDBI plays a crucial role in supporting the growth and development of MSMEs, which contribute significantly to India's economic development, employment generation, and industrial growth.

5.7. The National Bank for Agriculture and Rural Development (NABARD):

Is an apex development financial institution in India. It was established on July 12, 1982, by the Government of India with the main objective of promoting sustainable agriculture and rural development.

Key functions and roles of NABARD include:

1. Rural Credit: NABARD refinances and provides credit facilities to cooperative banks, regional rural banks, and other financial institutions to support agricultural and rural development activities.

2. Rural Infrastructure Development: NABARD finances and supports projects related to rural infrastructure, such as irrigation, rural roads, and agri-processing units, to improve the livelihoods of rural communities.

3. Microfinance: NABARD promotes and supports microfinance institutions (MFIs) to provide financial services to small and marginal farmers, rural artisans, and other rural poor.

4. Sustainable Agriculture: NABARD works towards promoting sustainable agricultural practices, including organic farming, watershed development, and water conservation.

5. Rural Innovation: NABARD encourages research and development activities in agriculture and rural sectors, promoting innovation and adoption of modern technologies.

6. Rural Development Programs: NABARD implements and supports various government rural development programs and initiatives aimed at poverty alleviation and inclusive growth.

7. Capacity Building: NABARD conducts training and capacity-building programs for farmers, rural entrepreneurs, and other stakeholders to enhance their skills and knowledge.

NABARD plays a vital role in ensuring rural credit flow, agricultural and rural development, and promoting financial inclusion in rural areas. It acts as a catalyst in transforming the rural landscape and improving the livelihoods of millions of people across India.

5.8. Microfinance:

Introduction: Microfinance is one of the popular terms in today's time. Came into existence in the 80s, it emerged as a great solution for poverty elevation and also for empowering women. It helps women become self-dependent.

Microfinance, also called microcredit, is the provision of small credit to the low-income individuals or groups who otherwise would have no other access to financial services. The term 'missing middle' is often used for this section of our society who lost out on formal credit for want of a collateral support. It is here that Microfinance steps in, providing 'micro' credit with no collateral whatsoever.

The last few years saw the micro-credit industry mainstreaming with the broader financial sector. Some of the largest NBFC-MFIs became Banks or Small Finance Banks (SFBs) and some were bought over by Banks and large NBFCs. Banks and NBFCs also started building their own micro-credit portfolio, through Business Correspondent partnerships. As a result of mainstreaming, micro-credit sector today is competitive and served by a diverse set of players - Banks, SFBs, NBFC-MFIs, BCs and NBFCs.

Outside of these microfinance providers, there exists a strong ecosystem of other stakeholders including the regulators, the Government, financial institutions, credit bureau, employee bureau, rating agencies and others which play an important role in the delivery of Microfinance.

Key Microfinance Data:

Industry Loan Portfolio	3,48,339 Cr
Active Loan Accounts	13 Cr
Number of Borrowers	6.6 Cr
Number of Microfinance Entities	202

Key Microfinance Highlights:

Almost 99% microfinance loans in India are provided to women from low-income households.

98% loans are provided through the Joint Liability Group (JLG) lending model wherein a group of customers, usually 5-10, individually come under JLG to take loans and agree to support and repay the loans if customers in the group face difficulty in making repayment. This group model brings efficiencies in operational costs and leverages social collateral towards underwriting and against the risks of defaults.

Microfinance loans are collateral free. Outflows on account of repayment of monthly loan obligations shall be subject to a limit of maximum 50 per cent of the monthly household income.

Microfinance industry has a diverse supply-side with multiple lenders (nearly 194) including Banks, Small Finance Banks, NBFC-MFIs and NBFCs.

The industry has an outreach in almost 632 districts of India. In terms of geographic spread, 76% of the loan portfolio is rural and 24% urban.

Loans are primarily for income generating activities but are also taken for household expenses like education, health, and housing.

Except non-profit MFIs, all lenders are regulated by the Reserve Bank of India (RBI).

Non-performing assets have remained under 1% over the years despite external shocks in recent past.

5.9. Microfinance in India:

Like many other countries, modern micro-credit/microfinance industry in India started in 1990s inspired by the Grameen Model of Prof Mohammad Yunus in Bangladesh. Overtime, as this model evolved and became successful, it boosted the confidence of customers, MFIs and other stakeholders and started to scale-up.

From 2005-2006, many non-profit MFIs converted into for-profit NBFCs and many new for-profit NBFCs also entered the micro-credit business, attracting private capital, commercialization, professionalism, and scale. This fuelled growth, competition, scale with a sharp focus on specialization in delivering micro-credit efficiently and profitably. As a result, within 5 years, the micro-credit industry in India increased multi-fold to reach an outstanding of nearly Rs 20,000 Cr. However, this period also witnessed the challenges around customer-protection including over-leverage, inadequate disclosures, lack of customer awareness, high pricing as well as risks of geographic concentration, ghosts' loans, local-level interferences and lack of regulations and oversight.

Recognizing this, Reserve Bank of India (Central Bank of India), introduced a new category of NBFCs called NBFC-MFIs in Dec 2011 with specific regulations for the micro-credit sector, focusing on customer protection. On the back of these regulations, the industry had a hugely successful decade.

Today, the micro-credit sector is diverse and competitive with over 100 regulated players – Banks, SFBs, NBFC-MFIs and NBFCs. To ensure a level playing field, in March 2022, the RBI introduced the harmonised guidelines creating an entity agnostic but activity-based regulation. A clear regulatory framework, a sound underlying business model, performance trends overtime, and potentially large un- met demand has attracted private capital to sustain the growth.

As a result, micro-credit in India remains one of the largest micro-credit sectors globally, quite unmatched in terms of its outreach with low-ticket loans, scale, diversity of supply-side, spread, efficiency, performance, customer-protection standards, and contribution of the private sector.

MICROFINANCE SECTOR OUTREACH

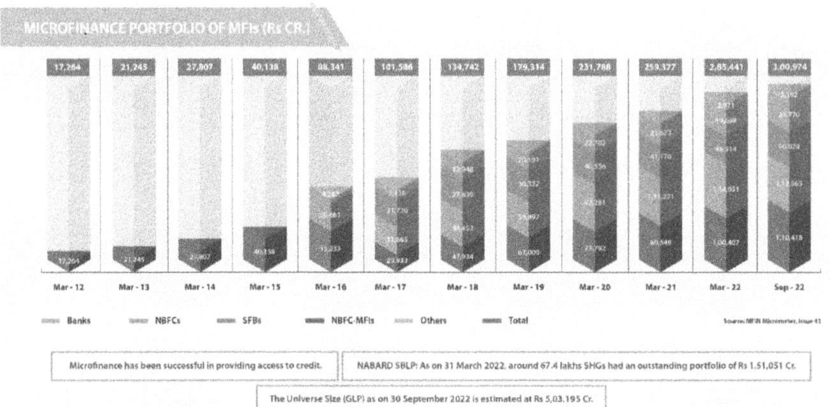

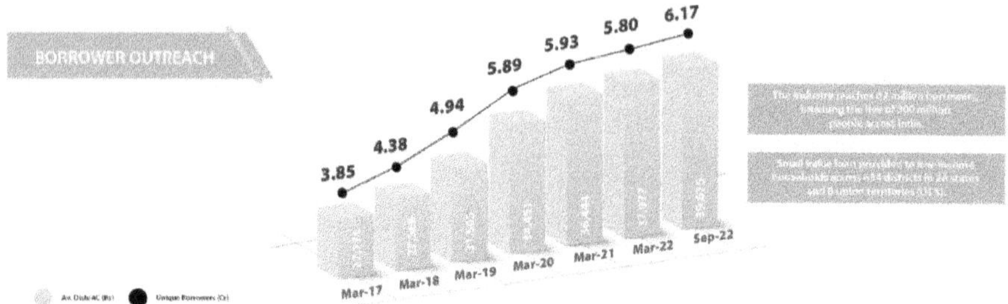

(Both photos courtesy mfin)*

Women Empowerment
Self Esteem
Digitalization
Rural Entrepreneurship
Income
Financial Inclusion
Financial Literacy
Sustainable Livelihood
Dignity
Financial Independence
Employment
Stability
Poverty alleviation

5.10. Industry Portfolio and Outreach:

The various categories of financial institutions engaged in the microfinance space in India include NBFC-MFIs, Banks, Small Finance Banks (SFBs), NBFCs and Others (including Non-profit MFIs).

As on 31 March 2023, 82 NBFC-MFIs are the largest provider of micro-credit with a loan amount outstanding of Rs 1,38,310 Cr, accounting for 39.7 % to total industry portfolio. 13 Banks hold the second largest share of portfolio in micro-credit with total loan outstanding of Rs 1,19,133 Cr, which is 34.2% of total micro-credit universe. SFBs have a total loan amount outstanding of Rs 57,828 Cr with total share of 16.6%. NBFCs account for another 8.5% and Other MFIs account for 1.0% of the universe.

Apart from MFIs, National Rural Livelihood Mission (NRLM) also contributes significantly to the microfinance universe through its SHG Bank Linkage Programme (SBLP). As of March 2023, around 83.4 lakhs SHG's had an outstanding portfolio of Rs 1,98,918 Cr with them.

Considering SHG outreach, the overall size of the universe in terms of GLP as on 31 March 2023 is roughly Rs 5,47,256 Cr.

As on: 31st March 2023

Types of Entity	No of Entities	Unique Borrowers (Cr)	Active Loan Accounts (Cr)	Portfolio O/s (Cr)
NBFC – MFIs	82	2.9	5.1	1,38,310
Banks	13	3.2	4.7	1,19,133
SFB	9	1.6	2	57,828
NBFC	69	0.9	1	29,440
Others	38	0.1	0.2	3,629
Total	**211**	**6.6**	**13**	**3,48,339**

5.11. Benefits of Microfinance:

To the Borrowers:

Microfinance is "a world in which as everyone, especially the poor and socially marginalized people and households have access to a wide range of affordable, high quality financial products and services, including not just credit but also savings, insurance, payment services, and fund transfers.

1. To the borrowers Financial Inclusion:

By bringing them into the folds of financial inclusion, Microfinance has ensured that the poor partake in the development of the nation.

2. Self-Sufficiency:

Innumerable stories illustrate how microfinance has made its customers self-sufficient through entrepreneurial activities, making their lives and that of their families, better.

3. Stability:

Access to steady and sustainable income as compared to one-time access to capital has helped borrowers by bringing in stability in their lives as against their prior vulnerability to the vagaries of life. Microfinance helped borrowers raise income, build assets and/or cushion themselves against external shocks.

4. Women Entrepreneurship:

Increase in the household incomes has improved self-esteem of woman, further motivating them, evident in the rise of many rural entrepreneurs.

5. Financial Literacy:

An understanding of financial matters is important before borrowers are entrusted with credit. Microfinance providers have focussed on financial literacy among borrowers to increase awareness about accessing credit, managing it, and utilising it wisely.

6. Digitization:

Microfinance has taken technology to the remotest parts of India. Be it mobile phones, or Apps or biometric devices, the rural woman is a happy digital customer, enjoying the ease of 'connectivity.

7. Crisis Support:

Behind the increased resilience of the borrower, is the solace provided by a microfinance provider. Time and again, microfinance providers have supported stressed borrowers in times of a calamity or crisis.

To the Nation:

Besides the obvious benefits of bringing a large section of the poor and unserved population of India into the folds of financial inclusion, the intangible benefits of Microfinance are immense.

The world has long been talking of sustainability of businesses, in which Microfinance has been a great contributor. By providing access to dependable credit through easily serviceable loans, income generating activities in rural India are now far more sustainable. Moreover, this sustainability of business has also enabled Microfinance to help the poor manage their poverty. With credit support of a regulated sector as against dependency on local moneylenders, the extreme poor now have a cushion or a so called 'safety net'. While the Prime Minister urged the nation to become digital, Microfinance can proudly claim to be one of the largest proponents of the movement by introducing newer and advanced digital technologies in rural India, truly contributing to the development of the nation. Focusing largely on women, microfinance has been a game changer rurally, empowering women and promoting entrepreneurial spirit.

An NCAER report analysed the contribution of the microfinance sector to the overall economy in terms of income or 'Gross Value Added', a measure of the national economic output and employment. The study points out that the present and potential contribution of microfinance to the macroeconomy is significant, especially considering its operations that focus on meeting the credit needs of the lower income households and smaller enterprises. Further, the promise of microfinance in meeting the credit needs of the poor and assisting them to overcome poverty has been at the core of the policy interest.

Microfinance also complements the efforts of public policies aimed at overall development and poverty reduction. Besides the economic impact of credit, there have also been social or non-economic benefits, one key area is women's empowerment. As per the study, the contribution of microfinance sector as a whole, including all MFIs and SHGs, is 2.03 per cent of GVA. In employment, the contribution of microfinance sector as a whole, inclusive of direct, indirect backward and forward linkages and including all MFIs and SHGs amounts to 128.46 lakh jobs.

The study also estimates that the contribution of the microfinance sector as a whole to the GVA is projected to reach 3.52 per cent of the GVA in 2025-26.

5.12. Indian and International forum's:

To further strengthen the microfinance universe and leverage from the combined learnings of various organizations in the sector, MFIN closely works with Associations and Forums in the space.

South Asian Micro Entrepreneurs Network (SAMN) is a regional network aiming at enhancing capacity, financing, and regional dialogue in the microfinance sector of South Asia. It is represented by leading apex institutions from the countries of the region along with the Agency for Technical Cooperation and Development (ACTED). Current SAMN Members include Afghanistan Microfinance Association (AMA), Credit Development Forum (CDF), Bangladesh, Centre for Microfinance (CMF), Nepal, Lanka Microfinance Practitioner's Association (LMFPA), Sri Lanka, Pakistan Microfinance Network (PMN) and Microfinance Institutions Network (MFIN) in India.

MFIN has a long-standing association with SAMN where together they have organised the SAMN Conclave, a platform that has, over the years, brought together various practitioners, policy makers and relevant stakeholders to brainstorm policy issues and exchange best practices. The Secretariat has curated customised research papers on Client Protection, Credit Bureaus etc.

Micro Units Development and Refinance Agency Bank (MUDRA) and the Governing Council of BFSI Sector Skill Council of India: MFIN CEO is currently on the Board of MUDRA & BFSI Sector Skill Council of India, engaging and steering support towards developments within the microfinance industry.

Sa-Dhan: MFIN enjoys a strong relationship with Sa-Dhan, also an SRO. Both the industry associations have been collaborating and putting their combined learning and efforts into crisis management, exemplified in their joint working during field stress in Assam and Covid 2019. The third edition of Code of Conduct and the Code for Responsible Lending was jointly revised and released during the Sa-Dhan National Conference held in September 2019.

Access Assist Development Services: MFIN has collaborated with Access Assist over the years by associating with the Inclusive Finance Summit. The Secretariat has been assisting Access in providing support services, knowledge resources and interaction across various forums to ensure that the contribution of microfinance within financial inclusion is well established.

5.13. The state-led microfinance movement in India began in the early 1980s as a response to the inadequate formal financial services available to the poor and marginalized sections of society, especially in rural areas. The government recognized the need to address financial inclusion and provide credit facilities to the unbanked population.

One of the pivotal moments in the state-led microfinance movement was the establishment of the National Bank for Agriculture and Rural Development (NABARD) in 1982. NABARD played a crucial role in promoting rural and agricultural development, including microfinance initiatives. It provided refinancing and credit facilities to cooperative banks and regional rural banks, which in turn extended financial services to rural and underserved areas.

MYRADA (Mysore Resettlement and Development Agency) is a well-known non-governmental organization (NGO) in India that works in the field of rural development and social empowerment. It was founded in 1968 in response to the challenges faced by the resettlement of refugees from Tibet in the Mysore region of Karnataka, India.

MYRADA's core mission is to promote sustainable livelihoods, rural development, and community empowerment, primarily focusing on marginalized and vulnerable populations in rural areas. Over the years, MYRADA has implemented various development projects and programs in sectors such as agriculture, natural resource management, water and sanitation, microfinance, and capacity-building.

Key areas of MYRADA's work include:

1. Watershed Development: MYRADA has been actively involved in implementing watershed development projects to improve water availability and agricultural productivity in drought-prone regions.

2. Livelihood Promotion: The organization focuses on promoting sustainable livelihoods through various interventions like farmer training, livelihood diversification, and promoting non-farm enterprises.

3. Women Empowerment: MYRADA places significant emphasis on women's empowerment and has implemented several projects to enhance their socio-economic status and leadership roles.

4. Community-Based Institutions: MYRADA promotes the formation and strengthening of community-based organizations, including self-help groups (SHGs), to foster self-reliance and participatory development.

5. Microfinance: MYRADA has played a key role in providing microfinance services to the rural poor, especially through the formation and support of women's SHGs.

MYRADA's work has made a positive impact on the lives of numerous rural communities, and it continues to be recognized for its commitment to sustainable development and social transformation:

5.14. After the success of the state-led microfinance movement in India, especially the SHG-Bank Linkage Program, the microfinance sector witnessed significant growth and diversification with the emergence of various Microfinance Institutions (MFIs) across the country. These MFIs were established to cater to the financial needs of the unbanked and underserved populations, particularly in rural areas. Let's explore the emergence of MFIs in India in more detail:

5.14.1. 1990s: The 1990s saw the establishment of several Non-Governmental Organizations (NGOs) and voluntary organizations that aimed to provide microcredit and other financial services to marginalized communities. Organizations like SKS Microfinance (now India Financial Inclusion Limited) and SHARE Microfin Limited were among the early MFIs to gain prominence.

5.14.2. Legal Framework: In the late 1990s, there was a push to formalize the microfinance sector by regulating and providing a legal framework for MFIs. In 1997, the Reserve Bank of India (RBI) issued guidelines for Non-Banking Financial Companies (NBFCs) engaged in microfinance activities, leading to the establishment of microfinance-specific NBFCs.

5.14.3. Microfinance Institutions Network (MFIN): In 2009, the Microfinance Institutions Network (MFIN) was formed as a self-regulatory organization to represent the interests of NBFC-MFIs and promote responsible microfinance practices.

5.14.4. Transformation to Small Finance Banks: With the enactment of the Microfinance Institutions (Development and Regulation) Act in 2010, the RBI introduced the concept of Small Finance Banks (SFBs). Several prominent MFIs converted themselves into SFBs to expand their product offerings and provide a full suite of banking services to their clients.

5.14.5. Diversification of Services: Over time, MFIs in India expanded their services beyond microcredit. They started offering savings products, insurance, remittance services, and financial literacy programs to cater to the diverse needs of their clients.

5.14.6. Impact Investing and Funding: The growth of MFIs in India attracted the attention of impact investors and development finance institutions, leading to increased funding and investments in the sector. This influx of capital enabled MFIs to scale up their operations and reach more clients.

5.14.7. Technology Integration: In recent years, technology has played a significant role in transforming the microfinance sector. Many MFIs have adopted digital platforms and mobile banking solutions to enhance operational efficiency and serve clients in remote areas.

Today, the microfinance sector in India continues to evolve and contribute to financial inclusion and poverty alleviation. Various MFIs, Small Finance Banks, and community-based institutions play a crucial role in providing financial services to millions of low-income individuals and micro-entrepreneurs, thereby empowering them and improving their socio-economic conditions.

5.15. Criteria for selection of SHG for bank Linkage programme:

The selection of Self-Help Groups (SHGs) for the Bank Linkage Program in India typically involves certain criteria to ensure the groups are financially viable, socially cohesive, and capable of managing credit responsibly. While specific criteria might vary among different financial institutions or organizations involved in the program, some common factors considered for selection are:

1. Regular Meetings: SHGs that conduct regular meetings and maintain proper records are preferred. A group that meets at least once a month and maintains accurate records of their financial transactions and activities is considered more organized and disciplined.

2. Membership: The SHG should have a minimum number of members, often ranging from 10 to 20 individuals. This ensures that the group is diverse enough to cater to the financial needs of its members and has adequate social cohesion.

3. Homogeneity: The members of the SHG should be from a similar socio-economic background or occupation to foster a sense of common purpose and mutual understanding.

4. Savings Culture: The SHG should have a consistent savings culture, and its members should contribute regularly to a common savings fund. A strong savings habit reflects financial discipline and the ability to manage funds responsibly.

5. Transparent Operations: The SHG should operate with transparency and accountability. This includes maintaining clear and accurate records, ensuring fair decision-making processes, and having an open atmosphere for discussion among members.

6. Creditworthiness: SHGs are often assessed for their creditworthiness based on their repayment history and past financial performance. A track record of timely repayments on previous loans (if any) demonstrates the group's creditworthiness.

7. Social Cohesion: The SHG members should have a strong social bond and trust among themselves, as this helps in maintaining group solidarity and joint liability.

8. Leadership: The SHG should have capable and responsible leaders who can guide the group effectively and represent its interests.

9. Business Plan: The SHG may be asked to present a viable business plan that outlines the purpose of the loan, its utilization, and the expected income-generating activities.

Financial institutions and agencies involved in the Bank Linkage Program use these criteria to assess the viability and creditworthiness of SHGs before providing them with formal financial services like credit and savings facilities. The goal is to ensure that the selected SHGs can use credit responsibly and improve their socio-economic conditions effectively.

5.16. Uniqueness of SHG bank Linkage programme:

The Self-Help Group (SHG) Bank Linkage Program in India is a unique and innovative approach to financial inclusion and poverty alleviation. Several factors contribute to the uniqueness of this program:

1. Grassroots Approach: The SHG Bank Linkage Program is based on a grassroots-level approach, empowering women in rural areas to come together and form self-help groups. It leverages the existing social networks and trust among group members to promote financial inclusion.

2. Women Empowerment: The program has a strong focus on women's empowerment. SHGs are predominantly women-centric, and the program aims to enhance their decision-making power, financial independence, and social standing.

3. Group Liability: SHG members are jointly liable for the repayment of loans taken by any individual member. This group liability encourages peer pressure and ensures a high rate of loan repayment, reducing the risk for financial institutions.

4. Microcredit Delivery: The SHG Bank Linkage Program facilitates the delivery of microcredit to the doorstep of underserved communities. This approach overcomes the barriers of distance and accessibility faced by rural borrowers in accessing formal financial services.

5. Savings Mobilization: In addition to credit, the program emphasizes the importance of savings mobilization within SHGs. Members contribute regular savings to a common fund, building a financial cushion and fostering a culture of thrift.

6. Integration with Formal Banking System: The program integrates informal self-help groups with the formal banking system. SHGs establish banking relationships with commercial banks, regional rural banks, and cooperative banks, gaining access to formal credit facilities.

7. Scalability and Replicability: The SHG Bank Linkage Program has demonstrated scalability and replicability. It has been successfully implemented across various states in India and has inspired similar initiatives in other countries, promoting financial inclusion on a global scale.

8. Social and Financial Transformation: The program goes beyond providing access to credit. It promotes social transformation by empowering women, enhancing financial literacy, and fostering community development.

9. Sustainable Impact: The SHG Bank Linkage Program has shown sustainable impact over the years, helping to alleviate poverty, improve living standards, and enhance economic opportunities for rural communities.

The unique features and success of the SHG Bank Linkage Program have made it a model for inclusive finance worldwide. It has contributed significantly to the growth of the microfinance sector in India and has been recognized as an effective tool for poverty reduction and social empowerment.

5.17. Advantage of SHG bank Linkage Program:

The Self-Help Group (SHG) Bank Linkage Program in India offers numerous advantages and benefits for both the participating SHGs and the financial institutions involved. Some of the key advantages of the program are:

1. Financial Inclusion: The program promotes financial inclusion by bringing unbanked and underserved populations into the formal financial system. It helps individuals in rural areas gain access to credit and savings facilities, which were previously unavailable to them.

2. Empowerment of Women: The SHG Bank Linkage Program has a strong focus on women's empowerment. By forming and participating in SHGs, women gain financial independence, decision-making power, and enhanced social status within their communities.

3. Peer Support and Group Liability: SHGs operate on the principle of group liability, where all members are jointly responsible for each other's loans. This creates peer pressure and ensures high repayment rates, reducing the risk for financial institutions.

4. Credit Access for Small Borrowers: The program targets small and marginalized borrowers who may not qualify for formal bank loans individually. By pooling resources within the group, SHG members can access larger loan amounts than they could as individuals.

5. Low Transaction Costs: Since SHGs are local and self-managed, the administrative and transaction costs for financial institutions are relatively low. This makes it cost-effective for banks to serve rural areas and extend microcredit.

5.18. Pilar's of SHG bank Linkage Program:

The SHG Bank Linkage Program was initially piloted in India by a few organizations and financial institutions to test its feasibility and effectiveness. The program's success during the pilot phase led to its subsequent expansion and widespread adoption. Some of the prominent pilots and key players of the SHG Bank Linkage Program include:

1. National Bank for Agriculture and Rural Development (NABARD): NABARD played a crucial role in piloting the SHG Bank Linkage Program in the early 1990s. It provided the necessary financial support, technical expertise, and guidance to test the linkage between SHGs and banks.

2. MYRADA: The Mysore Resettlement and Development Agency (MYRADA) was among the pioneering organizations that piloted the SHG Bank Linkage Program in the state of Karnataka. MYRADA's successful implementation served as a model for the expansion of the program.

3. National Dairy Development Board (NDDB): NDDB, through its subsidiary, Mother Dairy, piloted the SHG Bank Linkage Program in Gujarat. This pilot aimed to link dairy cooperative-based SHGs with formal banks.

4. NABFINS: NABARD Financial Services Limited (NABFINS) is a subsidiary of NABARD that piloted the SHG Bank Linkage Program in Tamil Nadu. NABFINS provides financial and technical assistance to SHGs for their linkage with banks.

5. Self-Employed Women's Association (SEWA): SEWA was instrumental in piloting the SHG Bank Linkage Program in the state of Gujarat. It played a significant role in promoting the program's women-centric approach.

6. SKS Microfinance (BFIL): SKS Microfinance (BFIL), which later became India Financial Inclusion Limited (BFIL), was among the first MFIs to pilot the SHG Bank Linkage Program in the state of Andhra Pradesh.

These organizations, along with the support of NABARD and other development agencies, conducted pilot projects to demonstrate the viability and impact of linking SHGs with formal banks. The successful outcomes of these pilots provided evidence of the program's effectiveness in promoting financial inclusion, women's empowerment, and community development. As a result, the program gained momentum, and various financial institutions, NGOs, and government agencies adopted and scaled it up across different states in India. Today, the SHG Bank Linkage Program is a well-established model for microfinance and financial inclusion, benefitting millions of individuals across the country.

5.19. Purpose of loan under SHG bank Linkage Programme:

The purpose of loans provided under the Self-Help Group (SHG) Bank Linkage Program is to support income-generating activities and meet the financial needs of the SHG members. These loans are typically small-ticket loans, tailored to the specific requirements of the individual members and the collective needs of the SHG. The primary purposes of loans under the SHG Bank Linkage Program are as follows:

1. Income Generation: One of the main objectives of providing loans is to facilitate income-generating activities for SHG members. These activities may include small businesses, agriculture, livestock rearing, handicrafts, and other livelihood ventures.

2. Small Business Expansion: SHG members may use the loans to expand their existing small businesses or start new ventures. This helps in increasing their income and improving their financial stability.

3. Agricultural and Allied Activities: Loans are often utilized by SHG members engaged in agriculture for purchasing inputs, seeds, fertilizers, and equipment, as well as for meeting expenses related to land preparation and irrigation.

4. Livestock Development: SHG members involved in livestock rearing may use the loans for purchasing livestock, improving animal husbandry practices, and expanding their livestock enterprises.

5. Working Capital Support: Loans are often provided as working capital support to members engaged in small trading and retail activities, enabling them to procure goods and maintain inventory.

6. Education and Healthcare Expenses: SHG members may also use loans to meet expenses related to education, healthcare, and emergencies.

7. Housing Improvement: In some cases, loans are provided to SHG members to improve their housing conditions, such as constructing or renovating their houses.

The loans under the SHG Bank Linkage Program are generally provided without the requirement of collateral, relying on the group's joint liability and peer support. Repayment of loans is usually on a regular basis, either weekly, fortnightly, or monthly, depending on the loan terms.

By providing loans for income-generating purposes, the program aims to uplift the socio-economic status of SHG members, empower women, and promote self-reliance among marginalized and underserved communities in rural areas. The SHG Bank Linkage Program has been successful in promoting financial inclusion and empowering women by providing them with access to formal credit and financial services.

5.20. Models under SHG bank Linkage Programme:

Under the Self-Help Group (SHG) Bank Linkage Programme in India, several models and approaches have been implemented to facilitate financial inclusion and empower marginalized communities. Some of the common models used under the SHG Bank Linkage Programme are:

1. SHG Joint Liability Group (JLG) Model: In this model, SHG members come together to form a Joint Liability Group. The group collectively applies for a loan from a formal financial institution. Each member of the group is jointly liable for the repayment of the loan, fostering peer support and ensuring higher repayment rates.

2. SHG Federations Model: In this model, several SHGs in a specific area or region are federated into a higher-level organization known as an SHG Federation. The federation acts as a link between the SHGs and the formal financial institutions. It helps in coordinating with banks, ensuring better access to credit, and providing support and training to SHGs.

3. Cluster-Based Model: In the cluster-based approach, multiple SHGs in a particular geographic area are linked with a single bank branch. The bank provides financial services to all the SHGs in that cluster, streamlining the linkage process and making it more efficient.

4. Individual Bank Linkage Model: In this model, individual SHG members are linked with formal financial institutions directly. Each member has an individual savings account and can access credit based on their creditworthiness and repayment history.

5. Promoting Institution Model: Under this model, SHG promoting institutions, such as NGOs or government agencies, play a significant role in facilitating the formation and capacity-building of SHGs. These institutions act as intermediaries, assisting SHGs in accessing financial services from formal banks.

6. Linkage with Small Finance Banks (SFBs): With the establishment of Small Finance Banks, some SHGs have direct linkages with these banks, which offer a broader range of banking services beyond microcredit.

7. Linkage with Cooperative Banks: Many SHGs are linked with cooperative banks, which are local financial institutions that play a significant role in rural areas.

Each model serves different contexts and regions, and the selection of the most appropriate model depends on factors such as the local financial ecosystem, the nature of the SHGs, and the objectives of financial inclusion and empowerment. The SHG Bank Linkage Programme has been instrumental in promoting inclusive finance, women's empowerment, and community development in India.

5.21. SHG Bank Linkage Model Advantages and Limitations:

The SHG Bank Linkage Model in India has brought significant advantages in promoting financial inclusion, empowering women, and fostering community development. However, like any program, it also has some limitations. Let's explore both the advantages and limitations:

Advantages:

1. Financial Inclusion: The SHG Bank Linkage Model has been instrumental in bringing the unbanked and underserved population into the formal banking system. It provides access to formal credit and savings facilities to those who were previously excluded from mainstream financial services.

2. Empowerment of Women: The program's women-centric approach has empowered women by providing them with a platform to pool their resources, make collective decisions, and access credit. It has enhanced their financial independence, decision-making abilities, and social status.

3. Peer Support and Group Liability: The model's joint liability feature encourages peer support and ensures a high rate of loan repayment. Group members collectively bear the responsibility for loan repayments, leading to lower default rates.

4. Low Transaction Costs: The program operates on a grassroots level, with self-managed SHGs, resulting in relatively lower administrative and transaction costs for financial institutions involved in the linkage.

5. Community Development: SHGs foster social cohesion and community development. They facilitate collective decision-making, address local issues, and undertake community development initiatives.

6. Sustainable Impact: The program's emphasis on building financial skills and social capital helps members continue to benefit even after completing their initial loan cycles, leading to sustainable socio-economic impact.

7. Scalability: The SHG Bank Linkage Model has demonstrated scalability and replicability. It can be expanded to serve a larger number of people in various regions, making it an effective tool for widespread financial inclusion.

Limitations:

1. Limited Coverage: Despite its successes, the SHG Bank Linkage Model has not reached all underserved areas and populations. In some regions, access to formal financial services remains inadequate.

2. Over-Reliance on Women: The program's focus on women empowerment sometimes leads to the exclusion of men from financial services, even though they might be in need of credit and other financial assistance.

3. Informal Nature of SHGs: Some SHGs may face challenges in maintaining proper records, adhering to financial regulations, and managing funds, which can affect their creditworthiness and restrict access to larger loans.

4. Limited Product Diversity: The SHG Bank Linkage Model primarily provides credit and savings services, but other financial products, such as insurance and pension schemes, may not be adequately integrated into the program.

5. Variability in SHG Performance: SHGs' performance can vary significantly based on factors such as the strength of social cohesion, leadership quality, and the commitment of group members.

6. Limited Scope for Individual Lending: The joint liability feature may limit individual access to credit for members who have different credit needs or risk profiles.

Despite its limitations, the SHG Bank Linkage Model has proven to be a successful approach in promoting financial inclusion and women's empowerment. Efforts to address its limitations can help in further enhancing its impact and reach.

5.22. Micro enterprise Development Program in SHG bank Linkage Model:

In the Self-Help Group (SHG) bank linkage model, the Micro Enterprise Development Program is integrated with the SHG approach. SHGs are small groups of individuals, typically women from similar socio-economic backgrounds, who come together to save money, access credit, and engage in income-generating activities.

The Micro Enterprise Development Program, in this context, focuses on providing support and training to SHG members to start and expand micro-enterprises. This support can include skill development, business management training, access to credit facilities through the SHG-bank linkage, and mentoring to help the members establish and sustain their businesses.

By combining the SHG bank linkage model with the Micro Enterprise Development Program, the aim is to empower marginalized communities, especially women, by enhancing their economic opportunities and promoting self-sufficiency. It has been a successful approach in promoting financial inclusion and socio-economic development in various regions, particularly in rural areas.

5.23. Performance under a SHG-bank linkage program:

SHG-bank linkage programs have shown promising results in various regions, particularly in India and some other developing countries. These programs aim to promote financial inclusion and socio-economic empowerment of women and marginalized communities by linking Self-Help Groups (SHGs) with formal financial institutions like banks.

The performance of SHG-bank linkage programs is often measured based on several key indicators:

1. **Increased Financial Inclusion:** These programs enable SHG members to access formal financial services, including savings accounts, credit facilities, and insurance products, which were previously out of reach for many.

2. **Empowerment of Women:** As many SHGs predominantly comprise women, the linkage programs have contributed to women's empowerment by providing them with a platform to save, access credit, and engage in income-generating activities.

3. **Savings Mobilization:** SHGs encourage regular savings among their members, and the linkage with banks helps mobilize these savings, making them accessible for productive purposes.

4. **Credit Disbursement:** SHG members gain access to credit through the bank linkage, allowing them to invest in various income-generating activities, agricultural ventures, or small businesses.

5. **Repayment Performance:** One crucial aspect of the program's success is the timely repayment of loans by SHG members. Good repayment rates indicate the effectiveness of the program and the disciplined financial behavior of the members.

6. Social Capital and Community Development: SHG-bank linkage programs also foster social capital within communities, encouraging collective decision-making and supporting social initiatives.

It's essential to note that the performance of these programs can vary depending on the implementation, geographical location, and the commitment of the involved stakeholders. To get the most recent and accurate performance data, it's recommended to consult official reports, research papers, or relevant organizations that are actively involved in implementing and evaluating SHG-bank linkage programs.

5.24. Qualitative Aspects of SHG Landing:

The qualitative aspects of Self-Help Group (SHG) lending refer to the non-financial or subjective factors that influence the effectiveness and impact of lending within SHGs. These aspects play a crucial role in determining the success and sustainability of SHG lending programs. Some of the key qualitative aspects include:

1. Social Cohesion: The strength of the group's social fabric and cohesion is vital for successful SHG lending. Strong interpersonal relationships, trust, and cooperation among SHG members promote timely repayments, mutual support, and collective decision-making.

2. Empowerment: SHG lending should empower members, especially women, by providing them with financial access, enhancing their decision-making capabilities, and enabling them to engage in income-generating activities.

3. Group Dynamics: The dynamics within the SHG, including leadership, participation, and communication, influence the effectiveness of the lending process. Efficient group functioning fosters transparency and accountability.

4. Capacity Building: Providing training and capacity-building opportunities to SHG members regarding financial literacy, business skills, and market linkages enhances their ability to manage loans and undertake income-generating activities.

5. **Inclusivity:** SHG lending should be inclusive, reaching out to the most marginalized and vulnerable sections of society. Inclusivity ensures that those who need financial support the most can benefit from the program.

6. **Social Capital:** SHG lending helps build social capital within communities, leading to collective action, increased social support, and community development initiatives.

7. **Repayment Culture:** Encouraging a strong repayment culture within SHGs is critical for sustainability. Members must be committed to repaying loans on time, which helps ensure the availability of credit for other members in need.

8. **Local Context:** Understanding and adapting the lending program to the local socio-economic context and specific needs of the community is crucial for its success.

9. **Supportive Ecosystem:** A supportive ecosystem involving NGOs, financial institutions, and government agencies can facilitate the success of SHG lending by providing guidance, resources, and policy support.

Considering and addressing these qualitative aspects is essential to maximize the positive impact of SHG lending on poverty reduction, women's empowerment, and community development.

5.25. Findings of NABARD study 2010 conducted in seven states in India:

The study findings of NABARD (2010) conducted in seven states in India revealed the following:

SHGs have helped to reduce the dependence on local moneylenders (upto 66% of the members are now free - either fully or partially from the clutches of local moneylenders in Tamil Nadu and as high as 92% in Karnataka).

Bankers continue to take long time to provide the first loan to SHGs and only a few groups were able to get bank loans after six months.

While NGOs and Government departments provided skill training to the SHG members, bankers as SHPIs were not very proactive in providing vocational training to members.

The training given by the SHPIs did not meet the skill requirements of the members for taking up suitable income generating activities.

There is laxity in enforcing group discipline like regular attendance and regular savings in the meetings.

Asset creation out of the SHG loan is seen in about 28 per cent cases while in other cases loans are used for consumption/purchase of utility items of household goods.

Competition among various SHPIs and emphasis on achieving targets also resulted in multiple memberships by SHG members.

5.26. Initiatives by NABARD:

NABARD (National Bank for Agriculture and Rural Development) has been actively involved in various initiatives aimed at promoting rural development and agriculture in India. Some of the key initiatives by NABARD include:

1. Rural Credit Initiatives: NABARD plays a significant role in providing credit support to rural areas through various schemes and programs. It refinances and supervises Regional Rural Banks (RRBs), State Cooperative Banks (SCBs), and other financial institutions to ensure adequate and affordable credit to farmers and rural entrepreneurs.

2. Self-Help Group (SHG) Bank Linkage Program: NABARD has been instrumental in promoting the SHG-bank linkage model, which empowers women and marginalized communities by enabling them to access credit and financial services through their self-formed groups.

3. Watershed Development Projects: NABARD supports watershed development projects to conserve water, increase agricultural productivity, and enhance rural livelihoods through sustainable land and water management practices.

4. Farmer Producer Organizations (FPOs): NABARD encourages the formation and capacity-building of Farmer Producer Organizations to promote collective farming, marketing, and value addition for small and marginal farmers.

5. Rural Infrastructure Development Fund (RIDF): NABARD manages RIDF, which finances critical rural infrastructure projects such as roads, bridges, irrigation systems, and rural electrification.

6. Financial Inclusion Initiatives: NABARD works towards extending financial services to the unbanked and underserved areas through initiatives like Financial Inclusion Fund (FIF) and facilitating the deployment of Point of Sale (POS) machines in rural areas.

7. Climate Change and Sustainable Agriculture: NABARD supports projects related to climate change adaptation, renewable energy, and sustainable agriculture practices to build resilience in rural communities.

8. Farmer Connect Initiatives: NABARD engages with farmers through Farmer Clubs, Farmers' Melas (fairs), and various extension services to disseminate agricultural knowledge and best practices.

9. Rural Entrepreneurship Development Programmes: NABARD provides training and skill development programs to rural youth and entrepreneurs to promote self-employment and livelihood opportunities.

5.27. Role of NABARD for other microfinance initiatives:

NABARD (National Bank for Agriculture and Rural Development) plays a significant role in supporting and coordinating various microfinance initiatives in India. Its role extends beyond its own microfinance programs to foster a conducive environment for microfinance institutions (MFIs) and other stakeholders in the microfinance sector. Some of the key roles of NABARD in supporting other microfinance initiatives are:

1. **Refinancing:** NABARD provides refinancing support to microfinance institutions, cooperative banks, and regional rural banks that extend microcredit to small farmers, rural entrepreneurs, and Self-Help Groups (SHGs). This ensures that these financial institutions have access to affordable funds to lend to the target beneficiaries.

2. **Capacity Building:** NABARD conducts training and capacity-building programs for microfinance institutions, SHGs, and other stakeholders to enhance their financial management skills, promote responsible lending practices, and improve overall operational efficiency.

3. **Regulatory Support:** NABARD collaborates with regulatory bodies and policymakers to advocate for supportive policies and regulations that promote responsible microfinance practices and protect the interests of borrowers.

4. **Monitoring and Evaluation:** NABARD monitors and evaluates the performance and impact of microfinance programs to assess their effectiveness and identify areas for improvement.

5. **Research and Knowledge Dissemination:** NABARD conducts research and studies related to microfinance and rural development to generate insights and share best practices with the microfinance sector and other stakeholders.

6. **Technology Adoption:** NABARD encourages the adoption of technology in microfinance operations, such as digital payment systems and mobile banking, to improve accessibility and efficiency of financial services in rural areas.

7. **Linkages and Partnerships:** NABARD facilitates linkages between microfinance institutions and banks, encouraging the flow of funds and resources to the microfinance sector. It also promotes partnerships between

MFIs and other development organizations to leverage resources and expertise.

8. Financial Inclusion: NABARD actively contributes to the government's financial inclusion agenda by supporting microfinance initiatives that extend financial services to the unbanked and underserved sections of society.

5.28. Joint Liability Groups in Microfinance:

Joint Liability Groups (JLGs) are an important mechanism in microfinance that allows individuals, typically from similar socio-economic backgrounds, to come together and access credit as a group. JLGs are formed to address the limitations faced by individual borrowers in the absence of collateral and credit history. These groups are prevalent in various microfinance initiatives and are commonly used in India.

Key characteristics and features of Joint Liability Groups in microfinance:

1. Group Formation: JLGs consist of 4 to 10 individuals who voluntarily come together to form a cohesive borrowing group. They may be friends, neighbors, or belong to the same community.

2. Joint Liability: In a JLG, the members share joint liability for the repayment of loans taken by any member of the group. If one member defaults on the loan, the other members become collectively responsible for repaying the outstanding amount.

3. Collateral Substitute: JLGs serve as a substitute for traditional collateral in microfinance lending. The collective responsibility of the group members reduces the risk for the lender and improves access to credit for the individual borrowers.

4. Individual Loans: While the group members are jointly liable, each member is eligible for an individual loan amount based on their credit needs and repayment capacity. The loan is used for income-generating activities or productive purposes.

5. Social Pressure and Peer Monitoring: The mutual trust and social pressure within the group create an environment of peer monitoring, ensuring that members are motivated to repay their loans promptly.

6. Regular Meetings: JLGs typically hold regular meetings to discuss loan utilization, repayment schedules, and other matters related to their collective financial activities.

7. Graduation to Higher Loans: Successful repayment and regularity in the group's financial activities can lead to higher loan amounts and improved creditworthiness for individual members.

JLGs have proven to be effective in promoting financial inclusion and empowering individuals, particularly in rural areas where access to credit is limited. They promote a sense of responsibility, self-discipline, and financial inclusion among the members, while also reducing the risks for lenders. As a result, Joint Liability Groups play a vital role in microfinance programs that aim to uplift communities and support small-scale entrepreneurs.

5.29. Microfinance Institutional Approach:

The Microfinance Institutional Approach refers to the strategy and structure adopted by microfinance institutions (MFIs) to provide financial services to the unbanked and underserved populations, especially in rural areas. It focuses on establishing specialized institutions dedicated to delivering microfinance services and products, aiming to promote financial inclusion and poverty alleviation. This approach has been instrumental in reaching out to millions of individuals who lack access to traditional banking services.

Key elements of the Microfinance Institutional Approach:

1. Targeted Clientele: MFIs primarily target low-income individuals, especially those engaged in microenterprises and small-scale businesses.

These clients often lack collateral and formal credit history, making them less attractive to traditional banks.

2. Financial Services: MFIs offer a range of financial services, including microloans, savings accounts, insurance products, and remittances. The services are tailored to meet the specific needs of the target clientele and support income-generating activities.

3. Group Lending: Many MFIs adopt the group lending model, such as Self-Help Groups (SHGs) or Joint Liability Groups (JLGs), to extend credit to their clients. Group-based lending enhances repayment discipline through social pressure and mutual support among group members.

4. Relationship-based Approach: MFIs emphasize building strong relationships with their clients by understanding their needs, offering personalized financial solutions, and providing financial literacy training.

5.30. Bank Partnership Model of Microfinance in India:

The Bank Partnership Model of Microfinance in India is a collaborative approach that involves microfinance institutions (MFIs) partnering with mainstream commercial banks to extend financial services to underserved and financially excluded populations. This model leverages the strengths of both MFIs and banks to reach a larger number of clients, especially in rural and semi-urban areas.

Key features of the Bank Partnership Model of Microfinance in India:

1. Refinancing and Funding: Under this model, commercial banks provide funds to MFIs through refinancing arrangements or direct credit lines. This allows MFIs to access the necessary capital to expand their lending operations.

2. Risk Sharing: Banks and MFIs share the credit risk associated with lending to low-income clients. While the MFIs have a better understanding of their clients and provide on-ground support, the banks bring in their financial expertise and resources.

3. **Leveraging Infrastructure:** Commercial banks have an established branch network and technology infrastructure, which can be utilized by MFIs to extend their services to remote areas more efficiently.

4. **Regulatory Compliance:** MFIs partnering with banks need to adhere to the regulations set forth by the Reserve Bank of India (RBI) and other regulatory bodies governing the microfinance sector.

5. **Product Diversification:** The partnership allows MFIs to offer a broader range of financial products and services, such as savings accounts and insurance, in addition to microloans.

6. **Capacity Building:** The collaboration between MFIs and banks often involves capacity-building initiatives to enhance the skills and knowledge of MFI staff, improve credit appraisal processes, and ensure adherence to best practices.

7. **Customer Base Expansion:** Through the bank partnership model, MFIs can access the bank's existing customer base, leading to potential cross-selling opportunities and increased outreach.

8. **Technology Integration:** Integration of technology and digital platforms between the bank and MFI can streamline processes, improve data management, and reduce operational costs.

The Bank Partnership Model of Microfinance in India has played a significant role in scaling up microfinance operations and reaching a wider segment of the population. It has contributed to financial inclusion by providing access to formal credit and other financial services to previously underserved communities. This collaboration between MFIs and banks has been mutually beneficial, allowing banks to fulfil their priority sector lending targets and MFIs to access resources and expertise to expand their outreach.

5.31. Bank Partnership Model, Business Correspondence Model in Indian Banking industry:

The Bank Partnership Model and the Business Correspondence Model are two important approaches in the Indian banking industry aimed at extending banking services to unbanked and underbanked populations, particularly in rural areas. Both models involve collaboration between banks and third-party entities to enhance financial inclusion.

1. Bank Partnership Model:

In the Bank Partnership Model, commercial banks partner with Microfinance Institutions (MFIs) or other Non-Banking Financial Companies (NBFCs) to expand their reach and provide financial services to underserved communities. Under this model, the bank extends credit lines or refinancing facilities to the partnering entity (MFI or NBFC), which then acts as a channel for the bank to deliver banking services to customers.

Key features of the Bank Partnership Model:

The partnering entity (MFI or NBFC) serves as a Business Correspondent (BC) on behalf of the bank.

The BC acts as an intermediary, facilitating account opening, cash deposits, withdrawals, and other banking transactions in areas where the bank doesn't have a physical presence.

The BC is responsible for onboarding customers, collecting necessary documents, and providing customer support.

The bank remains responsible for regulatory compliance and risk management while leveraging the BC's local knowledge and outreach.

2. Business Correspondence Model:

The Business Correspondence Model is a broader approach that involves partnerships between banks and various entities (individuals, entities, or non-bank entities) to act as business correspondents. These correspondents enable the delivery of basic banking services in areas where the bank has limited presence.

Key features of the Business Correspondence Model:

Business correspondents can include individuals (e.g., local kirana shop owners), banking agents, retail entities, NGOs, or other organizations.

Correspondents are appointed by the bank and authorized to conduct specified banking transactions on behalf of the bank.

They act as touchpoints for customers, offering banking services like account opening, deposits, withdrawals, and remittances.

The model helps banks extend their outreach to remote and financially underserved areas without the need to set up brick-and-mortar branches.

Both the Bank Partnership Model and the Business Correspondence Model have been instrumental in promoting financial inclusion in India. They leverage the strengths of different entities to bridge the gap between banks and the unbanked population, improving access to formal financial services and fostering economic development in underserved regions. These models have played a crucial role in expanding the reach of banking services and achieving the objectives of financial inclusion set by the Reserve Bank of India (RBI).

5.32. Nutrition value of microfinance in BPL families:

Microfinance can play a role in improving the nutrition of Below Poverty Line (BPL) families by providing them with access to financial services and resources. While microfinance itself does not directly address nutritional challenges, it can indirectly contribute to better nutrition through several mechanisms:

1. Income Generation: Microfinance loans enable BPL families to invest in income-generating activities, such as small businesses or agricultural ventures. Increased income can lead to improved purchasing power and better access to nutritious food.

2. Diversification of Livelihoods: With access to microfinance, BPL families may diversify their livelihood options, reducing their reliance on a single source of income. This diversification can improve overall economic stability and, in turn, enhance their ability to afford nutritious food.

3. Women's Empowerment: Microfinance programs often prioritize women borrowers, empowering them as decision-makers and income earners. Studies suggest that empowered women are more likely to invest in their families' nutrition and well-being.

4. Investment in Health and Education: Microfinance loans can also be utilized for investments in health and education. Improved health and education outcomes positively influence nutrition and well-being in BPL households.

5. Social Capital: Participation in microfinance groups, such as Self-Help Groups (SHGs), fosters social capital and community support. This can lead to knowledge-sharing on nutrition, health, and hygiene practices within the community.

While microfinance can have a positive impact on the nutrition of BPL families, it's essential to recognize that addressing nutritional challenges requires a multi-dimensional approach. Nutrition outcomes are influenced by factors such as education, healthcare, sanitation, and access to clean drinking water. Microfinance programs can be more effective in improving nutrition outcomes when integrated with other social development initiatives and targeted interventions focused on health and nutrition education.

5.33. Microfinance Institutional Structure in India:

The microfinance institutional structure in India comprises a diverse ecosystem of various entities that work together to provide financial services to low-income and underserved populations. The structure is designed to foster financial inclusion and promote socio-economic development in rural and semi-urban areas. Here are the key components of the microfinance institutional structure in India:

1. **Non-Banking Financial Companies:** Microfinance Institutions (NBFC-MFIs): NBFC-MFIs are specialized financial institutions that focus on providing microfinance services to the target population. They are registered as NBFCs with the Reserve Bank of India (RBI) and follow specific regulations for microfinance operations.

2. **Self-Help Groups (SHGs):** SHGs are small groups of individuals, primarily women, who come together to save money regularly and provide mutual support. They act as primary units for microfinance operations and are linked with banks to access credit and other financial services.

3. **Regional Rural Banks (RRBs):** RRBs are government-owned banks operating at the regional level. They play a vital role in providing financial services to rural areas, including microfinance lending to individuals and SHGs.

4. **Commercial Banks:** Commercial banks, both public and private sector, are crucial players in the microfinance sector. They partner with NBFC-MFIs and NGOs as well as directly lend to SHGs and individuals through the Joint Liability Group (JLG) model.

5. **Non-Governmental Organizations (NGOs):** Several NGOs in India are actively involved in microfinance initiatives. They often act as intermediaries between funding agencies and beneficiaries, facilitating financial services and capacity-building for the target population.

6. **National Bank for Agriculture and Rural Development (NABARD):** NABARD is a development bank that plays a significant role in promoting rural and agricultural development, including supporting microfinance initiatives through refinancing and capacity-building programs.

7. **Small Finance Banks:** Small Finance Banks are specialized banks that primarily serve the unbanked and underbanked population, including

microfinance borrowers. They have a mandate to focus on financial inclusion and provide a wide range of financial services.

8. Microfinance Networks and Associations: Various microfinance networks and associations, such as Sa-Dhan and Microfinance Institutions Network (MFIN), work towards the development and strengthening of the microfinance sector in India. They provide a platform for knowledge-sharing, advocacy, and capacity-building.

The microfinance institutional structure in India is multi-faceted, comprising a combination of formal financial institutions, self-help groups, and non-governmental organizations working together to address the financial needs of the underserved population and promote inclusive growth.

The Role of Stakeholders in Developing the Microfinance Sector Like Government, Regulatory Agency, Apex Bodies, Banks, Donors, MFOs, Community Based Service Providers, Support Organizations:

The development of the microfinance sector involves the collective efforts of various stakeholders, each playing a crucial role in promoting financial inclusion and empowering underserved communities.

5.34. Here's the role of each stakeholder:

1. Government:

Formulating Policy and Regulatory Framework: Governments set the policy and regulatory framework for the microfinance sector to ensure transparency, consumer protection, and responsible lending practices.

Allocating Funds: Governments may allocate funds or create special funds to support microfinance initiatives and promote financial inclusion.

Supporting Capacity Building: Governments may support capacity-building programs to enhance the skills and knowledge of microfinance institutions and service providers.

2. Regulatory Agencies:

Monitoring and Supervision: Regulatory agencies oversee the operations of microfinance institutions, ensuring compliance with regulations and safeguarding the interests of clients.

Setting Prudential Norms: Regulatory agencies set prudential norms, such as capital adequacy and loan portfolio quality, to maintain the stability and sustainability of microfinance institutions.

3. Apex Bodies:

Representation and Advocacy: Apex bodies like industry associations represent the collective interests of microfinance institutions, engage in advocacy efforts, and liaise with the government and regulatory agencies.

4. Banks:

Refinancing and Funding: Banks provide refinancing facilities and credit lines to microfinance institutions, helping them expand their operations and reach underserved populations.

Partnering with Microfinance Institutions: Banks collaborate with microfinance institutions through the Bank Partnership Model to extend financial services to unbanked and underbanked communities.

5. Donors:

Funding Support: Donors provide financial assistance to microfinance institutions and support organizations to enhance their capacity and outreach.

Research and Innovation: Donors often fund research and innovative projects in the microfinance sector to identify best practices and effective strategies.

6. Microfinance Institutions (MFIs):

Service Delivery: MFIs are at the forefront of delivering microfinance services, including microloans, savings, and insurance, to the target population.

Client Outreach: MFIs work towards reaching out to the unbanked and underserved communities, identifying their financial needs, and customizing services accordingly.

Capacity Building: MFIs invest in capacity building for their staff and clients, focusing on financial literacy, business skills, and client empowerment.

7. Community-Based Service Providers:

Grassroots Outreach: Community-based service providers, such as NGOs and SHGs, have strong ties with local communities and play a crucial role in identifying beneficiaries and facilitating financial services at the grassroots level.

8. Support Organizations:

Training and Technical Assistance: Support organizations offer training and technical assistance to microfinance institutions, helping them improve their operations and management practices.

Research and Knowledge Sharing: Support organizations conduct research, collect data, and share knowledge and best practices to enhance the effectiveness of microfinance initiatives.

5.35. Constraints in mainstreaming of microfinance industries and challenges faced by the microfinance sector:

Mainstreaming of microfinance industries and the microfinance sector, in general, has made significant progress in promoting financial inclusion and empowering underserved communities. However, several constraints and challenges persist, hindering its full integration into the mainstream financial system. Some of the key constraints and challenges include:

1. Financial Sustainability: Many microfinance institutions (MFIs) struggle to achieve financial sustainability due to the high operational costs of serving the low-income population, coupled with the challenges of reaching remote and rural areas.

2. Limited Access to Funding: MFIs often face difficulties in accessing long-term and affordable funding, especially from formal financial institutions, which impacts their ability to scale up operations and expand outreach.

3. Over-Indebtedness: In some cases, clients may become over-indebted as they access multiple loans from different MFIs or informal sources, leading to repayment difficulties and credit risk for MFIs.

4. Interest Rate Regulations: Interest rate caps imposed by regulators may limit the ability of MFIs to cover operational costs, affecting their financial viability and restricting the availability of credit to clients.

5. Governance and Risk Management: Some MFIs face challenges in implementing strong governance practices and robust risk management systems, which can lead to poor loan portfolio management and financial losses.

6. Customer Protection and Transparency: Ensuring adequate consumer protection and transparent disclosure of terms and conditions is critical to building trust among clients and promoting responsible lending practices.

7. Market Saturation: In some regions, microfinance markets may become saturated with multiple MFIs serving the same client base, leading to increased competition and potential over-lending.

8. Economic and Political Instability: Economic downturns or political instability in certain regions can adversely impact microfinance operations, leading to increased default rates and repayment challenges.

9. Limited Financial Literacy: Low levels of financial literacy and awareness among clients can hinder their effective utilization of microfinance services and hinder financial inclusion efforts.

10. Technology and Digital Divide: Technological challenges, including limited internet connectivity and access to digital platforms, can impede the adoption of digital financial services and hinder the scaling of microfinance operations.

Addressing these constraints and challenges requires a multi-faceted approach involving collaboration between governments, regulators, MFIs, banks, donors, and support organizations. Strengthening regulatory frameworks, enhancing capacity-building initiatives, promoting responsible lending practices, improving access to funding, and investing in financial education are among the strategies to overcome these hurdles and ensure sustainable growth and impact in the microfinance sector.

5.36. Current challenges of microfinance sector in India:

Microfinance sector in India faced several challenges. While the specific challenges may evolve over time, some common ones included:

1. COVID-19 Pandemic Impact: The COVID-19 pandemic presented significant challenges to the microfinance sector, leading to disruptions in loan repayments and borrower livelihoods, especially in vulnerable communities.

2. Over-Indebtedness: The issue of over-indebtedness continued to be a concern, as some borrowers took loans from multiple sources without adequate capacity to repay, leading to repayment stress for borrowers and financial risk for microfinance institutions (MFIs).

3. Interest Rate Regulations: Interest rate caps imposed by regulators may limit the profitability of MFIs, affecting their financial sustainability and ability to expand services to underserved areas.

4. Funding Constraints: Access to affordable and long-term funding remained a challenge for many MFIs, particularly smaller institutions, impacting their ability to expand outreach and scale up operations.

5. Governance and Risk Management: Ensuring robust governance practices and effective risk management systems remained essential for the sustainable growth of MFIs and to protect the interests of clients.

6. Customer Protection: Ensuring adequate customer protection and transparent disclosure of terms and conditions remained crucial to building trust and confidence among clients.

7. Digital Transformation: The shift towards digital financial services and digital lending required investments in technology infrastructure and financial literacy initiatives to bridge the digital divide among clients.

8. Economic Slowdown: The economic slowdown and uncertainty in certain regions affected the financial health of borrowers and impacted repayment behaviour, leading to potential asset quality deterioration for MFIs.

9. Regulatory Environment: Adapting to evolving regulatory requirements and ensuring compliance with changing regulations remained a challenge for the microfinance sector.

10. Social Impact and Responsible Lending: Striking a balance between financial sustainability and social impact while maintaining responsible lending practices remained a challenge for MFIs.

5.37. Borrower unfriendly products and procedures in microfinance:

In the microfinance sector, there have been instances of borrower-unfriendly products and procedures that can negatively impact the clients and borrowers. These practices can result in financial distress, over-indebtedness, and potential exploitation. Some borrower-unfriendly practices in microfinance include:

1. High Interest Rates: Some microfinance institutions (MFIs) charge excessively high interest rates, leading to a heavy burden on borrowers and making it difficult for them to repay loans (In Some Cases).

2. Multiple Borrowing: Inadequate borrower credit assessment can result in borrowers taking loans from multiple sources without considering their repayment capacity, leading to over-indebtedness and repayment difficulties (In Some Cases).

3. Coercive Loan Recovery Practices: Aggressive loan recovery practices, including harassment, threats, and public shaming, can create stress for borrowers (In Some Cases).

4. Inflexible Repayment Terms: Some microfinance products may have rigid repayment schedules that do not consider the seasonal or cyclical nature of borrowers' income, making it challenging for them to repay on time (In Some Cases).

5. Group Pressure: In group-based lending models like Joint Liability Groups (JLGs) or Self-Help Groups (SHGs), group pressure to repay loans can lead to social tensions and conflicts among members (In Some Cases), in current senecio after COVID-19 JLG is not working.

6. Inadequate Financial Literacy: Insufficient financial literacy and awareness programs can hinder borrowers' understanding of financial products and their rights and responsibilities.

Addressing these issues requires a multi-pronged approach that involves industry-wide efforts (Majority of points are followed by maximum Microfinance Institutions, which are mentioned below) including:

Strengthening regulation and supervision to ensure that microfinance products and procedures are customer-centric and transparent.

Encouraging responsible lending practices and fair pricing of loans to avoid excessive burden on borrowers.

Promoting financial literacy initiatives to empower borrowers with the knowledge to make informed financial decisions.

Implementing client protection principles to safeguard borrowers' interests and promote ethical lending practices.

Promoting greater transparency in loan terms and conditions to enhance borrower understanding and prevent hidden charges.

Establishing effective grievance redressal mechanisms to address borrower complaints and ensure timely resolution of issues.

By addressing borrower-unfriendly practices and promoting responsible lending, the microfinance sector can much better serve its mission of financial inclusion and poverty alleviation while safeguarding the interests of the borrowers.

5.38. Inflexibility and delay in banks regarding microfinance loans:

Inflexibility and delays in banks regarding microfinance loans can be significant challenges for borrowers, especially those from low-income and underserved communities who heavily rely on timely access to credit for their livelihoods. Some common reasons for these issues include:

1. **Lengthy Approval Processes:** Banks may have complex and time-consuming loan approval processes, involving extensive documentation and multiple layers of scrutiny. This can lead to delays in disbursing funds to borrowers.

2. **Risk Perception:** Banks may perceive microfinance lending as higher risk due to the absence of formal credit histories and limited financial documentation of borrowers, leading to cautiousness and slower loan processing.

3. **Bureaucratic Hurdles:** In large banking institutions, bureaucratic procedures and lack of decentralized decision-making can cause delays in loan processing and disbursement.

5. **Lack of Local Presence:** In areas where banks do not have a physical presence, the loan processing may rely on external agents or business correspondents, leading to communication gaps and delays.

6. Credit Assessment Practices: Traditional credit scoring models used by banks may not be suitable for assessing the creditworthiness of microfinance borrowers, leading to prolonged evaluation and decision-making.

7. Limited Understanding of Microfinance: Some bank staff may have limited knowledge or experience in microfinance operations, resulting in inefficient handling of microfinance loan applications.

To address these issues, banks can take several measures to improve flexibility and reduce delays in microfinance loan processes:

1. Simplify Loan Procedures: Banks can streamline and simplify loan approval processes to make them more borrower-friendly and efficient.

2. Adapt Risk Assessment: Implement tailored risk assessment models for microfinance borrowers, considering alternative credit evaluation methods, social indicators, and repayment history with microfinance institutions.

3. Offer Flexible Repayment Terms: Banks can design microfinance loan products with flexible repayment terms that align with the borrowers' cash flows and income patterns.

4. Local Presence and Partnerships: Banks can establish branches or partner with microfinance institutions and business correspondents to improve local outreach and understanding of borrower needs.

5. Invest in Technology: Embrace technology to digitize loan processing, reduce paperwork, and enhance efficiency in disbursing microfinance loans.

6. Capacity Building: Provide training to bank staff on microfinance principles, social performance management, and client protection to improve their understanding of the sector and borrower requirements.

By implementing borrower-friendly practices and overcoming these challenges, banks can enhance their effectiveness in providing microfinance loans, contribute to financial inclusion, and support the socio-economic development of underserved communities.

5.39. High transaction costs in microfinance can be a significant challenge for both microfinance institutions (MFIs) and borrowers, particularly in rural and remote areas. These costs can arise from various factors and can impact the overall efficiency and viability of microfinance operations. Here are some key components of transaction costs in microfinance:

1. Transport Cost: In rural areas, where many microfinance clients reside, the lack of nearby MFI branches or access points may require clients to travel long distances to access financial services. This incurs transport costs for both the clients and MFIs.

2. Incidental Cost: Incidental costs include expenses related to paperwork, documentation, verification, and client education. These costs can add up, especially when serving a large number of clients with small loan amounts.

3. Opportunity Cost: Opportunity cost refers to the potential earnings or benefits that borrowers forego when they spend time on obtaining microfinance services instead of engaging in income-generating activities.

4. Intermediary Cost: Intermediary costs can arise when MFIs work with local agents or business correspondents to reach clients in remote areas. These agents may charge a fee for their services, contributing to transaction costs.

Addressing high transaction costs in microfinance requires a combination of strategies:

1. Digital Solutions: Embracing digital technology can help reduce transaction costs by offering cost-effective and efficient service delivery. Digital platforms can enable online applications, electronic verification, and mobile banking services.

2. Branchless Banking: Implementing branchless banking or agent banking models can bring services closer to the clients, reducing their travel costs and making services more accessible.

3. Group Lending: Utilizing group lending models like Self-Help Groups (SHGs) or Joint Liability Groups (JLGs) can help lower transaction costs as group members provide mutual support and act as intermediaries.

4. Training and Capacity Building: Providing financial literacy and capacity-building programs to clients can enhance their understanding of financial services, reducing errors in documentation and verification.

5. Partnerships and Collaboration: MFIs can collaborate with other organizations, such as NGOs, to share operational costs and extend services in cost-effective ways.

6. Innovation and Cost Efficiency: Continuous innovation in microfinance operations and cost-efficient practices can help MFIs optimize resources and streamline processes.

7. Flexible Loan Products: Offering flexible loan products with appropriate repayment schedules can reduce opportunity costs for borrowers.

By addressing high transaction costs, the microfinance sector can become more sustainable and better equipped to serve the financial needs of low-income populations, especially in remote and underserved areas.

5.40. High transaction costs in microfinance can be a significant challenge for both microfinance institutions (MFIs) and borrowers, particularly in rural and remote areas. These costs can arise from various factors and can impact the overall efficiency and viability of microfinance operations. Here are some key components of transaction costs in microfinance:

1. Transport Cost: In rural areas, where many microfinance clients reside, the lack of nearby MFI branches or access points may require clients to travel long distances to access financial services. This incurs transport costs for both the clients and MFIs.

2. Incidental Cost: Incidental costs include expenses related to paperwork, documentation, verification, and client education. These costs can add up, especially when serving a large number of clients with small loan amounts.

3. Opportunity Cost: Opportunity cost refers to the potential earnings or benefits that borrowers forego when they spend time on obtaining microfinance services instead of engaging in income-generating activities.

4. Intermediary Cost: Intermediary costs can arise when MFIs work with local agents or business correspondents to reach clients in remote areas. These agents may charge a fee for their services, contributing to transaction costs.

Addressing high transaction costs in microfinance requires a combination of strategies:

1. Digital Solutions: Embracing digital technology can help reduce transaction costs by offering cost-effective and efficient service delivery. Digital platforms can enable online applications, electronic verification, and mobile banking services.

2. Branchless Banking: Implementing branchless banking or agent banking models can bring services closer to the clients, reducing their travel costs and making services more accessible.

3. Group Lending: Utilizing group lending models like Self-Help Groups (SHGs) or Joint Liability Groups (JLGs) can help lower transaction costs as group members provide mutual support and act as intermediaries.

4. Training and Capacity Building: Providing financial literacy and capacity-building programs to clients can enhance their understanding of financial services, reducing errors in documentation and verification.

5. Partnerships and Collaboration: MFIs can collaborate with other organizations, such as NGOs, to share operational costs and extend services in cost-effective ways.

6. Innovation and Cost Efficiency: Continuous innovation in microfinance operations and cost-efficient practices can help MFIs optimize resources and streamline processes.

7. **Flexible Loan Products:** Offering flexible loan products with appropriate repayment schedules can reduce opportunity costs for borrowers.

By addressing high transaction costs, the microfinance sector can become more sustainable and better equipped to serve the financial needs of low-income populations, especially in remote and underserved areas.

5.41. Social obligations and non-business opportunities in microfinance:

Microfinance goes beyond a purely profit-driven business model; it also encompasses social obligations and non-business opportunities aimed at promoting financial inclusion, poverty reduction, and socio-economic development. Some key aspects of social obligations and non-business opportunities in microfinance include:

1. **Financial Inclusion:** One of the primary social obligations of microfinance is to extend financial services to the unbanked and underbanked populations, providing them with access to credit, savings, insurance, and other financial products.

2. **Poverty Reduction:** Microfinance aims to alleviate poverty by empowering low-income individuals and households through access to capital for income-generating activities and improving their economic prospects.

3. **Women Empowerment:** Microfinance often prioritizes women borrowers and encourages their participation in income-generating activities, promoting gender equality and women's economic empowerment.

4. **Social Impact:** Microfinance institutions (MFIs) are committed to creating positive social impact beyond financial services. They may engage in community development initiatives, capacity-building programs, and promoting sustainable livelihoods.

5. **Financial Literacy and Education:** MFIs invest in financial literacy training for their clients, educating them about money management,

savings, and responsible borrowing, enhancing their financial decision-making capabilities.

6. Client Protection: Ensuring client protection and responsible lending practices is an essential non-business aspect of microfinance, safeguarding the interests of borrowers and promoting ethical practices.

7. Social Performance Management: MFIs measure and manage their social performance, focusing on their outreach to the poor and impact on clients' lives, alongside financial sustainability metrics.

8. Non-Financial Services: Some microfinance institutions offer non-financial services, such as health services, education support, and vocational training, to address the holistic needs of their clients.

9. Vulnerable Group Targeting: MFIs may design special loan products or outreach programs to cater to vulnerable groups, such as disabled individuals or refugees, providing them with opportunities for socio-economic improvement.

10. Community Engagement: MFIs actively engage with the communities they serve, involving them in decision-making processes and considering their feedback and needs in designing financial products and services.

Microfinance plays a significant role in promoting inclusive economic growth and fostering social development. Its social obligations and non-business opportunities help uplift marginalized communities, empower women, and contribute to sustainable development goals. By integrating these social dimensions into their operations, microfinance institutions contribute to positive change and make a meaningful impact on the lives of their clients and the communities they serve.

5.42. Financing to alternatives MFIs:

Financing to alternative microfinance institutions (MFIs) would involve providing financial support to each MFI through different means. There are several options for financing MFIs, and the choice of funding sources would depend on various factors, including the MFI's size, structure, mission, and the amount of funding required. Here are two common alternatives for financing MFIs:

1. Debt Financing:

Debt financing involves providing loans to the MFIs, which they can use to expand their lending operations or meet their financial needs.

This can be done through traditional banks, financial institutions, or specialized microfinance funds that offer funding to MFIs at competitive interest rates.

The MFI will have to repay the loan amount along with interest over an agreed-upon period.

Debt financing is a common and straightforward option for MFIs to raise capital for their operations.

2. Equity Financing:

Equity financing involves investors (individuals or institutions) purchasing ownership shares or equity stakes in the MFI in exchange for capital infusion.

This form of financing allows the MFI to raise funds without taking on additional debt.

Equity investors become shareholders in the MFI and may have voting rights and the potential to share in the MFI's profits.

Equity financing is often sought by larger MFIs looking to scale up their operations or by socially responsible investors who align with the MFI's mission.

Both debt financing and equity financing have their advantages and considerations. Debt financing provides a straightforward way to raise funds, but it comes with the obligation to repay the borrowed amount and interest. On the other hand, equity financing allows the MFI to bring in long-term capital without the pressure of repayment, but it involves sharing ownership and decision-making with investors.

Other financing alternatives for MFIs may include grants from philanthropic organizations, blended finance models combining debt and equity, and access to deposits from clients (if allowed by regulatory frameworks). MFIs often use a mix of these financing options based on their specific needs and the prevailing financial market conditions.

Chapter - 6

Legal and Governance Framework

6.1. Regulatory Framework of Microfinance in the World:

The regulatory framework for microfinance varies across countries. It typically involves a mix of financial, legal, and operational regulations to ensure the stability and inclusivity of microfinance institutions. These regulations can cover aspects such as capital requirements, interest rate caps, client protection, reporting standards, and more. Different countries have tailored approaches based on their economic, social, and regulatory environments.

The regulatory framework for microfinance varies extensively worldwide due to differing economic, legal, and social contexts. While not possible to provide a comprehensive overview of every country's regulation's, I can highlight some key aspects that are commonly found in regulatory frameworks:

1. Legal Recognition: Many countries define microfinance institutions (MFIs) in their legal systems, outlining their roles, responsibilities, and eligibility criteria.

2. Licensing and Registration: MFIs often need to obtain licenses or register with relevant regulatory bodies to ensure they meet certain standards and operate legally.

3. **Capital Requirements:** Regulations may require MFIs to maintain a minimum level of capital to ensure their financial stability and ability to manage risks.

4. **Interest Rate Caps:** Some countries impose caps on interest rates to prevent predatory lending and ensure fair treatment of borrowers.

5. **Consumer Protection:** Regulatory frameworks often include measures to protect borrowers, such as clear disclosure of terms, fair lending practices, and mechanisms for dispute resolution.

6. **Reporting and Transparency:** MFIs are usually required to submit regular financial and operational reports to regulatory authorities, promoting transparency and accountability.

7. **Governance and Management:** Regulations may stipulate governance standards and requirements for board composition and management practices.

8. **Risk Management:** Regulatory frameworks may outline guidelines for risk assessment, management, and mitigation to ensure the stability of MFIs.

9. **Supervision and Oversight:** Regulatory bodies often monitor MFIs' compliance with regulations, conduct inspections, and take corrective actions when necessary.

10. **Social Performance:** Some regulatory frameworks encourage or mandate MFIs to report on their social impact alongside financial performance.

11. **Digital Financial Services:** As technology evolves, regulatory frameworks are adapting to address digital financial services, ensuring their security and inclusivity.

The specifics of regulatory frameworks can vary significantly based on each country's context and priorities. For detailed and up-to-date information about the microfinance regulatory framework in a specific country or region, it's advisable to refer to official government sources, financial regulatory bodies, and international organizations.

Here we are reading the regulation of Microfinance in Indian context, as this book is written specific for the knowledge of Microfinance to Indian Microfinance practitioners.

In Indian context there are companies for Microfinance are registered under Companies Act, Societies Registration Act (for nonprofit organization) both are mandatorily required to take certificate from Reserve bank of India under the category of NBFC-MFI.

After A.P. Crisis the significant policies are made for Microfinance, after A.P. Crisis RBI was constituted a committee in the chairmanship of Sri Y H Malegam in 2010 which we know as Malegam Committee for Microfinance. The key notes on Malegam Committee is mentioned hear.

6.2. Malegam Committee:

The Reserve Bank of India formed a sub-committee in order to study the Microfinance sector regulated by the bank.

The Expert Committee comprises of the following members:

1. Shri Y.H. Malegam, Director, Central Board of Reserve Bank of India, Mumbai - Chairman

2. Shri K. Madhava Rao, Ex-Chief Secretary, Government of Andhra Pradesh, Hyderabad - Member

3. Shri U. C. Sarangi, Additional Chief Secretary, Government of Maharashtra, Mumbai - Member

4. Dr. S. K. Goel, Principal Secretary, Government of Maharashtra, Mumbai - Member

5. Shri K. Elumalai, Director, Indira Gandhi National Open University, New Delhi - Member

6. Shri H. K. Patil, President, National Federation of Co-op. Urban Banks, New Delhi - Member

7. Dr. M. L. Abhyankar, Director, Cosmos Co-operative Bank Ltd., Pune - Member

8. Shri A. Udgata, Chief General Manager-in-Charge, Urban Banks Department, RBI, Central Office, Mumbai - Member Secretary

RBI had constituted the Malegam Committee, the name of eight members of committee are mentioned above. Based on this committee's recommendations, the RBI has issued a series of guidelines, notifications and directives, starting with the creation of a separate category of NBFC-MFIs. The regulatory guidance extends to capital requirement, qualifying asset category, asset classification and provisioning norms, pricing of credit, fair practices in lending, transparency and disclosure in interest rate, avoidance of multiple lending and excessive debt, recovery practices, corporate governance and improvement in efficiency through information technology. The two micro finance industry associations, namely Sa-Dhan and MFIN (Micro) Finance Institutions Network) have evolved a unified code of conduct for their members. The much- awaited Microfinance Institutions (Development and Regulation) Bill, 2012 was tabled in the Indian Parliament in May 2012 and is referred to the Parliamentary standing committee on finance.

6.3. Recommendations of Malegam Committee:

Microfinance institutions in India have made significant progress during the last three decades in terms of outreach and penetration in unbanked areas. Over the last two decade the model of microfinance Institutions have grown at impressive speed. These MFIs have attracted large volume of bank credit support and also an increasing interest in equity investments. The advent of NBFCs in the Microfinance sector appears to have resulted in a significant increase in reach and the credit made available to the sector. Between 31 March 2007 and 31 March 2010, the number of outstanding loan accounts serviced by the MFIS is reported to have increased from

10.04 million to 26.7 million and outstanding loans from about Rs. 3800 crore to Rs. 18,344 crore. While this growth is impressive, the specific areas of concern in the Indian context have been identified. They are as follows:

Areas of concern:

- Unjustified high rate of interest
- Multiple lending
- Upfront collection of security deposits
- Coercive methods of recovery
- Over-borrowing
- Ghost borrowers
- Lack of transparency in interest rates and other charges

This high growth of MFIS has encountered serious setbacks in the last few years due to adverse consequences of the Andhra Pradesh crisis. The MFI sector, more particularly for the profit model, which was in limelight for its rapid growth and success in Financial Inclusion was suddenly seen in a bad light because a wide spread criticism of MFIS. The reason for the criticism was due to the exorbitantly high profits earned by MFIs, which was on account of high leverage of bank loans and high rates of interest. But what pushed the sector to the crisis are the coercive money collection practices. It was seen that certain MFIs which followed the Grameen model had incentivized collection which ran into unethical practices. These practices got highlighted with the media reporting of suicides among microfinance clients in Andhra Pradesh - the state that has the largest chunk of MFI lending. This prompted the Andhra Pradesh Government to bring in the Andhra Pradesh Microfinance Institutions (Regulation of Money Lending) Ordinance 2010. As a result, repayment of all MFI in Andhra Pradesh almost came to a halt. As more than 50 per cent of MFIs exposure is in Andhra Pradesh alone, the business of MFI got adversely affected. Banks and SIDBI had about Rs. 19000 crore exposures to MFIs which came to risk under circumstances. Banks had extended CDR to the MFI's which has been of little avail as the loan losses has been almost total.

6.4. Background of Andhra Pradesh Microfinance Crisis 2010:

[MFIs have emerged as important stakeholders in the Microfinance sector in lending to the poor people: The advent of the Microfinance sector appears to have resulted in a significant increase in outreach and the credit made available to the sector. Between 2007-10 the number of outstanding loan accounts served by MFIs was reported to have increased from 10,04 million to 26.7 million and outstanding loans from about Rs. 3800 Cr. to Rs. 18344 Cr. The incessantly flourishing MFI industry providing credit to the doorsteps of the poor has however also been correlated with excessively high interest rate, use of coercive methods for recovery, number of suicides by the credit beneficiaries etc. It was alleged that in Andhra Pradesh many microfinance clients committed suicides because of high handedness of MFI staff to recover loans. This led the state government of Andhra Pradesh to enact the AP MFI Act 2010 which had suddenly put brakes to the expanding MFI industry. The provisions of the ordinance require that each MFI to register themselves with district administration to keep records of all their clients, not to give loan to SHG members if they have already taken loan from other SHGs (to control over indebtedness) without prior permission of district collectors and so on.]

In view of the above-mentioned development, RBI had set up a committee of its Board members under the chairmanship of Shri. Y.H. Malegam to study the issues and concerns in Micro finance sector. The committee reviewed the definition of MF and MFI, examined the alleged malpractices by MFIs especially with respect to high interest rate and methods of recovery, specified the scope of regulation by RBI of these MFIs and suggested a proper regulatory framework. It also examined the prevalent money lending legislation and other relevant items at the state level, and suggested redressal machinery.

The Committee has recommended that a NBFC-MFI may be defined as "a company (other than a company licensed under section 25 of the Companies Act, 1956) which provides financial services predominantly to low-income borrowers with loans of small amounts, for short terms, on unsecured basis, mainly for income generating activities with repayment schedules which are more frequent than those normally stipulated by commercial banks and which further conforms to the regulations specified".

The committee has also arrived at the concept of qualifying asset of NBFC which will decide if it is an MFI. Accordingly, not less than 90 per cent of its (NBFC-MFI's) total assets (other than cash and bank balances and money market instruments) are in the nature of 'qualifying assets' it will be deemed an NBFC-MFI. Qualifying asset shall mean a loan which satisfies the following criteria:

The loan is given to a member of a household whose annual income does not exceed Rs. 50,000/-

The amount of loan does not exceed Rs. 25000/- and the total outstanding indebtedness of the borrower including this loan also does not exceed Rs. 25000/- The tenure of the loan is not less than 12 months where the loan amount does not exceed Rs. 15000/- and 24 months in other cases with a right to the borrower of prepayment without penalty in all cases. The loan is without collateral.

The aggregate amount of loans given for income generating purposes is not less than 75 per cent of the total loans given by the MFIs. The loan repayable by weekly, fortnightly or monthly installments at the choice of the borrower The income it derives from other services is in accordance with the regulation specified. An NBFC which does not qualify as a NBFC-MFI should not be permitted to give loans to the microfinance sector which in the aggregate exceed 10 per cent of its total assets. Interest rate related recommendations The committee has recommended that there should be a interest 'margin cap' of 10 per cent in respect of those MFIs which have an outstanding loan portfolio at the beginning of the year of Rs. 100Cr. and a 'margin cap' of 12 per cent in respect of MFIs which have an outstanding loan portfolio at the beginning of the year of an amount not exceeding Rs. 100Cr. There should also be a cap of 24 per cent on individual loans. This means that the NBFC-MFIs cannot charge more than 22% or 24% p.a ROI and that on a reducing balance method too.

The committee recommends that (Transparency related issues) There should be only three components in the pricing of the loan namely (a) a processing fee not exceeding 1 per cent of the gross amount (ii) the interest charge and (iii) the insurance premium. Only the actual cost of insurance should be recovered and no administrative charges should be levied. Every MFI should provide to the borrower a loan card which shows (i) the rate of interest (ii) the other terms and conditions attached to the loan (iii) information which adequately identifies the borrower and (iv) acknowledgment by the MFI of payments of installments received and the final discharge. The card should show this information in the local language understood by the borrower.

The effective rate of interest charged by the MFI should be prominently displayed in all its offices and in the literature issued by it.

There should be adequate regulations regarding the manner in which insurance premium is computed and collected and policy proceeds disposed of. There should not be any recovery of security deposit. Security deposits already collected should be returned.

6.5. There should be a standard form of loan agreement.

Committee also recommends that (About multiple lending, over borrowing and ghost borrowers) MFIs should lend to an individual borrower only as a member of a JLG and should have the responsibility of ensuring that the borrower is not a member of another JLG. A borrower cannot be a member of more than one SHG/JLG. Not more than two MFIS should lend to the same borrower. This would require the NBFC to have full details of the borrower. There must be a minimum period of moratorium between the grant of the loan and the commencement of its repayment. Recovery of loan given in violation of the regulations should be deferred till all prior existing loans are fully repaid. Ghost borrowers generally arise in two sets of circumstances:

When the borrower on record is a benami for the real borrower and Fictitious loans are recorded in the books, The first type of Ghost borrower is often used as a device for multiple lending or over borrowing. This can be cured only by a better discipline in the system of identification and creation of data base of borrowers and better follow up by the field worker.

The second type of Ghost Borrower can pose much greater systemic problem as it would create fictitious repayments and thus hide the actual level of delinquencies. The committee recommends that all sanctioning and disbursement of loans should be done only at a central location and more than one individual should be involved in this function. In addition, there should be close supervision of the disbursement function. The committee has recommended that a Credit Information Bureau be established for MFT one or more Credit Information Bureaus be established and be operational as soon as possible and all MFIs be required to become members of such bureau. In the meantime, the responsibility to obtain information from potential borrowers regarding existing borrowings should be on the MFI.

As regards Coercive Methods of Recovery the committee recommends that the responsibility to ensure that coercive methods of recovery are not used should rest with the MFI and they and their management should be subject to severe penalties if such methods are used the regulator should monitor whether MFIs have a proper Code of Conduct and proper systems for recruitment, training and supervision of field staff to ensure the prevention of coercive methods of recovery.

Field staff should not be allowed to make recovery at the place of residence or work of the borrower and all recoveries should only be made at the Group level at a central place to be designated. MFIs should consider the experience of banks that faced similar problems in relation to retail loans in the past and profit by that experience. Each MFI must establish a proper Grievance Redressal Procedure.

The institution of independent Ombudsmen should be examined and based on such examination; an appropriate mechanism may be recommended by RBI to lead banks.

6.6. Customer Protection Code:

The regulator should publish a Client Protection Code for MFIS and mandate its acceptance and observance by MFIS. This Code should incorporate the relevant provisions of the Fair Practices Guidelines prescribed by the Reserve Bank for NBFCs. Similar provision should also be made applicable to banks and financial institutions which provide credit to the microfinance sector.

Improvement of efficiencies MFIs should review their back-office operations and make the necessary investments in Information Technology and systems to achieve better control, simplify procedure and reduce cost. Support to SHGs/JLGS under both the SHG Bank Linkage Programme (SBLP) model and the MFI model, greater resources should be devoted to professional inputs both in the formation of SHGs and JLGS as also in the imparting of skill development and training and generally in handholding after the group is formed. This would be in addition to and complementary to the efforts of the State Governments in this regard. The architecture suggested by the Ministry of Rural Development should also be explored funding of MFIs assignment and securitization disclosure should be made in the financial statements of MFIs of the outstanding loan portfolio which has been assigned or securitized and the MFI continues as an agent for collection. The amounts assigned and securitized must be shown separately. Where assignment or securitization is with recourse the full value of the outstanding loan portfolio assigned or securitized should be considered as risk-based assets for calculation of capital adequacy. Where the assignment or securitization is without recourse but credit enhancement has been given, the value of the credit enhancement should be deducted from the Net Owned Funds for the purpose of calculation of capital adequacy. Before acquiring assigned or securitized loans, banks should ensure that the loans have been made. The MFI should continue to enjoy "priority sector lending" status. However, advances to MFIs which do not comply with the regulation should be denied 'priority sector lending' status. It may also be necessary for the RBI to revisit its existing guidelines for lending to the priority sector. While regulations are important, they cannot by themselves be the sole instruments to reduce interest rates charged by MFIs or improve the service provided to borrowers. Ultimately this can only be done through greater competition both within the MFIs and from other agencies operating in the Microfinance Sector. The Committee therefore recommends that bank lending to the Microfinance sector both through the SHG-Bank Linkage program and directly should be significantly increased and this should result in a reduction in the lending interest rates. Priority Sector Status owned Funds should be in the form of Tier I Capital. Need for Competition the provisioning for loans should not be maintained for individual loans but an MFI should be required to maintain at all times an aggregate provision for loan losses which shall be the higher of (1) I per cent of the outstanding loan portfolio or (ii) 50% of the aggregate loan installments which are overdue for more than 90 days and less than 180 days and 100% of the aggregate loan installments which are overdue for 180 days or more. NBFC-MFIs be required to maintain Capital Adequacy Ratio of 15% and all of the Net Corporate size all NBFC-MEIs should have a minimum Net Worth of Rs. 5Cr. Corporate governance Every MFI be required to have a system of Corporate Governance in accordance with rules to be specified by the regulator Maintenance of solvency in accordance with the terms of the specified regulations. Creation of one or more "Domestic Social Capital Funds" may be examined in consultation with SEBI. MFIs should be encouraged to issue preference capital with a ceiling on the coupon rate and this can be treated as part of Tier II capital subject to capital adequacy norms.

6.7. Monitoring of compliance

The primary responsibility for ensuring compliance with the regulations should rest with the MP itself and its management must be penalized in the event of non-compliance. Industry associations must ensure compliance through the implementation of the code of conduct with penalties for non-compliance.

Banks also must play a part in compliance by surveillance of MFIs through their branches. The RBI should have the responsibility for off-site and on-site supervision of the MFIs but the on-site supervision may be confined to the larger MFIs and be restricted to the functioning of the organizational arrangements and systems with some supervision of the branches. It should also include supervision of the industry associations in so far as their compliance mechanism is concerned Reserve Bank should also explore the use of outside agencies for inspection.

The RBI should have the power to remove from office the CEO and/ or a director in the event of persistent violation of the regulations quite apart from the power to deregister an MFI and preve from operating in the microfinance sector. The Reserve Bank should considerably enhance its existing supervisory organization dealing with NBFC-MFIS Moneylenders Acts NBFC-MFIs should be exempted from the provisions of the Money-Lending Acts as interest margin caps and increased regulations are recommended.

6.8. The Micro Finance Institutions (Development and Regulation) Bill 2012:

The Central Government has drafted a 'Micro Finance Institutions (Development and Regulation) Bill 2012' will apply to all microfinance organizations other than (a) banks (b) Co-operative societies engaged primarily in agricultural operations or industrial activity or purchase or sale of any goods and such other activities (c) NBFCs other than licensed under section 25 of the Companies Act, 1956 (d) Co-operative societies not accepting deposits from anybody except from its members having voting rights or from those members who will acquire voting rights after a stipulated period of their making deposits as per the law applicable to such co-operative societies, The Bill is being debated, off the parliament for a long time now. The Bill refined and it was tabled in the Parliament in 2012 as the Micro Finance Institutions (Development and Regulation) Bill, 2012. It is hoped that the Act will provide for all entities covered by the Act to be registered with the regulator. Possibly entities where aggregate loan portfolio does not exceed Rs. 10 Cr. may be exempted from registration. Further as RBI regulates NBFC it has been suggested that if

NABARD is designed as the regulator under the proposed Act, there must be close co-ordination between NABARD and RBI in the formulation of the regulations applicable to the regulated entities. Another important suggestion is that the micro finance entities governed by the proposed Act should not be allowed to do the business of providing thrift services. Microfinance is not a single tool but a combination of tools. MFIs around the world serve different types of clients, operate in diverse environments and offer different combination of services.

There have been many surveys, both in India and abroad as to the impact of microfinance on the lives of the poor people it is intended to reach. The results have been both conflicting and confusing. These surveys report many success stories but they also voice many apprehensions that microfinance has in some cases created credit dependency and cyclical debt. Doubts have also been expressed as to whether lending agencies have in all cases remained committed to the goal of fighting poverty or whether they are solely motivated by financial gain. Mere extension of micro credit unaccompanied by other social measures will not be an adequate anti-poverty tool.

While the lender has the responsibility to provide timely and adequate credit at a fair price in a transparent manner, the borrower also has the responsibility to honor his/her commitments for payment of interest and repayment of principal. A financial system ultimately depends on the circulation of funds within the system. If the recovery culture is adversely affected and free flow of funds is interrupted the system will break down. This will affect the borrowers themselves as the slow-down of recovery will inevitably reduce the flow of fresh funds into the system.

6.9. The comparison between Malegam Committee recommendations and RBI guidelines is presented here:

Comparison between Malegam Committee recommendations and RBI guidelines, Particulars, Qualifying assets, Loan amount, Malegam Committee Recommendations, The loan given to a borrower who is a member of a household whose annual income does not exceed Rs. 50,000/-, The amount of loan does not exceed Rs. 25,000/and the total outstanding indebtedness of the borrower including this loan also does not exceed Rs. 25,000/-, Pricing of interest, There should be a 'margin cap' of 10% in respect of MFIs which have an outstanding loan portfolio at the beginning of the year of Rs.100 crore and a 'margin cap' of 12 per cent in respect of MFIs which have an outstanding loan portfolio at the beginning of the year of an amount not exceeding Rs.100 Cr. There should also be a cap 24% on individual loans. RBI Guidelines, Loan disbursed by an MFI to a borrower with a rural household annual income not exceeding Rs. 60,000 or urban and semi urban household income not exceeding Rs. 1,20,000/-, Loan amount not to exceed Rs. 35,000/- in the first cycle and Rs. 50,000/- in subsequent cycles. Total indebtedness of the borrower not to exceed Rs. 50,000/-, Banks should ensure a margin cap of 12 per cent and an interest rate cap of 26 per cent for their lending to be eligible to be classified as priority sector loans, Tenure of loan, The tenure of the loan is not less than 12 months where the loan amount does not exceed Rs. 15000 and 24 months in other cases with a right to the borrower of prepayment without penalty in all cases, Tenure of loan not to be less than 24 months for loan amount in excess of Rs. 15000/- without prepayment penalty. Loan extended without collateral consequent to Malegam Committee recommendations, the RBI has issued a series of guidelines. notifications and directives, starting with the creation of a separate category of NBFC-MFIS. The regulatory guidance extends to capital requirement, qualifying asset category, asset classification and provisioning norms, pricing of credit, fair lending practices, transparency and disclosure in interest rate, avoidance of multiple lending excessive debt, recovery practices, corporate governance and improvement in efficiency through information technology.

Priority sector lending is a policy initiative, which requires banks to allocate a percentage of their portfolios to investment in specified priority sectors at a reduced interest rate. Currently, the loans from microfinance institutions registered as NBFC-MFIs are designated as a priority sector. In order to register as an NBFC-MFI, an institution must meet requirements specified by the RBI. In December 2011, the RBI opened up the external commercial borrowings (ECBS) channel to NBFC-MFIS, something that was previously open only to non-profit MFIs. The network organizations, support institutions, research and policy advocacy groups have been working to bring microfinance back to track and prepare it for orderly and responsible growth. The lead initiative taken by SIDBI towards carrying out the Code of Conduct Assessments of MFIs has helped pave the way for ensuring effective client protection principles in the operations. Recognizing the importance of systematic compilation of credit information of clients for effective monitoring and follow-up, RBI has made it mandatory for NBFC-MFIs to register with at least one credit information company. The need of a Microfinance Credit Bureau Infrastructure in India was triggered mainly by two factors.

Regulatory changes brought in by RBI allowing MFIs to register as NBFC-MFIS, and making it mandatory for NBFC-MFIS to register with at least one credit information company (CIC) and 2. The strong need in the industry to know about the other liabilities of its borrowers and their performance on those, in this backdrop. High Mark Credit Information Services (High Mark) launched the country's first Microfinance Credit Bureau in March 2011. The data captured in High Mark's database is of individuals who have been given credit through JLG, SHG or direct lending. (Microfinance credit bureaus have been operational, and are successfully helping the MFIs in screening multiple borrowing by customers from MFIs).

Microfinance Institutions irrespective of legal forms, seek to create social benefits and promote financial inclusion by providing financial services to clients of financially un-served and underserved households. Over time, the Microfinance sector has become an integral part of the financial infrastructure for the vulnerable sections of society in India. Hence it is important to define core values and fair practices for the microfinance sector so as to ensure that microfinance services through MFIs are provided in a manner that benefits clients and is ethical and dignified.

Code of conduct for Microfinance Institutions included (i) The core values of Microfinance (ii) Code of conduct for Microfinance Institutions (The Code) (iii) Client Protection Guidelines for MFIs (iv) Institutional Conduct guidelines.

6.10. The core values of Microfinance are stated as follows:

1. **Integrity:** To provide low-income clients women and men and their families, with access to financial services that are client focused and designed to enhance their wellbeing and are delivered in a manner that is ethical, dignified, transparent, equitable and cost effective.

2. **Quality of Service:** To ensure quality services to clients, appropriate to their needs and delivered efficiently in a convenient and timely manner. To maintain high standards of professionalism based on honesty, nondiscrimination and customer centricity.

3. **Transparency:** To provide complete and accurate information to clients regarding all products and services offered. To create awareness and enable clients and all other stakeholders to understand the information provided with respect to financial services offered and availed.

4. **Fair Practices:** To ensure that clients are protected against fraud and misrepresentation deception or unethical practices. To ensure that all practices related to lending and recovery of loans are fair and maintain respect for client's dignity and with an understanding of client's vulnerable situation. Privacy of client information to safeguard personal information of clients, allowing disclosures and exchange of relevant information with authorized personnel only, and with the knowledge and consent of clients.

5. **Integrating social values into operations:** To ensure high standards of governance and management to monitor and report social as well as financial data.

6. **Feedback and grievance redressal mechanism:** To provide clients formal and informal channels for feedback and suggestions to consistently

assess the impact of services in order to enhance competencies and serve clients better to provide a formal grievance redressal mechanism for clients Code of Conduct for Micro finance Institutions, All MFIs are required to follow all regulatory norms as well as consumer protection practices (specifically RBI's Guidelines on Fair practices for NBFCs) laid down by the government and the regulators in both letter and spirit. The Code of Conduct lays down additional requirements to enhance and improve sector practices. The Code of Conduct is to be followed by all MFIs regardless of their form.

6.11. Application of the Code:

The Code applies to the following activities undertaken by Microfinance Institutions providing credit services to clients, individually or in groups Recovery of credit provided to clients Collection of thrift from clients, wherever applicable Providing insurance and pension services, remittance services or any other related products and services Formation of any type of community collectives including Self Help groups, Joint Liability groups and their federations Business development services including marketing of products or services made or extended by the eligible clients or for any other purpose for the welfare and benefit of clients.

6.12. Micro Finance Institutions must agree to:

Promote and strengthen the Microfinance movement in the country by bringing low-income clients to the mainstream financial sector build progressive, sustainable and client-centric systems and practices to provide a range of financial services (consistent with regulation) to clients promote cooperation and coordination among themselves and other agencies in order to achieve higher operating standards and avoid unethical competition in order to serve clients better in order to adhere to the core values of Microfinance, the Code of Conduct as mentioned below must be abided by all institutions providing microfinance services.

6.13. Code of Conduct

Integrity and ethical behavior of MFIs must design appropriate policies and operating guidelines to treat the clients and employees with dignity MFIs must incorporate transparent and professional governance system to ensure that staff and persons acting on their behalf are oriented and trained to put this Code into practice MFIs must educate clients on the code of Conduct and its implication.

6.14. Transparency

MFIs must disclose all terms and conditions to the clients for all services offered. Disclosure must be made prior to disbursement in accordance with the Reserve Bank of India's fair practices code, in any one of the following ways.

a. Individual sanction letter
b. Loan card
c. Loan schedule
d. Passbook
e. Through group/centre meetings (details can be printed in a paper and all borrowers can sign on the same as acknowledgement of their acceptance)
f. MFIs must communicate all the terms and conditions for all products/services offered to clients in the official regional language or a language understood by them.
g. At the minimum.

6.15. The MFI must disclose the following terms:

a. Rate of interest on a reducing balance method
b. Processing fee
c. Any other charges or fees howsoever described
d. Total charges recovered for insurance coverage and risks covered.

MFIs must communicate in writing charges levied for all financial services rendered. Fee on noncredit products/services will be collected only with prior declaration to the client h) MFIs must declare all interest and fees payable as an all-inclusive Annual Percentage Rate (APR) and equivalent monthly rate

MFIs must follow RBI's guidelines with respect to interest charges and security deposit j) Formal records of all transactions must be maintained in accordance with all regulatory and statutory norms and borrowers' acknowledgement/acceptance of terms and conditions must form a part of these records.

6.16. Client protection:

1. Fair Practices:

MFIs must ensure that the provision of microfinance services to eligible clients is as per RBI guidelines. MFIs must obtain copies of relevant documents from clients, as per standard KYC norms. Additional documents sought must be reasonable and necessary for completing the transaction.

Product should not be bundled. The only exception to bundling may be made with respect to credit life, life insurance and life-stock insurance products, which are typically offered bundled with loans. The terms of insurance should be transparently conveyed to the client and must comply with RBI and Insurance Regulatory and development authority (IRDA) norms. Consent of the client must be taken in all cases.

2. Avoiding over indebtedness:

MFIs must conduct proper due diligence as per their internal credit policy to access the need and repayment capacity of client before making a loan and must only make loans, commensurate with the client's ability to repay. If a client has loans from two separate lenders, then irrespective of the source of the loans, a MFI shall not be the third lender to that client... MFIs must not, under any circumstances, breach the total debt limit for any client as prescribed by RBI or Central/State government.

6.17. Appropriate interaction and collection practices:

MFIs must have clearly defined guidelines for employee interaction with clients. MFIs must ensure that all staff and persons acting on behalf of the MFI

1. Use courteous language maintain decorum, and respectful of cultural sensitivity during all interaction with clients.
2. Do not indulge in any behavior that in any manner would suggest any kind of threat or violence
3. Do not contact clients at odd hours as per the RBI guidelines for loan recovery agents.
4. Do not visit clients at inappropriate occasions such as bereavement, sickness etc to collect dues

MFIs must provide a valid receipt (in whatever form decided by the MFI) for each and every payment received from the borrower.

MFIs must have a detailed board approved process for dealing with clients, at each stage of default MFIs must not collect shortfalls in collections from employees and their HR policies must categorically denounce this practice. An exception can however be made in proven cases of frauds by employees.

6.18. Privacy of client information:

MFIs must keep personal client information strictly confidential. Client information may be disclosed to a third party subject to the following conditions:

(a) Client has been informed about such disclosure and permission has been obtained in writing (b) The party in question has been authorized by the clients to obtain client information from the MFI. (c) It is legally required to do so. (d) This practice is customary amongst financial institution and available for a close group basis (such as a credit bureau).

6.19. Governance:

MFIs must incorporate a formal governance system, that is transparent and professional, and adopt the following best practices of corporate governance:

MFIs must observe high standard of governance by inducting persons with good and sound reputation as members of Board of Directors/Governing Body.

MFIS must endeavor to induct independent person to constitute at least one third of the governing board, and the Board must be actively involved in all policy formulation and other important decisions.

MFIs must have a Board approved debt restructuring product/programme for providing borrowers facing repayment stress.

MFIs will appoint an audit committee of the Board with an independent director as Chairperson.

MFIs must ensure transparency in the maintenance of books of accounts and reporting/presentation and disclosure of financial statements by qualified auditor/s.

MFIs must put in best efforts to follow the Audit and Assurance Standard issued by the Institute of Chartered Accountants of India (ICAI).

MFIs must place before the Board of Directors a compliance report indicating the extent of compliance with this Code of Conduct, specifically indicating any deviation and reasons therefore, at the end of every financial year.

6.20. Recruitment:

1. The Code covers all MFI staff:

As a matter of free and fair requirement practice, there will be no restriction on hiring of staff from other MFIs by legitimate means in the public domain like general requirement advertisement in local newspapers, web advertisements, walk-in interviews etc.

Whenever an MFI recruits' staff from another MFI, it will be mandatory to seek a reference check from the previous employer. The reference check will be sought from current employer only after an offer is made and an offer letter is issued to the prospective employee. MFIs should respond to the reference check request another MFI within two weeks MFIs must honor a one-month notice period from an outgoing employee. No MFI shall recruit an employee of another MFI irrespective of the grader level of the employee. without the relieving letter from the previous MF1 employer. An exception can however be made in instance where the previous employer (MFI) fails to respond to the reference check request within 30 days. All MFIs must provide such relieving letter to the outgoing employee in case she or he has given proper notice, handed over the charge and settled all the dues towards the MF1, except in proven cases of fraud or gross misconduct by the employee. Whenever an MFI recruits from another MP1, at a level up to the branch manager position, the said employee shall not be assigned to the same area he/she was serving at the previous employer, for the period of one year.

2. Client Education:

MFIS must have a dedicated process to raise clients' awareness of the options, choices and responsibilities vis-à-vis financial products and services available. New clients must be informed about the organization's policies and procedures to help them understand their rights as borrowers.

MFIs must ensure regular checks on client awareness and understanding of the key terms and conditions of the products/services offered//availed (As part of the internal audit systems or through some other regular monitoring)

3. Data sharing:

MFIs will agree to share complete client data with all RBI approved Client Bureaus, as per the frequency of data submission prescribed by the Credit Bureaus.

4. Feedback/Grievance Redressal Mechanism:

MFIs must establish dedicated feedback and grievance redressal mechanisms to correct any error and handle/receive complaints speedily and efficiently.

MFIs must inform clients about the existence and purpose of these mechanisms and how to access them. MFIs must designate at least one grievance redressal official to handle complaints and/or note any suggestion from the clients and make his/her contact numbers easily accessible to clients. Each MFI will have an appropriate mechanism for ensuring compliance with the Code of Conduct Where complainants are not satisfied with the outcome of the investigation conducted by the concerned MFI into their complaint, they shall be notified of their right to refer the matter to the grievance redressal mechanism established by the industry Association.

5. Client Protection guidelines for Microfinance Institutions (CPG):

The CPG states that all MFIS, regardless of their form: Shall display the client protection code in all branches and offices, in plain view. Shall endeavor to provide microfinance services to all eligible clients, as per RBI guidelines. Shall educate clients, staff, and any person acting on their behalf on the code of conduct and its implementation. Shall disclose all terms and conditions to the client for all products, services offered, prior to disbursement in any of the following ways.

a. individual sanction letter.
b. loan card.
c. loan schedule
d. pass book
e. through Group/Centre meetings (details can be printed on a paper and all borrowers can sign on the same as acknowledge of their acceptance) Shall communicate all the terms and conditions for all products/services in the official regional language or a language understood by clients.

Shall disclose the following terms:

a. rate of interest on a reducing balance method.
b. processing fee.
c. any other charges or fees howsoever described.
d. total charges recovered for insurance coverage and risk covered. Shall communicate in writing, charges levied for all financial services rendered.

Shall not collect fee on non-credit product/services without prior declaration to the client. Shall declare all interest and fees payable as an all-inclusive APR and equivalent monthly rate. Shall follow RBI's guidelines with respect to interest charges and security deposits. Shall obtain copies of relevant documents from clients as per standard KYC norms. Additional documents sought must be reasonable and necessary for completing the transaction. Shall not bundle products, except for credit life, life insurance and Livestock insurance products. The terms of insurance should be transparently conveyed to the customer and must comply with RBI and IRDA norms. Consent of the client must be taken in all cases. Shall conduct proper due diligence to assess the need and the repayment capacity of clients making a loan and must only make loans commensurate with the client's ability to repay. Shall not be the 3rd lender to a client if the client has loans from two other lenders (irrespective the source of loan). Shall not breach the total debt limit for any client as prescribed by the RBI or Central/State Government. Shall ensure that all employees follow company guidelines for interaction with clients. Shall ensure that all staff and persons acting for the MFI or on behalf of the MFI.

a. use courteous language, maintain decorum, and/or respectful of cultural sensitivities during all interactions with clients.
b. do not indulge in any behavior that in any manner that would suggest any kind of threat or violence to clients.
c. do not contact clients at odd hours as per the RBI guidelines for loan recovery agents.

(d) do not visit clients at inappropriate occasions such as bereavement, sickness etc. to collect dues Shall provide a valid receipt (in whatever form decided by the MFI) for each and every payment received from the borrower.

Shall follow approved company procedure to deal with clients default sensitively. Shall follow the debt restructuring mechanism adopted by the MFI for borrowers under liquidity stress. Shall keep personal client information strictly confidential.

Shall disclose client information to a third party only under the following conditions:

a. Client has been informed about such disclosure and permission has been obtained in writing.
b. The party in question has been authorized by the client to obtain client information from the MFI.
c. It is legally required to do so.
d. This practice is customary amongst financial institution and available for a close group on reciprocal basis (such as a credit bureau)

Shall follow company approved process to raise client awareness of the options, choices and responsibilities vis-à-vis financial products and services available.

Shall inform all new clients about the organization's policies and procedures.

Shall inform clients about the existence and purpose of feedback mechanism and how to access them.

6.21. Institutional conduct guidelines for Micro Finance Institutions (ICG)):

The ICG states that all MEIs regardless of their form Shall have an appropriate mechanism for ensuring compliance with the code of conduct. Shall have appropriate policies and operating guidelines to treat clients and employees with dignity. Shall maintain formal records of all transactions in accordance with all regulatory and statutory norms and borrowers' acknowledgement/acceptance of terms/conditions must form a part of these records. Shall have detailed board approved process for dealing with clients at each stage of default Shall not collect shortfalls in collection from employees except in proven cases of frauds by employees Shall have a Board approved debt restructuring product/program for providing relief to borrowers facing repayment stress. Shall seek a reference check from previous employer for any new hire. Shall provide within two week the replies to the reference check correspondence for another MFI. Shall honor a one-month notice period from an outgoing employee. Shall not recruit an employee of another MFI without the relieving letter from the previous MFI employer except where the previous employer (MFI) fails to respond to the reference check request within 30 days. Shall not assign a new employee recruited from another MFI, to the same area he/she was serving at the previous employer for a period of one year. This restriction applies to positions up to the branch manager level. Shall have a dedicated process to raise client's awareness of options, choices, rights and responsibilities as a borrower and shall conduct regular checks on client awareness and understanding of the key terms and conditions of the products/service offered/availed. Shall agree to share complete client data with all RBI ap proved credit bureaus, as per the frequency of data submission prescribed by the Credit Bureaus. Shall establish dedicated feedback and grievances redressal mechanism to correct any error and handle/receive complaints speedily and efficiently. Shall designate an official to handle complaints and/or note any suggestions from the clients and make his/her contact numbers easily accessible to clients.

6.22. Legal Formats and Governance:

In relation to the vast demand, there is limited coverage of potential microfinance clients. Credit to the poor is provided through the formal financial system, semi-formal and informal institutions. In that backdrop. it is important to understand the laws and regulations that shape the financial sector. Laws and regulations cause costs as well as create opportunities for entrepreneurs and/or investors who supply micro-finance. Laws and regulations balance the interests of different groups of the stakeholders. Stakeholders are all those concerned of a given enterprise. The most important stakeholders of micro-finance are actual and potential clients, supplying institutions/companies and their owners (called "shareholders" because they put capital in the form of shares into the company), their managements and their staff, and regulating agencies. The most important regulating agencies are Reserve Bank of India (RBI), Government of India, Ministry of Finance, and State governments.

The Legal formats of MFIs that are provided by Indian laws can be classified by the profit motive. There are Not-For-Profit Entities such as trusts, societies and Section 25 companies. The for-Profit enterprises are Non-Banking Financial Companies (NBFCs). Co-operatives are also for profit but are Mutual-Benefit enterprises, Cooperatives are formed and owned by members to support their own activities. This includes Mutually Aided Co-operative Societies (MACSS), Multi State Co-ops, credit and non-credit co-operative societies, Producer Companies; Co-operative Banks.

Laws are made by Governments. The formal and central law-makers are Parliament and State Legislatures (elected representatives of the people). Debate on the law takes place inside and outside Parliament.

Ministries have an important role in formulating laws, as the officials are consulted by the politicians. In view of this, practitioners-owners and senior leaders of industry of microfinance institutions need engage in lobbying i.e. consulting and counseling bureaucrats and politicians about what they feel important for the sector. As the political debate results in such a number of laws covering various types of financial institutions, the legal provisions of one law are sometimes contradictory to the provisions of another law.

The understanding of following important laws or Acts may be useful to the microfinance professionals.

- Reserve Bank of India Act, 1934
- Companies Act, 1956 (Covers banks, NBFCs and S 25 companies)
- Societies Registration Act of 1860
- Mutually Aided Co-operative Societies Acts of various states
- Indian Trusts Act-1882
- Banking Regulation Act 1949
- The Multi-State Co-operative Societies Act 2002
- Banking Companies (Acquisition and Transfer of Undertakings) Act, 1970/1980: Relates to nationalization of banks; includes Local Area Banks (LAB)
- Bankers' Books Evidence Act Banking Secrecy Act
- Negotiable Instruments Act, 1881
- National Bank for Agriculture and Rural Development Act, 1981
- The Regional Rural Banks Act, 1976, and the Co-operative Societies Act, 1904, cover RRBs and co-operatives respectively.

6.23. RBI Guideline on Digital Landing on 14th March 2022, is mentioned here as it is:

भारतीय रिज़र्व बैंक
RESERVE BANK OF INDIA

www.rbi.org.in

RBI/DOR/2021-22/89

DoR.FIN.REC.95/03.10.038/2021-22 March 14, 2022

(Updated as on July 25, 2022)

All Commercial Banks (including Small Finance Banks,

Local Area Banks and Regional Rural Banks) excluding Payments Banks All Primary (Urban) Co-operative Banks/State Co-operative Banks/District Central Co-operative Banks

All Non-Banking Financial Companies (including Microfinance Institutions and Housing Finance Companies)

Madam/Dear Sir,

Master Direction – Reserve Bank of India (Regulatory Framework for Microfinance Loans) Directions, 2022

1. Please refer to paragraph 8 of the Statement on Developmental and Regulatory Policies announced as a part of the Bi-monthly Monetary Policy Statement for 2020-21 dated February 5, 2021, regarding review of the regulatory framework for microfinance.

2. A consultative document on regulation of microfinance loans was issued for public comments on June 14, 2021. Based on the feedback received, it has now been decided to put in place the directions for microfinance loans which are enclosed.

3. Frequently asked questions (FAQs) on these directions are available at following link Reserve Bank of India - Frequently Asked Questions (rbi.org.in)

Yours faithfully,

(J.P. Sharma)

Chief General Manager

विनियमन विभाग, केंद्रीय कार्यालय, दूसरी मंजिल, मुख्य भवन, शहीद भगत रोड, किला, मुंबई-400 001 ईमेल:cgmicdor@rbi.org.in

Department of Regulation, Central Office, 2nd Floor, Main Building, Shaheed Bhagat Road, Fort, Mumbai-400 001 Email: cgmicdor@rbi.org.in

---

हिंदी आसान है इसका प्रयोग बढ़ाइए

DoR.FIN.REC.95/03.10.038/2021-22 March 14, 2022

6.24. Master Direction - Reserve Bank of India (Regulatory Framework for Microfinance Loans) Directions, 2022

In exercise of the powers conferred by Section 21, Section 35A and Section 56 of the Banking Regulation Act, 1949; Chapter IIIB of the Reserve Bank of India Act, 1934; and Sections 30A and Section 32 of the National Housing Bank Act, 1987, the Reserve Bank, being satisfied that it is necessary and expedient in the public interest so to do, hereby, issues the directions hereinafter specified.

1. Short Title and Commencement

1.1 These directions shall be called the Reserve Bank of India (Regulatory Framework for Microfinance Loans) Directions, 2022.

1.2 These directions shall be effective from April 01, 2022, subject to stipulations as at paragraphs 5.3 and 9.3.

2. Applicability

2.1 The provisions of these directions shall apply to the following entities:

i. All Commercial Banks (including Small Finance Banks, Local Area Banks, and Regional Rural Banks) excluding Payments Banks;
ii. All Primary (Urban) Co-operative Banks/State Co-operative Banks/District Central Co-operative Banks; and
iii. All Non-Banking Financial Companies (including Microfinance Institutions and Housing Finance Companies).

2.2 The entities mentioned at points 2.1(i) to 2.1(iii) above are hereafter referred to as 'Regulated Entities (REs)' for the purpose of these directions.

3. Definition of Microfinance Loan

3.1 A microfinance loan is defined as a collateral-free loan given to a household having annual household income up to ₹3,00,000. For this purpose, the household shall mean an individual family unit, i.e., husband, wife and their unmarried children.

3.2 All collateral-free loans, irrespective of end use and mode of application/processing/disbursal (either through physical or digital channels), provided to low-income households, i.e., households having annual income up to ₹3,00,000, shall be considered as microfinance loans.

3.3 To ensure collateral-free nature of the microfinance loan, the loan shall not be linked with a lien on the deposit account of the borrower.

3.4 The REs shall have a board-approved policy to provide the flexibility of repayment periodicity on microfinance loans as per borrowers' requirement.

4. Assessment of Household Income

4.1 Each RE shall put in place a board-approved policy for assessment of household income. An indicative methodology for assessment of household income is provided in **Annex I.**

4.2 Self-regulatory organisations (SROs) and other associations/agencies may also develop a common framework based on the indicative methodology. The REs may adopt/modify this framework suitably as per their requirements with approval of their boards.

4.3 Each RE shall mandatorily submit information regarding household income to the Credit Information Companies (CICs). Reasons for any divergence between the already reported household income and assessed household income shall be specifically ascertained from the borrower/s before updating the assessed household income with CICs.

5. Limit on Loan Repayment Obligations of a Household

5.1 Each RE shall have a board-approved policy regarding the limit on the outflows on account of repayment of monthly loan obligations of a household as a percentage of the monthly household income. This shall be subject to a limit of maximum 50 per cent of the monthly household income.

5.2 The computation of loan repayment obligations shall take into account all outstanding loans (collateral-free microfinance loans as well as any other type of collateralized loans) of the household. The outflows capped at 50 per cent of the monthly household income shall include repayments (including both principal as well as interest component) towards all existing loans as well as the loan under consideration.

5.3 Existing loans, for which outflows on account of repayment of monthly loan obligations of a household as a percentage of the monthly household income exceed the limit of 50 per cent, shall be allowed to mature. However, in such cases, no new loans shall be provided to these households till the prescribed limit of 50 per cent is complied with.

5.4 Each RE shall provide timely and accurate data to the CICs and use the data available with them to ensure compliance with the level of indebtedness. Besides, the RE shall also ascertain the same from other sources such as declaration from the borrowers, their bank account statements and local enquiries.

6. Pricing of Loans

6.1 Each RE shall put in place a board-approved policy regarding pricing of microfinance loans which shall, inter alia, cover the following:

i. A well-documented interest rate model/approach for arriving at the all-inclusive interest rate;
ii. Delineation of the components of the interest rate such as cost of funds, risk premium and margin, etc. in terms of the quantum of each component based on objective parameters;
iii. The range of spread of each component for a given category of borrowers; and
iv. A ceiling on the interest rate and all other charges applicable to the microfinance loans.

6.2 Interest rates and other charges/fees on microfinance loans should not be usurious. These shall be subjected to supervisory scrutiny by the Reserve Bank.

6.3 Each RE shall disclose pricing related information to a prospective borrower in a standardised simplified factsheet (in accordance with the illustration provided in **Annex II**).

6.4 Any fees to be charged to the microfinance borrower by the RE and/or its partner/agent shall be explicitly disclosed in the factsheet. The borrower shall not be charged any amount which is not explicitly mentioned in the factsheet.

6.5 The factsheet shall also be provided for other loans (i.e., collateralized loans) extended to borrowers from low-income households.

6.6 There shall be no pre-payment penalty on microfinance loans. Penalty, if any, for delayed payment shall be applied on the overdue amount and not on the entire loan amount.

6.7 Each RE shall prominently display the minimum, maximum and average interest rates charged on microfinance loans in all its offices, in the literature (information booklets/pamphlets) issued by it and details on its website. This information shall also be included in the supervisory returns and subjected to supervisory scrutiny.

6.8 Any change in interest rate or any other charge shall be informed to the borrower well in advance and these changes shall be effective only prospectively.

6.9 As part of their awareness campaigns, SROs/other industry associations may publish the range of interest rates on microfinance loans charged by their members operating in a district. SROs/other industry associations may also sensitize their members against charging of usurious interest rates.

6.10 RBI would also make available information regarding interest charged by REs on microfinance loans.

7. Guidelines on Conduct towards Microfinance Borrowers

7.1 General

7.1.1 A fair practices code (FPC) based on these directions shall be put in place by all REs with the approval of their boards. The FPC shall be displayed by the RE in all its offices and on its website. The FPC should be issued in a language understood by the borrower.

7.1.2 There shall be a standard form of loan agreement for microfinance loans in a language understood by the borrower.

7.1.3 Each RE shall provide a loan card to the borrower which shall incorporate the following:

i. Information which adequately identifies the borrower;
ii. Simplified factsheet on pricing;
iii. All other terms and conditions attached to the loan;
iv. Acknowledgements by the RE of all repayments including instalments received and the final discharge; and
v. Details of the grievance redressal system, including the name and contact number of the nodal officer of the RE.

7.1.4 All entries in the loan card should be in a language understood by the borrower.

7.1.5 Issuance of non-credit products shall be with full consent of the borrowers and fee structure for such products shall be explicitly communicated to the borrower in the loan card itself.

7.2 Training of Staff

7.2.1 Each RE shall have a board-approved policy regarding the conduct of employees and system for their recruitment, training and monitoring. This policy shall, inter alia, lay down minimum qualifications for the staff and shall provide necessary training tools to deal with the customers. Training to employees shall include programs to inculcate appropriate behavior towards customers. Conduct of employees towards customers shall also be incorporated appropriately in their compensation matrix.

7.2.2 Field staff shall be trained to make necessary enquiries regarding the income and existing debt of the household.

7.2.3 Training, if any, offered to the borrowers shall be free of cost.

7.3 Responsibilities for Outsourced Activities

7.3.1 Outsourcing of any activity by the RE does not diminish its obligations and the onus of compliance with these directions shall rest solely with the RE.

7.3.2 A declaration that the RE shall be accountable for inappropriate behaviour by its employees or employees of the outsourced agency and shall provide timely grievance redressal, shall be made in the loan agreement and also in the FPC displayed in its office/branch premises/website

7.4 Guidelines related to Recovery of Loans

7.4.1 Each RE shall put in place a mechanism for identification of the borrowers facing repayment related difficulties, engagement with such borrowers and providing them necessary guidance about the recourse available.

7.4.2 Recovery shall be made at a designated/central designated place decided mutually by the borrower and the RE. However, field staff shall be allowed to make recovery at the place of residence or work of the borrower if the borrower fails to appear at the designated/central designated place on two or more successive occasions.

7.4.3 RE or its agent shall not engage in any harsh methods towards recovery. Without limiting the general application of the foregoing, following practices shall be deemed as harsh:

i. Use of threatening or abusive language
ii. Persistently calling the borrower and/or calling the borrower before 9:00 a.m. and after 6:00 p.m.

iii. Harassing relatives, friends, or co-workers of the borrower
iv. Publishing the name of borrowers
v. Use or threat of use of violence or other similar means to harm the borrower or borrower's family/assets/reputation
vi. Misleading the borrower about the extent of the debt or the consequences of non- repayment

7.4.4 Each RE shall have a dedicated mechanism for redressal of recovery related grievances. The details of this mechanism shall be provided to the borrower at the time of loan disbursal.

7.5 Engagement of Recovery Agents

7.5.1 Recovery agents shall mean agencies engaged by the RE for recovery of dues from its borrowers and the employees of these agencies.

7.5.2 The REs shall have a due diligence process in place for engagement of recovery agents, which shall, inter alia, cover individuals involved in the recovery process. REs shall ensure that the recovery agents engaged by them carry out verification of the antecedents of their employees, which shall include police verification. REs shall also decide the periodicity at which re-verification of antecedents shall be resorted to.

7.5.3 To ensure due notice and appropriate authorization, the RE shall provide the details of recovery agents to the borrower while initiating the process of recovery. The agent shall also carry a copy of the notice and the authorization letter from the RE along with the identity card issued to him by the RE or the agency. Further, where the recovery agency is changed by the RE during the recovery process, in addition to the RE notifying the borrower of the change, the new agent shall carry the notice and the authorization letter along with his identity card.

7.5.4 The notice and the authorization letter shall, among other details, also include the contact details of the recovery agency and the RE.

7.5.5 The up-to-date details of the recovery agencies engaged by the RE shall also be hosted on the RE's website.

8. Qualifying Assets Criteria

8.1 Under the earlier qualifying assets criteria1, a Non-banking Financial Company - Microfinance Institution (NBFC-MFI) is required to have minimum 85 per cent of its net assets2 as 'qualifying assets'. The definition of 'qualifying assets' of NBFC-MFIs is now being aligned with the definition of 'microfinance loans' given at paragraph 3 above. The minimum requirement of microfinance loans for NBFC-MFIs also stands revised to 75 per cent of the total assets.

8.2 Under the earlier guidelines, an NBFC that does not qualify as an NBFC-MFI, cannot extend microfinance loans exceeding 10 per cent of its total assets. The maximum limit

[1] In order to be classified as a 'qualifying asset', a loan is required to satisfy the following criteria:

i. Loan which is disbursed to a borrower with household annual income not exceeding ₹1,25,000 and ₹2,00,000 for rural and urban/semi-urban households, respectively;
ii. Loan amount does not exceed ₹75,000 in the first cycle and ₹1,25,000 in subsequent cycles;
iii. Total indebtedness of the borrower does not exceed ₹1,25,000 (excluding loan for education and medical expenses);
iv. Minimum tenure of 24 months for loan amount exceeding ₹30,000;
v. Collateral free loans without any prepayment penalty;
vi. Minimum 50 per cent of aggregate amount of loans for income generation activities; and
vii. Flexibility of repayment periodicity (weekly, fortnightly or monthly) at borrower's choice.

[2] Net assets have been defined as total assets other than cash, bank balances and money market instruments on microfinance loans for such NBFCs (i.e., NBFCs other than NBFC-MFIs) now stands revised to 25 per cent of the total assets.

9. Exemption for 'Not for Profit' Companies engaged in Microfinance Activities

9.1 The definition of microfinance loans for 'not for profit' companies (registered under Section 8 of the Companies Act, 2013) is now aligned with the revised definition of microfinance loans viz., collateral-free loans to households with annual household income up to ₹3,00,000, provided the monthly loan obligations of a household does not exceed 50 per cent of the monthly household income.

9.2 Exemptions from Sections 45-IA[3], 45-IB[4] and 45-IC[5] of the RBI Act, 1934 have been withdrawn for those 'not for profit' companies engaged in microfinance activities that have asset size of ₹100 crore and above.

9.3 'Not for profit' companies that are not eligible for the exemptions mentioned at paragraph 9.2 above, are required to register as NBFC-MFIs and adhere to the regulations applicable to NBFC-MFIs. Such companies shall submit the application for registration as an NBFC-MFI to the Reserve Bank within three months of the issuance of this circular. Those companies that currently do not comply with the regulations prescribed for NBFC-MFIs, shall submit a board-approved plan, with a roadmap to meet the prescribed regulations, along with their application for registration.

10. Net Owned Fund (NOF) Requirement

Existing NBFC-MFIs shall adhere to the NOF glidepath indicated under paragraph 3.1 (a) of the Circular dated October 22, 2021 on 'Scale Based Regulation (SBR): A Revised Regulatory Framework for NBFCs' as given below:

NBFCs	Current NOF	By March 31, 2025	By March 31, 2027
NBFC-MFI	₹5 crore (₹2 crore in NE Region)	₹7 crore (₹5 crore in NE Region)	₹10 crore

[3] 45-IA: Requirement of registration as an NBFC

[4] 45-IB: Maintenance of a certain percentage of outstanding deposits in approved securities by deposit taking NBFCs

[5] 45-IC: Transfer of 20 per cent of net profit to reserve fund

Annex I

(cf. Para 4.1 of these Directions)

Indicative Methodology for Household Income Assessment

1. For undertaking the income assessment of a low-income household, information related to following parameters may be captured by the lender:

(i) Parameters to capture household profile

a) Composition of the household

i. Number of earning members
ii. Number of non-earning members

b) Type of accommodation (owned/rented, etc.)

c) Availability of basic amenities (electricity, water, toilet, sewage, LPG connection, etc.)

d) Availability of other assets (land, livestock, vehicle, furniture, smartphone, electronic items, etc.)

(ii) Parameters to capture household income

a) Primary source of income

i. Sector of work (Agriculture & allied activities, trading, manufacturing, services, etc.)
ii. Nature of work (Self-employed or salaried, regular or seasonal, etc.)
iii. Frequency of income (daily/weekly/monthly)
iv. Months/days of employment over last one year
v. Self-reported monthly income
vi. Average monthly income (to be derived from (iv) & (v) above)

b) Other sources of income

i. Remittance
ii. Rent/Lease
iii. Pension
iv. Government transfer
v. Scholarship
vi. Others (specify details)

c) The income assessment as above may be carried out for all earning members with respect to all sources (primary or secondary) of income. While assessing income of all members from all sources, it may be ensured that there is no double counting of income such as counting of salary income of one migrant member also as remittance income for the household.

d) While the income computation may be done on a monthly basis, the income assessment for all members and sources may be carried out over a period of minimum one year to ascertain the stability of the household income.

(iii) Parameters to capture household expenses

a) Regular monthly expenses (food, utilities, transport, house/shop rent, clothing, regular medical costs, school/college fees, etc.)

b) Irregular expenses over last one year (medical expenses, house renovation, purchase of household goods, functions, etc.)

2. Self-reported income at 1(ii) above may be corroborated with the profile of household at 1(i) and household expenses at 1(iii). Further, household income may also be verified from other sources (bank account statements of the borrowers, group members, other references in the vicinity, etc.).

Annex II

(cf. Para 6.3 of these Directions)

Illustrative Factsheet on Pricing of Microfinance Loans

(to be provided in a language (vernacular language) understood by the borrower)

Date: XXX **Lender's Name:** XXX **Applicant Name:** XXX

Sr. No.	Parameter	Details
(i)	Loan amount (amount disbursed to the borrower) (in Rupees)	20,000
(ii)	Total interest charge during the entire tenure of the loan (in Rupees)	3,274
(iii)	Other up-front charges (break-up of each component to be given below) (in Rupees)	400
(a)	Processing fees (in Rupees)	160
(b)	Insurance charges (in Rupees)	240
(c)	Others (if any) (in Rupees)	-
(iv)	Net disbursed amount ((i)-(iii)) (in Rupees)	19,600
(v)	Total amount to be paid by the borrower (sum of (i), (ii) and (iii)) (in Rupees)	23,6746
(vi)	Effective annualized interest rate (in percentage) (computed on net disbursed amount using IRR approach and reducing balance method)	17.07%
(vii)	Loan term (in months)	24
(viii)	Repayment frequency by the borrower	Monthly
(ix)	Number of instalments of repayment	24
(x)	Amount of each instalment of repayment (in Rupees)	970

Details about Contingent Charges		
(xi)	Borrower shall not be charged any penalty on prepayment of loan at any time.	
(xii)	Penal charges in case of delayed payments (if any)	
(xiii)	Other charges (if any)	

Detailed Repayment Schedule

Instalment No.	Outstanding Principal (in Rupees)	Principal (in Rupees)	Interest (in Rupees)	Instalment (in Rupees)
1	20,000	720	250	970
2	19,280	729	241	970
3	18,552	738	232	970
4	17,814	747	223	970
5	17,067	756	213	970
6	16,310	766	204	970
7	15,544	775	194	970
8	14,769	785	185	970
9	13,984	795	175	970
10	13,189	805	165	970
11	12,384	815	155	970
12	11,569	825	145	970
13	10,744	835	134	970
14	9,909	846	124	970
15	9,063	856	113	970
16	8,206	867	103	970
17	7,339	878	92	970
18	6,461	889	81	970
19	5,572	900	70	970
20	4,672	911	58	970
21	3,761	923	47	970
22	2,838	934	35	970

23	1,904	946	24	970
24	958	958	12	970

The difference in repayment amount calculated from the total of instalments given under the detailed repayment schedule i.e., ₹23,280 (=970*24) (excluding ₹400 (other up-front charges)) vis-à-vis the amount of ₹23,674 (₹20,000 (loan amount) + ₹3,274 (Interest charges) + ₹400 (other up-front charges) mentioned under (v) is due to rounding off the instalment amount of ₹969.73 to ₹970 under the detailed repayment schedule.

6.25. The New Guidelines in lay man language:

1. Applicability

- All Commercial Banks (including Small Finance Banks, Local Area Banks and Regional Rural Banks) excluding Payments Banks
- All Primary (Urban) Co-operative Banks/State Co-operative Banks/District Central Co-operative Banks
- All Non-Banking Financial Companies (including Microfinance Institutions and Housing Finance Companies)

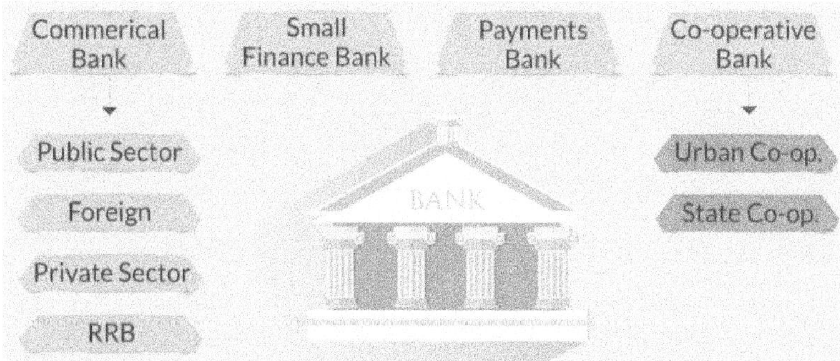

2. Positive Impact on us (on Microfinance Company's):

- All banks, SFBs and NBFC-MFIs also have to mandatorily obey these guidelines.
- A perfect level-playing filed for us as NBFC MFI
- A better credit underwriting hence better decision while disbursing

3. The Guidelines are very simple based on:

- Household Income
- Cash Flow and
- Indebtedness Limit

4. Important to know:

- How to Calculate the Household Income
- How to Calculate the Cash Flow

5. Important for MFI'S:

- A better Credit Underwriting
- Correct Disbursement = Timely Repayment
- More Profitability

6. Household Income Assessment:

Household Income: Household income limit has been revised and the current limit is Rs.300000/Annum/Family.

Parameters to capture household profile:

- Composition of the household
- Number of earning members
- Number of non-earning members

Type of accommodation (owned/rented, etc.)

- Availability of basic amenities (electricity, water, toilet, sewage, LPG connection, etc.)
- Availability of other assets (land, livestock, vehicle, furniture, smartphone, electronic items, etc.)

7. Parameters to capture household income:

7.a. Primary source of income

Sector of work (Agriculture & allied activities, trading, manufacturing, services, etc.)

Nature of work (Self-employed or salaried, regular or seasonal, etc.)

Frequency of income (daily/weekly/monthly)

Months/days of employment over last one year

Self-reported monthly income

Average monthly income (to be derived from (iv) & (v) above)

- Other sources of income
    - Remittance
    - Rent/Lease
    - Pension
    - Government transfer
    - Scholarship
    - Others (specify details)

8. Cash Flow: FOIR (Fixed Obligation to Income Ratio) Calculation

- Cash flow will be calculated based on:
- Earning of the family from the heads mentioned in the Household Income
- Total EMI Obligations to be calculated at the backend by running CBs of all the adult members of the HH.
- While calculating income points mentioned below will be taken
- into consideration:
- Nature of Work- Self-employed or salaried, regular or seasonal, etc.
- Frequency of Income- daily/weekly/monthly
- Month/days of employment in last one year

MFI's staff has to collect KYC from borrower, co-borrower and adult children. For borrower two KYCs (including VID must) and from coborrower VID collection is must and one KYC each for each adult children (VID is preferable)

9. Cautionary: Data inputs related to accommodation types, amenities, income and expense have to be as accurate as possible; any manipulation will be subject to Audit and Disciplinary Actions.

10. Earning Members of Family: Borrower, Co-borrower and all adult Unmarried children of Household

11. Indebtedness Limit & Lenders Count:

As per revised RBI guidelines, there is no capping indebtedness limit and lender's count limit but we are continuing with this as an internal check mechanism

From 1st of April'22, the loan amount of customer will be finalized basis Cash flow and income assessment. Maximum EMI of the customer should not go beyond 50% of the household income.

Illustration-1:

Ragini: Works as cook in 2 houses and earns 5000 per month has a loan of EMI 1500/month Dinesh (Husband): Has own Barbar shop and earns 15000/month has a loan EMI 3500/per month, Geeta (Daughter): Earns Rs. 2000/per month from tuitions and has no running loan:

Household Income:

Ragini: 5000 per month + Dinesh: 15000/month + Geeta: 2000/month

Total: 22000/month i.e. 2,64,000 per year

Monthly Loan Liability/EMI:

Ragini: 1500 per month Dinesh: 3500/month

Total: 5000/month

Household Income: 22000/month

EMI: 5000/month

Total EMI should not go beyond 50% of the household income.

Total EMI should not go beyond 50% of 22000 i.e. Rs. 11000/-

Next Loan EMI should not go beyond (Rs. 11000 – Rs. 5000) i.e. **<=Rs. 6000**

Loan Amount Finalization:

From 1st of April'22, the Loan Size of customer will not be only on the basis customer indebtedness. It will primarily dependent on FOIR <= 50%. Indebtedness limit will be the secondary filter.

The total EMI including the EMI of loan that any MFI is going to offer must not be more than 50 per cent of the customer's monthly household income.

Illustration-2:

Rina: Works in a local factory as semi-skilled labour and earns Rs. 9795 per month has a loan of EMI 2500/month

Kamlesh: owns an auto earns 10000/month has a loan EMI 7500/month

Sonu (Son): Works at a grocery shop and earns 4000/month and has no running loan

Household Income:

Rina: 9795/m + Kamlesh: 10000/m + Sonu: 4000/m

Total Rs. 23795/m so Rs. 2,85,540/year

Loan Liability/EMI:

Rina: 2500 per month Kamlesh: 7500/month

Total: 10000/month,

Household Income: 23795/month EMI: 10000/month.

Total EMI should not go beyond 50% of the household income.

Total EMI should not go beyond 50% of 23795 i.e. Rs. 11897/-.

Next Loan EMI should not go beyond (Rs. 11897 – Rs. 10000) **Rs. 1897/-.**

Loan amount will depend after checking the EMI Limit as per FOIR.

6.26. Summarisation:

1. RBI Policy on Credit Decisioning:

i. 'Family' definition (situation wise guidance to be provided)
ii. Capturing the income of all the earning members of the family (of borrower) by asking detailed questions
iii. Capture household expenses by asking parameter wise questions.
iv. Identify all the adult members of the 'family' to run Credit Bureau.
v. FOIR Calculation at the backend.

2. What MFI's Staff(s) needs to do at the time of Verification?

i. Sincerely inquire and capture income information of the borrower, co- borrower, and other unmarried adults of the family. Reject application if the family has >25K monthly income.
ii. Sincerely inquire and capture information regarding household expenses.
iii. Collect KYCs of borrower, Co-borrower and other unmarried adults of the family.
iv. Sincerely inquire and capture asset Profile & PPI information.

3. What Branch Head (First Line Manager of Field Staff) needs to do at the time of Cross Verification?

i. Cross Verify the income, expenses and Asset/PPT info captured by the Field Statt of Microfinance.
ii. Reject (Do not approve) the application if the information captured are unreasonable.
iii. Provision to modify Income, and Expense data. Recalculate FOIR if data have been modified.

iv. Take a responsible decision while sanctioning a loan (w.r.t. go/no-go and loan amount); it is possible to sanction lower amount than the FOIR decided amount.

6.27. Legal and Regulatory Framework in Microfinance:

The legal and regulatory framework in microfinance plays a crucial role in ensuring consumer protection, promoting financial inclusion, and maintaining the stability of the microfinance sector. The specific legal and regulatory environment can vary from one country to another, but some common elements include:

1. **Legal Entity Registration:** Microfinance institutions (MFIs) are required to register as legal entities, such as non-profit organizations, non-governmental organizations (NGOs), or non-banking financial companies (NBFCs), depending on the country's regulations.

2. **Licensing and Authorization:** MFIs typically need to obtain licenses or authorization from the relevant regulatory authorities to operate as microfinance providers. This process involves meeting specific criteria and fulfilling prudential norms.

3. **Capital Adequacy:** Regulatory frameworks often specify minimum capital requirements that MFIs must maintain to ensure financial stability and solvency.

4. **Interest Rate Regulation:** Some countries impose interest rate caps on microfinance loans to protect borrowers from excessive interest rates and prevent predatory lending practices.

5. **Consumer Protection:** Legal and regulatory frameworks incorporate consumer protection measures, such as transparent disclosure of terms and conditions, fair treatment of clients, and grievance redressal mechanisms.

6. **Reporting and Disclosure Requirements:** MFIs are typically required to submit periodic reports to regulatory authorities, disclosing their financial and operational performance. This fosters transparency and accountability.

7. **Social Performance Management:** Some regulatory frameworks encourage or require MFIs to adopt social performance management practices, focusing on their outreach to the poor and impact on clients' lives.

8. **Risk Management:** Regulations may outline risk management guidelines to ensure MFIs assess and manage credit, operational, and liquidity risks effectively.

9. **Reserve and Liquidity Requirements:** MFIs may need to maintain reserves or meet liquidity requirements to safeguard the interests of depositors and borrowers.

10. **Group-Based Lending Norms:** In countries where group-based lending models, such as Self-Help Groups (SHGs) or Joint Liability Groups (JLGs), are prevalent, specific regulations may be in place to govern their operations.

It's important to note that the legal and regulatory framework in microfinance must strike a balance between promoting financial inclusion and consumer protection while maintaining the financial viability and sustainability of MFIs. The effectiveness of the framework largely depends on its implementation, enforcement, and continuous adaptation to evolving market conditions and the needs of the microfinance sector.

6.28. mfin, in detail:

Tere is a well-known organization in India called "Microfinance Institutions Network" (MFIN) that is not a regulatory body but a self-regulatory organization (SRO) representing the non-banking financial company-microfinance institutions (NBFC-MFIs) in India, here are the details about MFIN:

1. Microfinance Institutions Network (mfin):

MFIN is an industry association representing the NBFC-MFIs operating in India.

It was established in October 2009 to act as a platform for advocacy, capacity-building, and self-regulation of its member MFIs.

MFIN aims to promote responsible lending practices, protect the interests of clients, and facilitate the growth and development of the microfinance sector in India.

The organization works closely with regulatory bodies and other stakeholders to address challenges and opportunities in the microfinance industry.

2. Functions and Activities of MFIN:

1. Advocacy and Representation: MFIN represents the collective interests of its member MFIs to various stakeholders, including government authorities, policymakers, regulators, and financial institutions.

2. Self-Regulation: MFIN has developed a Code of Conduct for its member MFIs, which outlines responsible lending practices, client protection principles, and ethical behaviours.

3. Data Collection and Reporting: MFIN collects data from its member MFIs to create comprehensive reports and publications on the performance and trends in the Indian microfinance sector.

4. Capacity Building: MFIN organizes training programs, workshops, and seminars to enhance the skills and knowledge of microfinance professionals and strengthen the sector's capabilities.

5. Research and Policy Advocacy: MFIN conducts research studies and policy analysis to contribute to evidence-based policymaking and promote a conducive regulatory environment for microfinance.

6. Investor Facilitation: MFIN helps connect potential investors with member MFIs, facilitating investments in the microfinance sector.

It is important to note that while MFIN serves as an industry association and self-regulatory body, the formal regulatory authority for microfinance institutions in India is the Reserve Bank of India (RBI). The RBI regulates and supervises the operations of NBFC-MFIs and other financial institutions providing microfinance services to ensure compliance with regulations and consumer protection.

MFIN is indeed an industry association and a self-regulatory organization (SRO) representing the non-banking financial company-microfinance institutions (NBFC-MFIs) in India. It does not have regulatory authority but functions as a platform for advocacy, capacity-building, and self-regulation of its member MFIs.

6.29. Sa-dhan, in detail, as association of microfinance:

"Sa-Dhan" is an association of microfinance, well-known organization in the Indian microfinance sector. Sa-Dhan is an association of community development finance institutions in India and serves as a Self-Regulatory Organization (SRO) for the microfinance sector.

1. Here are the details about Sa-Dhan:

Sa-Dhan is an association of community development finance institutions in India, primarily comprising Microfinance Institutions (MFIs), Non-Governmental Organizations (NGOs), and other entities engaged in microfinance and financial inclusion initiatives.

It was founded in 1999 and registered under the Societies Registration Act.

Sa-Dhan's main objective is to promote the growth and development of the microfinance sector while ensuring responsible lending practices and client protection.

The organization works closely with various stakeholders, including policymakers, regulators, government agencies, and financial institutions, to advocate for favourable policies and regulations that support financial inclusion and the sustainable development of the microfinance sector.

2. Functions and Activities of Sa-Dhan:

3. Advocacy and Representation: Sa-Dhan represents the collective interests of its member MFIs and community finance institutions to policymakers, regulators, and other stakeholders. It advocates for a conducive regulatory environment that fosters financial inclusion and responsible microfinance practices.

4. Capacity Building: Sa-Dhan conducts training programs, workshops, and seminars to enhance the capacity of microfinance professionals and improve the effectiveness of microfinance operations.

5. Research and Knowledge Sharing: Sa-Dhan undertakes research and data analysis to generate insights into the microfinance sector's performance and impact. It disseminates knowledge through publications and reports to promote evidence-based policymaking.

6. Responsible Finance Initiatives: Sa-Dhan promotes responsible finance practices among its members, emphasizing client protection, social performance management, and transparency in microfinance operations.

7. Social Performance Management: The organization supports its members in adopting social performance management practices, ensuring that they align their activities with social objectives and impact.

8. Code of Conduct and Standards: Sa-Dhan has developed a Code of Conduct for its member MFIs, outlining the principles of responsible lending and ethical behaviours.

As a prominent SRO in the Indian microfinance sector, Sa-Dhan plays a vital role in shaping the industry, facilitating collaboration, and ensuring that the sector's growth is balanced with the welfare of clients and borrowers.

6.30. Inappropriate forms of organizations, legal constraints of microfinance:

In the microfinance sector, inappropriate forms of organizations and legal constraints can hinder the effective delivery of financial services to the target population and impact the sustainability and impact of microfinance initiatives. Here are some key issues related to inappropriate forms of organizations and legal constraints in microfinance:

1. **Unregulated Informal Providers:** In some countries, informal moneylenders or unregulated microfinance providers may exploit vulnerable borrowers by charging exorbitant interest rates and employing coercive loan recovery practices.

2. **Lack of Legal Recognition:** Microfinance institutions (MFIs) operating in certain countries may face challenges in obtaining legal recognition or obtaining appropriate licenses from regulatory authorities, impacting their ability to operate formally and access funding.

3. **Inflexible Regulatory Frameworks:** Overly stringent regulations or inadequate legal frameworks for microfinance can hinder the growth of MFIs and limit their ability to innovate and cater to the diverse needs of clients.

4. **Limited Scope for Innovation:** Legal constraints that restrict the types of financial products and services MFIs can offer may impede their capacity to respond to changing client demands and emerging market opportunities.

5. **Collateral Requirements:** Legal requirements for MFIs to demand collateral for microfinance loans can exclude many low-income individuals from accessing credit, as they often lack traditional assets to pledge as security.

6. **Interest Rate Caps:** While consumer protection is important, rigid interest rate caps imposed by regulations may limit the ability of MFIs to cover operational costs, impacting their financial viability and ability to serve underserved populations.

7. **Ambiguity in Legal Definitions:** Unclear or ambiguous definitions of microfinance activities and institutions can lead to regulatory challenges and hamper the growth of the microfinance sector.

8. **Reporting and Compliance Burden:** Excessive reporting requirements and compliance burdens may impose additional costs on MFIs, especially smaller institutions, diverting resources from serving clients.

6.31. Inappropriate forms of organizations, legal constraints of microfinance:

In the microfinance sector, inappropriate forms of organizations and legal constraints can hinder the effective delivery of financial services to the target population and impact the sustainability and impact of microfinance initiatives. Here are some key issues related to inappropriate forms of organizations and legal constraints in microfinance:

1. **Informal and Unregulated Moneylenders:** In many regions, informal moneylenders operate outside the formal regulatory framework, charging exorbitant interest rates and employing coercive loan recovery practices. Borrowers may fall into a debt trap due to the lack of consumer protection and oversight.

2. **Limited Legal Recognition:** Some microfinance institutions (MFIs) may face challenges in obtaining legal recognition or appropriate licenses from regulatory authorities, hindering their ability to operate formally and access funding from formal financial channels.

3. **Restrictive Legal Frameworks:** Inflexible or overly restrictive regulations can stifle the growth and innovation of MFIs, limiting their ability to meet the diverse financial needs of clients and adapt to changing market conditions.

4. **Interest Rate Caps:** While consumer protection is important, rigid interest rate caps imposed by regulations may limit the ability of MFIs to cover operational costs, leading to reduced lending to the target population.

5. **Reporting and Compliance Burden:** Excessive reporting requirements and compliance burdens may impose additional costs on MFIs, especially smaller institutions, diverting resources from serving clients effectively.

6. **Barriers to Innovation:** Legal constraints that restrict the types of financial products and services MFIs can offer may impede their capacity to respond to changing client demands and emerging market opportunities.

6.31. Lack of commercial orientation in microfinance of India:

The lack of commercial orientation in microfinance in India refers to the limited focus on generating profits or financial sustainability by some microfinance institutions (MFIs). Historically, microfinance emerged as a social and development-oriented initiative to provide financial services to the unbanked and underserved populations, particularly those living in poverty. While the social mission of microfinance remains essential, commercial orientation is also crucial for the long-term viability and scalability of MFIs. Here are some reasons for the lack of commercial orientation in Indian microfinance:

1. Social Mission Dominance: Many microfinance institutions in India are driven primarily by a social mission to uplift the poor and financially excluded. This emphasis on social goals might lead to a lesser focus on financial sustainability and commercial viability.

2. Subsidized Interest Rates: Some MFIs offer microfinance products with subsidized interest rates, making it challenging to cover operational costs and achieve profitability.

3. Dependency on External Funding: MFIs in India often rely on grants, subsidies, or concessional loans from governments, donors, or development agencies. While these funding sources can support social objectives, they may not promote self-sufficiency.

4. Limited Access to Formal Funding: Access to affordable and long-term funding from formal financial institutions can be a challenge for many MFIs, especially smaller ones, limiting their capacity to grow and diversify their operations.

5. Regulatory Constraints: Some regulatory frameworks may impose interest rate caps or other restrictions that can hinder MFIs' ability to charge market-based rates and achieve financial sustainability.

6. Mission Drift: In some cases, MFIs may face the risk of mission drift, where commercial pressures may lead them to focus more on profit-making activities than serving their original target client base.

6.33. To address the lack of commercial orientation while maintaining the social mission of microfinance, a balanced approach is required:

1. Financial Inclusion and Profitability: MFIs should balance their social objectives with the need for financial viability. This can be achieved by offering a mix of financial and non-financial services while ensuring responsible lending practices.

2. Access to Formal Funding: Improving access to formal funding sources like banks, capital markets, and impact investors can help MFIs diversify their funding base and achieve financial sustainability.

3. Market-Based Interest Rates: Allowing market-based interest rates based on the risk profile of clients can enable MFIs to cover costs and generate sufficient returns to support their operations.

4. Robust Governance and Risk Management: Implementing strong governance practices and risk management systems can ensure financial stability and transparency.

5. Impact Measurement: Tracking and reporting social impact alongside financial performance can demonstrate the dual mission of MFIs and attract socially responsible investors.

By embracing a commercial orientation while staying true to their social mission, microfinance institutions in India can achieve financial self-sufficiency, expand outreach, and make a more significant contribution to poverty alleviation and inclusive economic growth.

6.34. The microfinance, isolated and scattered:

Microfinance in some regions or areas can indeed be isolated and scattered, especially in remote or underserved locations. This isolation and scattered nature of microfinance can create challenges and limitations for both microfinance institutions (MFIs) and the target population they aim to serve. Here are some key characteristics and implications of isolated and scattered microfinance:

1. **Limited Access to Financial Services:** The isolation of microfinance services means that many individuals in remote or rural areas may have limited or no access to formal financial services. This lack of access can hinder economic opportunities and financial inclusion.

2. **High Transaction Costs:** Providing financial services in isolated and scattered areas can be costlier due to the need for physical outreach, travel, and communication. High transaction costs may discourage MFIs from expanding their operations in such regions.

3. **Challenges in Monitoring and Supervision:** For MFIs, monitoring and supervising scattered operations can be logistically challenging, leading to potential difficulties in ensuring adherence to responsible lending practices and client protection measures.

4. **Limited Economies of Scale:** Isolated and scattered microfinance operations may struggle to achieve economies of scale, making it harder for MFIs to sustainably cover operational costs.

5. **Inadequate Infrastructure:** Poor infrastructure in isolated areas, such as limited road connectivity and unreliable communication networks, can further hinder the delivery of financial services.

6. **Risk Management Challenges:** The geographical dispersion of clients may expose MFIs to a diverse set of risks, including credit risk, operational risk, and security concerns.

6.35. Addressing the challenges of isolated and scattered microfinance requires innovative solutions and collaborative efforts:

1. **Technology Adoption:** Leveraging digital technology and mobile banking can help bridge the gap and provide financial services to clients in remote areas.

2. **Branchless Banking:** Implementing branchless banking or agent banking models can bring financial services closer to the clients and reduce transaction costs.

3. **Partnerships and Networking:** Collaborating with local community organizations, NGOs, and government agencies can help reach underserved populations effectively.

4. **Capacity Building:** Building the capacity of local staff and agents to provide financial services can improve outreach and ensure responsible financial practices.

5. **Policy Support:** Policymakers can support the expansion of microfinance in isolated areas through targeted policies, regulatory flexibility, and financial incentives.

By proactively addressing the challenges of isolation and scattering, microfinance institutions can expand their reach, enhance financial inclusion, and contribute to the socio-economic development of underserved communities.

6.36. Lack of poor governance and accountability in Indian microfinance:

The lack of poor governance and accountability in Indian microfinance has been a concern in the sector and has garnered attention in recent years. Poor governance and accountability practices can lead to various issues that impact the clients, the institutions themselves, and the overall credibility of the microfinance industry. Here are some of the key implications of poor governance and accountability in Indian microfinance:

1. **Client Exploitation:** Weak governance can lead to client exploitation, such as aggressive lending practices, over-indebtedness, and coercive loan recovery methods, harming the financial well-being of borrowers.

2. **Mission Drift:** Poor governance may result in mission drift, where microfinance institutions (MFIs) prioritize profit-making over social impact, deviating from their original goal of serving the underserved.

3. **Misallocation of Resources:** Inadequate accountability may lead to the misallocation of resources, where funds meant for client services are diverted for other purposes, impacting the quality of financial services provided.

4. **Lack of Transparency:** Weak accountability can lead to a lack of transparency in financial reporting and decision-making processes, raising concerns among investors and stakeholders.

5. **Regulatory and Legal Compliance Issues:** Poor governance can lead to non-compliance with regulatory requirements, exposing MFIs to legal and reputational risks.

6. **Erosion of Trust:** Clients and investors may lose trust in the microfinance sector if governance and accountability issues persist, affecting the sector's overall credibility.

6.37. Addressing the lack of poor governance and accountability in Indian microfinance requires concerted efforts from multiple stakeholders:

1. **Strengthening Corporate Governance:** MFIs should establish robust governance structures, independent boards, and transparent decision-making processes to ensure accountability.

2. Social Performance Management: Emphasizing social performance management can help MFIs stay focused on their mission and measure their social impact, aligning financial goals with social objectives.

3. Client Protection Measures: Implementing client protection principles and ethical practices can safeguard borrowers from exploitation and ensure fair treatment.

4. Transparent Reporting: MFIs should maintain transparent financial reporting to demonstrate their financial health and accountability to investors, clients, and regulators.

5. Regulatory Oversight: Regulatory bodies should enforce compliance with governance and accountability standards and take appropriate actions against institutions that fail to adhere to them.

6. Investor Due Diligence: Investors in the microfinance sector should conduct thorough due diligence on MFIs to assess their governance practices before making investments.

6.38. RBI's "know your customer" (KYC):

The "Know Your Customer" (KYC) guidelines issued by the Reserve Bank of India (RBI) are aimed at preventing financial institutions from being used for illegal activities like money laundering and fraud. These guidelines require banks and other financial entities to establish the identity of their customers, understand their financial dealings, and assess the potential risk involved.

Under the KYC norms:

1. Customer Identification Process: Banks must verify the identity and address of customers before establishing a business relationship. This typically involves collecting documents such as identification proofs, photographs, and address proofs.

2. Customer Due Diligence: Financial institutions need to understand the nature of the customer's activities, source of funds, and expected transactions. Enhanced due diligence is applied for high-risk customers.

3. Risk Categorization: Customers are categorized into low, medium, and high-risk categories based on factors like their occupation, income, and transaction patterns.

4. Ongoing Monitoring: Banks need to regularly monitor their customers' transactions to identify any unusual or suspicious activities that might indicate money laundering or other illicit activities.

5. Reporting Suspicious Transactions: If a bank suspects a transaction to be suspicious or related to illegal activities, they are required to report it to the appropriate authorities.

6. Record Keeping: Banks are mandated to maintain records of customer identification data and transaction details for a specified period.

The KYC guidelines are crucial not only for preventing financial crimes but also for maintaining the integrity of the financial system and ensuring customer protection. These guidelines are regularly updated by the RBI to align with evolving international standards and to address emerging risks in the financial sector. Along with RBI SEBI, IRDA, TRAI and other entity's who have the relation with Individuals are also Follow the KYC guidelines.

For formal regulation of microfinance institutions in India, the Reserve Bank of India (RBI) is the regulatory authority responsible for overseeing NBFC-MFIs and other financial institutions providing microfinance services. The RBI sets regulations, guidelines, and prudential norms for the microfinance sector to ensure compliance, consumer protection, and financial stability. It plays a critical role in maintaining the integrity and sustainability of the microfinance industry in India.

Chapter - 7

Financial Inclusion in Microfinance

The primary objective of financial inclusion is to ensure that all individuals and businesses have access to affordable and appropriate financial products and services. This includes services like banking, savings, credit, insurance, and investments. Financial inclusion aims to promote economic growth, reduce poverty, and enhance social stability by providing equal opportunities for people to participate in the financial system, regardless of their income level or location.

The objective of financial inclusion in microfinance is to provide access to essential financial services, such as credit, savings, insurance, and payment options, to individuals and businesses who are traditionally underserved or excluded from the formal banking sector. This helps empower them economically and improves their overall financial well-being.

Microfinance's approach aims to empower underserved individuals and businesses by granting them access to vital financial services, ultimately leading to improved financial stability and overall well-being.

7.1. Introduction of Financial Inclusion:

Financial inclusion refers to the process of ensuring that all individuals and businesses, regardless of their income level or location, have access to a wide range of affordable and appropriate financial services. These services include basic banking, savings accounts, credit facilities, insurance coverage, and investment opportunities. The goal of financial inclusion is to promote economic development, reduce poverty, and enhance social equity by providing everyone with the tools and resources they need to effectively manage their finances, plan for the future, and participate in economic activities. This concept acknowledges that access to financial services is a fundamental right that can significantly impact individuals' quality of life and contribute to overall societal progress.

7.2. Financial inclusion from the angle of individuals:

From the perspective of individuals, financial inclusion means having access to a variety of financial services that are designed to meet their diverse needs and circumstances. This includes having access to basic banking services such as savings and recuring accounts, as well as being able to borrow money through affordable loans or credit options. Additionally, financial inclusion entails having access to insurance products that provide protection against unforeseen events, as well as access to investment opportunities that allow individuals to grow their wealth over time.

For individuals, financial inclusion goes beyond just having access to these services. It also means having the knowledge and capability to effectively use these services to manage their finances, plan for the future, and improve their overall economic well-being. It empowers individuals to make informed financial decisions, build a safety net for themselves and their families, and participate more actively in economic activities.

In essence, financial inclusion on the individual level aims to provide the tools and opportunities necessary for people to achieve financial stability, improve their living standards, and work towards their long-term goals.

7.3. Financial inclusion from the angle of families:

Viewed from the perspective of families, financial inclusion encompasses a broader scope of access to financial services that benefit not just individual members, but the entire household unit. Financial inclusion for families means having access to services that cater to their collective needs and aspirations.

This includes access to banking services that allow families to manage their finances efficiently, save for future expenses, and access credit when needed. Insurance products provide families with a safety net against unexpected events, protecting their financial well-being. Investment opportunities enable families to grow their wealth over time, supporting long-term goals such as education, homeownership, and retirement planning.

Moreover, financial inclusion for families also involves financial literacy and education, ensuring that all family members are equipped with the knowledge and skills to make informed financial decisions. This contributes to overall financial stability, better planning for the future, and the ability to manage financial challenges as a cohesive unit.

Financial inclusion for families means enabling households to access a range of financial services that support their collective financial health, while also empowering them with the education to make sound financial choices together.

7.4. Financial inclusion from the angle of small and medium business house (SMBs):

From the perspective of small and medium-sized businesses (SMBs), financial inclusion entails access to a comprehensive suite of financial services that cater to their unique needs and challenges. These services contribute to the growth and sustainability of SMBs, which are often engines of economic development and employment generation.

Financial inclusion for SMBs involves access to credit and financing options that are tailored to their size and operational requirements. This allows them to invest in expansion, purchase inventory, and fund day-to-day operations. Additionally, access to payment solutions, including digital payment platforms, enables smoother transactions and enhances business efficiency.

SMBs also benefit from insurance products that safeguard against business-related risks and unexpected events. Having access to savings and investment opportunities helps SMBs accumulate capital for future growth and navigate economic fluctuations.

Furthermore, financial education and advisory services are crucial components of financial inclusion for SMBs. These resources empower business owners with the knowledge to make informed financial decisions, manage cash flows effectively, and strategize for long-term success.

In essence, financial inclusion for small and medium-sized businesses aims to provide them with the financial tools, services, and knowledge needed to thrive, expand, and contribute to local economies.

7.5. Financial inclusion from the angle of society:

Viewed from the perspective of society as a whole, financial inclusion has far-reaching implications that extend beyond individual and business benefits. Financial inclusion contributes to a more equitable and prosperous society by addressing systemic inequalities and fostering economic growth at all levels.

1. Poverty Reduction: Financial inclusion helps lift individuals and families out of poverty by providing them with opportunities to save, invest, and access credit. This enables them to start small businesses, improve their living conditions, and plan for the future.

2. Economic Growth: When more individuals and businesses have access to financial services, economic activity increases. SMBs can expand, create jobs, and stimulate local economies, leading to broader economic growth and development.

3. Reduced Inequality: Financial inclusion helps bridge the gap between different income groups, reducing income inequality. It empowers marginalized and underserved populations to participate in economic activities, thereby reducing disparities in wealth and access to resources.

4. Social Stability: Access to financial services can contribute to social stability by providing individuals and families with tools to manage financial shocks and uncertainties. This can lead to reduced vulnerability and increased resilience against economic downturns.

5. Women's Empowerment: Financial inclusion often has a positive impact on gender equality. When women have access to financial services, they can improve their economic status, make independent financial decisions, and contribute more actively to their families and communities.

6. Education and Healthcare: Financial inclusion can facilitate access to education and healthcare services. Families can save for educational expenses, and individuals can access affordable insurance coverage, ultimately improving human capital and well-being.

7. Digital Inclusion: As financial services become more digital, financial inclusion also contributes to digital inclusion. Access to digital financial tools can lead to improved digital literacy and access to other online services.

8. Entrepreneurship and Innovation: Financially inclusive societies foster entrepreneurship and innovation. Individuals have the means to turn their ideas into viable businesses, driving economic dynamism and fostering innovation.

In summary, financial inclusion benefits society by promoting economic development, reducing inequality, enhancing social stability, empowering marginalized groups, and fostering a more inclusive and prosperous community.

7.6. Financial inclusion from National perspective:

From a national perspective, financial inclusion is a strategic imperative that has significant implications for a country's overall economic growth, stability, and social development. Governments and policymakers recognize the importance of ensuring that all segments of the population have access to financial services, and they implement initiatives to promote financial inclusion for various reasons:

1. **Economic Growth**: Financially included individuals and businesses contribute to increased economic activity. As more people have access to credit, savings, and investment opportunities, they can engage in entrepreneurial activities, which in turn stimulate economic growth and job creation.

2. **Reduced Poverty:** Financial inclusion plays a crucial role in poverty reduction. When individuals can access financial services, they have better tools to save money, invest in education and healthcare, and build assets that improve their quality of life.

3. **Financial Stability:** A more inclusive financial system enhances overall stability. When a wider range of individuals and businesses participate in the formal financial sector, economic shocks are better absorbed, and there is reduced reliance on informal and potentially unstable financial arrangements.

4. **Social Equity:** Promoting financial inclusion aligns with principles of social equity and fairness. It ensures that historically marginalized or underserved populations gain access to the same financial opportunities as others, reducing disparities and promoting a more inclusive society.

5. **Enhanced Government Services:** Financial inclusion can facilitate efficient and transparent delivery of government services. Digital payment systems, for instance, streamline distribution of subsidies, pensions, and other social benefits, reducing leakage and improving service delivery.

6. **Financial Literacy and Education:** National financial inclusion efforts often include financial education programs. Educating citizens about financial matters enhances their understanding of financial products, helps them make informed decisions, and safeguards them against potential financial pitfalls.

7. **Digital Transformation:** Financial inclusion often involves leveraging technology to reach underserved populations. This contributes to the broader digital transformation of a country, promoting technology adoption, digital literacy, and access to digital services beyond finance.

8. Entrepreneurial Ecosystem: A financially inclusive environment fosters entrepreneurship. By providing access to credit and financial services, aspiring entrepreneurs have the means to start and grow businesses, contributing to innovation and economic diversification.

From a national perspective, financial inclusion is a critical element for promoting economic development, reducing inequality, ensuring financial stability, and building a more inclusive and resilient society. It's a holistic approach that benefits both individuals and the nation as a whole.

7.7. Financial inclusion, as per World Bank:

The World Bank defines financial inclusion as "individuals and businesses having access to useful and affordable financial products and services that meet their needs—transactions, payments, savings, credit, and insurance—delivered in a responsible and sustainable way." This definition emphasizes the importance of providing a wide range of financial services that are accessible, affordable, and tailored to the needs of all individuals and businesses, especially those who are traditionally underserved or excluded from the formal financial sector. The goal of financial inclusion, as per the World Bank, is to empower people economically and improve their overall well-being while fostering sustainable and responsible financial practices.

7.8. Financial inclusion, as per C. Rangrajan committee:

The C. Rangarajan Committee, officially known as the "Committee on Financial Inclusion" in India, defines financial inclusion as "the process of ensuring access to financial services and timely and adequate credit where needed by vulnerable groups such as weaker sections and low-income groups at an affordable cost." The committee's definition underscores the importance of extending financial services, including credit, to marginalized and economically disadvantaged sections of society in a cost-effective manner. This definition aligns with the broader goal of promoting inclusive economic growth and reducing inequalities by enabling access to financial resources for those who are traditionally excluded from the formal financial system.

7.9. Financial inclusion, as per United Nations:

The United Nations does not have an official definition of financial inclusion, but it recognizes the importance of financial inclusion in promoting sustainable development and reducing poverty. Financial inclusion, according to the United Nations, refers to the availability and equality of opportunities to access and use a variety of financial services responsibly and sustainably, regardless of an individual's or a community's income level.

The United Nations emphasizes that financial inclusion encompasses a range of services, including savings, credit, insurance, payments, and remittance facilities, and it aims to ensure that these services are accessible, affordable, and relevant to all segments of society. The goal of financial inclusion, within the framework of the United Nations' Sustainable Development Goals (SDGs), is to contribute to poverty reduction, economic growth, and improved overall well-being, particularly for vulnerable and marginalized populations.

7.10. Financial inclusion, as per Asian development Bank:

The Asian Development Bank (ADB) defines financial inclusion as "making available a full suite of quality financial services at affordable costs to all segments of the population, including the low-income, underserved, and unbanked, who currently lack access to formal financial services." The ADB's definition highlights the need to provide a comprehensive range of financial services that are accessible, affordable, and relevant to individuals and businesses across different income levels, especially those who have been historically excluded from the formal financial sector.

The ADB emphasizes that financial inclusion involves not only access to basic financial services such as savings and credit but also extends to insurance, payments, and other essential financial products. The goal is to create an inclusive financial ecosystem that contributes to poverty reduction, economic growth, and improved livelihoods for all members of society, particularly those who are financially underserved or marginalized.

7.11. Scope of Financial Inclusion:

The scope of financial inclusion is broad and multifaceted, encompassing various dimensions and stakeholders. Here are some key aspects that define the scope of financial inclusion:

1. **Access to Services:** Financial inclusion involves providing access to a wide range of financial services, including savings accounts, credit facilities, insurance products, payment systems, and investment opportunities.

2. **Population Segments:** The scope covers individuals and groups traditionally underserved by the formal financial sector, such as low-income households, rural communities, women, youth, migrants, and other vulnerable or marginalized populations.

3. **Geographical Reach:** Financial inclusion aims to extend services to both urban and rural areas, ensuring that remote and underserved regions have equal access to financial products and services.

4. **Diverse Financial Needs:** The scope includes addressing the diverse financial needs of people, ranging from basic transactional services to more complex services like credit for business expansion, insurance coverage, and retirement planning.

5. **Affordability:** Financial inclusion emphasizes affordability, ensuring that financial services are provided at reasonable costs to prevent exclusion due to high fees or charges.

6. **Technology and Innovation:** With the digital transformation of financial services, the scope of financial inclusion includes leveraging technology to offer digital financial products and expand access through mobile banking and digital payment platforms.

7. Financial Literacy and Education: A comprehensive approach to financial inclusion includes initiatives to enhance financial literacy and education, enabling individuals to make informed decisions and use financial services effectively.

8. Regulatory Environment: Financial inclusion requires a conducive regulatory environment that promotes innovation while ensuring consumer protection and stability within the financial system.

9. Public and Private Sector Collaboration: Collaboration among governments, financial institutions, non-governmental organizations (NGOs), fintech firms, and other stakeholders is essential to achieve comprehensive financial inclusion.

10. Global Perspective: Financial inclusion is a global concern, as evidenced by international efforts and organizations working to address issues related to access to financial services on a global scale.

11. Impact on Development: The scope of financial inclusion extends to its role in promoting economic development, poverty reduction, gender equality, entrepreneurship, and social stability.

The scope of financial inclusion encompasses a wide range of services, segments of the population, technological advancements, educational efforts, and collaborative initiatives that collectively work toward providing equal and affordable access to financial resources for all individuals and businesses.

7.12. Components of Financial Inclusion:

Financial inclusion is composed of several interrelated components that work together to ensure access to a comprehensive range of financial services for all individuals and businesses. Here are the key components:

1. Access to Banking Services: This involves providing individuals and businesses with the ability to open and maintain basic banking accounts, facilitating transactions, savings, and payment services.

2. Credit and Loans: Ensuring access to credit facilities that cater to various needs, including personal loans, business loans, and microcredit, allowing individuals and businesses to invest, expand, and manage cash flows.

3. Savings and Investments: Offering accessible savings accounts and investment options that allow individuals to save for future expenses, emergencies, and long-term goals, as well as to grow their wealth.

4. Insurance Services: Providing access to insurance products, such as life, health, and property insurance, which protect individuals and businesses from unexpected financial shocks.

5. Payment Systems: Enabling secure and efficient payment mechanisms, including digital payment platforms, mobile money, and electronic fund transfers, to facilitate transactions and reduce reliance on cash.

6. Financial Literacy and Education: Promoting financial literacy through educational programs and resources to empower individuals with the knowledge and skills needed to make informed financial decisions.

7. Regulatory Framework: Establishing regulatory policies that promote financial inclusion while ensuring consumer protection, fair practices, and stability within the financial sector.

8. Technology and Innovation: Leveraging technological advancements, including mobile banking, fintech solutions, and digital wallets, to extend the reach of financial services to remote and underserved areas.

9. Infrastructure Development: Building the necessary physical and digital infrastructure, such as banking outlets, ATMs, and reliable internet connectivity, to expand access to financial services.

10. Government and Policy Support: Creating an enabling environment through policies, initiatives, and collaborations that support financial inclusion goals and address barriers to access.

11. Data and Analytics: Utilizing data-driven insights to identify trends, gaps, and opportunities for improving the delivery of financial services and tailoring them to specific needs.

12. Social and Cultural Awareness: Recognizing cultural and social factors that may influence financial behavior and preferences, and designing services that are culturally sensitive and relevant.

13. Partnerships and Collaboration: Fostering partnerships among governments, financial institutions, fintech companies, NGOs, and international organizations to pool resources and expertise.

The components of financial inclusion encompass a comprehensive range of financial services, policies, technological advancements, educational efforts, and collaborative initiatives that collectively work towards ensuring that everyone has access to and benefits from the formal financial system.

7.13. Extent of Financial Inclusion:

The extent of financial inclusion varies widely across countries and regions and is influenced by a range of factors, including economic development, regulatory environment, technological infrastructure, cultural norms, and policy initiatives. Here's an overview of the extent of financial inclusion:

1. Global Disparities: Financial inclusion levels vary significantly between developed and developing countries. In many developed countries, a higher percentage of the population has access to formal financial services. However, in lower-income and developing regions, significant portions of the population remain financially excluded.

2. Urban-Rural Divide: In many countries, there is an urban-rural divide in financial inclusion. Urban areas tend to have better access to financial services, while rural areas often face challenges due to limited infrastructure and geographical barriers.

3. Income Inequality: Financial inclusion can also be influenced by income inequality. Low-income individuals and families may face more barriers to accessing formal financial services compared to wealthier segments of the population.

4. **Gender Disparities:** Women often face greater challenges in accessing financial services due to social norms, cultural factors, and legal restrictions. Gender disparities can hinder financial inclusion efforts.

5. **Technological Advancements:** The extent of financial inclusion is increasingly affected by technology. Digital financial services, mobile banking, and fintech innovations have the potential to rapidly expand access to financial services, especially in regions with limited physical infrastructure.

6. **Regulatory Environment:** The regulatory environment plays a critical role in determining the extent of financial inclusion. Supportive regulations can encourage financial institutions to reach underserved populations, while restrictive regulations may hinder expansion.

7. **Policy Initiatives:** Governments, central banks, and international organizations often implement policies and initiatives to promote financial inclusion. These can include setting up microfinance institutions, creating financial literacy programs, and launching digital payment systems.

8. **Cultural and Social Factors:** Cultural norms and social factors can influence people's attitudes toward formal financial services. Building trust and designing services that align with cultural practices can impact the extent of financial inclusion.

9. **Mobile and Digital Connectivity:** The prevalence of mobile phones and internet connectivity can significantly impact the reach of financial services, particularly in regions where traditional brick-and-mortar banking infrastructure is limited.

10. **Partnerships and Collaboration:** Collaborations between governments, financial institutions, NGOs, and fintech companies can accelerate financial inclusion efforts by combining resources, expertise, and innovative solutions.

11. Economic Growth: Higher economic growth often correlates with improved financial inclusion. As economies develop, financial infrastructure tends to expand, leading to increased access to services.

12. Data Availability: Reliable data on financial inclusion metrics, such as account ownership, credit usage, and insurance coverage, help gauge the extent of progress and areas that need improvement.

The extent of financial inclusion is a complex and multifaceted issue influenced by a combination of economic, regulatory, technological, cultural, and policy factors. Efforts to improve financial inclusion aim to bridge gaps and ensure that all individuals and businesses have access to the benefits of formal financial services.

7.14. Extent of Financial Inclusion in Indian context:

Financial inclusion efforts in India have made significant progress but continue to face challenges. Here's an overview of the extent of financial inclusion in the Indian context:

1. Jan Dhan Yojana: The Pradhan Mantri Jan Dhan Yojana (PMJDY) launched in 2014 aimed to provide every household with access to a bank account. The program has achieved substantial success in bringing previously unbanked individuals into the formal financial system.

2. Bank Account Penetration: The PMJDY led to a substantial increase in the number of bank accounts in India. However, while account penetration has improved, challenges remain in ensuring that these accounts are actively used for financial transactions and services beyond account opening.

3. Direct Benefit Transfers: The government's push for Direct Benefit Transfers (DBT) has leveraged the Jan Dhan accounts to directly transfer subsidies and benefits to beneficiaries. This has reduced leakages and improved targeting.

4. Digital Payments: Initiatives like Unified Payments Interface (UPI) and India Bill Payment System (BBPS) have accelerated the adoption of digital payments. Mobile wallets, digital payment apps, and other fintech solutions have increased access to financial services, especially in urban areas.

5. Microfinance Institutions (MFIs): Microfinance institutions have played a significant role in extending credit to underserved populations, particularly in rural areas. However, the high interest rates charged by some MFIs and instances of over-indebtedness have raised concerns.

6. Regional Disparities: While financial inclusion has improved, regional disparities persist. Rural areas and certain states continue to lag behind urban centers in terms of access to formal financial services.

7. Financial Literacy: Enhancing financial literacy remains crucial for effective financial inclusion. Many individuals, especially in rural and low-income areas, lack awareness of financial products and services.

8. Gender Gap: Despite efforts, a gender gap in financial inclusion persists, with fewer women having access to formal financial services. Gender-specific initiatives are necessary to address this gap.

9. Formal Credit: While credit availability has improved, challenges exist in terms of providing affordable and timely credit to small and medium-sized enterprises (SMEs) and rural entrepreneurs.

10. Regulatory Support: Regulatory initiatives, like differentiated banking licenses for small finance banks and payments banks, have contributed to expanding financial services to underserved areas.

11. Challenges: Challenges such as inadequate banking infrastructure in remote areas, lack of proper documentation, and a reliance on informal financial services continue to hinder full financial inclusion.

12. Technology Adoption: Increasing mobile and internet penetration has provided opportunities for digital financial services, but there are concerns about ensuring cybersecurity and privacy.

India has made significant strides in improving financial inclusion through policy initiatives, technological advancements, and awareness campaigns. While progress has been notable, ensuring active usage of financial services, addressing regional disparities, enhancing financial literacy, and narrowing the gender gap remain ongoing challenges. For the most current and detailed information, I recommend referring to the latest reports and updates from relevant Indian government departments and financial institutions.

7.15. Need for Financial Inclusion:

Financial inclusion is crucial because it ensures that all individuals and businesses have access to a wide range of financial services, including banking, credit, insurance, and investments. This helps to empower marginalized and underserved populations, reduce poverty, promote economic growth, and enhance overall financial stability within a society.

7.16. Detailed explanation of the need for financial inclusion:

1. **Reducing Poverty and Inequality:** Financial inclusion provides marginalized and low-income individuals with access to formal financial services. This enables them to save, borrow, and invest, leading to increased income, asset accumulation, and improved economic prospects. This, in turn, helps in reducing poverty and bridging income inequality gaps.

2. **Economic Growth and Development:** Access to financial services encourages entrepreneurship and business development. Small and medium-sized enterprises (SMEs) often struggle due to lack of access to credit and other financial resources. When they are included, they can contribute significantly to economic growth and job creation.

3. **Strengthening Financial Stability:** When a larger portion of the population is included in the formal financial system, it reduces their reliance on informal and often riskier financial channels. This can lead to greater financial stability by reducing vulnerabilities associated with unregulated financial activities.

4. **Promoting Savings and Investment:** Access to savings accounts and investment options encourages people to save and plan for their future. Financial inclusion allows individuals to protect themselves from unexpected financial shocks and invest in their long-term goals.

5. **Enabling Digital Transactions:** In today's digital age, financial inclusion also means digital financial inclusion. Access to digital payment systems and mobile banking services empowers individuals to participate in the modern economy and facilitates transactions even in remote areas.

6. **Empowering Women:** Financial inclusion can have a particularly positive impact on gender equality. Women often face more significant barriers to accessing financial services, and when they are included, they can gain greater control over their finances, access credit for business ventures, and improve their overall economic status.

7. **Access to Insurance and Risk Management:** Financially inclusive systems also provide access to insurance services, which help individuals and communities manage risks associated with health, agriculture, disasters, and other unforeseen events.

8. **Government Social Welfare Programs:** Governments can deliver social welfare benefits more efficiently and transparently by using digital payment systems. This reduces leakages and ensures that benefits reach those who need them most.

9. **Enhancing Financial Literacy:** As financial services become more accessible, there's an opportunity to improve financial literacy and educate individuals about making informed financial decisions, managing debt, and planning for retirement.

10. **Unlocking Human Potential:** When people have access to financial resources, they can invest in education, health, and skills development. This can contribute to the overall human development of a society.

Financial inclusion is not only a matter of social justice but also a driver of economic growth and stability. It allows individuals and communities to participate fully in the economy, improving their quality of life and fostering broader societal progress.

7.17. Need for Financial Inclusion in Indian context:

In the Indian context, financial inclusion is particularly crucial due to the diverse socio-economic landscape and the following reasons:

1. Vast Unbanked Population: India has a large population, a significant portion of which lacks access to formal banking services. Millions of people, especially in rural and remote areas, still do not have a bank account. Financial inclusion ensures that these individuals can access basic financial services, such as savings accounts and credit facilities.

2. Poverty Alleviation: India has a significant population living below the poverty line. Financial inclusion provides them with opportunities to save, invest, and access credit, enabling them to escape the cycle of poverty and improve their living conditions.

3. Rural Development: A significant percentage of India's population resides in rural areas. Access to financial services can boost rural development by facilitating agricultural loans, helping farmers invest in better farming practices, and supporting rural entrepreneurship.

4. Women's Empowerment: Gender disparity in financial access exists in India. Financial inclusion can empower women by giving them control over their finances, enabling them to start businesses, invest, and make independent financial decisions.

5. Digital Transformation: India's push towards a digital economy can be accelerated through financial inclusion. Mobile banking and digital payment platforms allow even those without physical bank branches in their vicinity to access financial services.

6. Government Benefit Distribution: Financial inclusion can streamline the distribution of government subsidies and welfare payments.

Direct benefit transfers to bank accounts reduce leakages and ensure that benefits reach intended beneficiaries.

7. **Micro, Small, and Medium Enterprises (MSMEs):** MSMEs are vital contributors to India's economy. Financial inclusion provides them with access to credit, enabling growth, innovation, and job creation.

8. **Financial Literacy:** As financial inclusion expands, it's an opportunity to promote financial literacy and educate people about responsible borrowing, saving, and investment practices.

9. **Reducing Informal Economy:** A significant portion of India's economy operates in the informal sector. Financial inclusion can help transition businesses and workers from informal to formal channels, improving economic stability and contributing to tax revenue.

10. **Economic Growth:** By including more people in the formal financial system, India can unlock their economic potential, leading to higher savings, investments, and overall economic growth.

In India, financial inclusion has been a priority, as evidenced by initiatives like the Jan Dhan Yojana (financial inclusion program) and digital payment platforms like UPI (Unified Payments Interface). These efforts are not only aimed at bringing more people into the financial fold but also at leveraging financial inclusion as a means to achieve broader economic and social goals.

7.18. Approaches to financial inclusion according to Dr. C. Rangrajan:

Dr. C. Rangarajan, an Indian economist and former Governor of the Reserve Bank of India, has emphasized various approaches to achieving financial inclusion in India. Some of these approaches include:

1. **Branch Expansion:** Dr. Rangarajan has stressed the importance of expanding the network of bank branches, especially in rural and remote areas. This would bring banking services closer to the unbanked and

underserved populations, making it easier for them to access financial services.

2. Use of Technology: Embracing technology is a key aspect of financial inclusion. Dr. Rangarajan has highlighted the role of mobile banking, internet banking, and other digital payment methods in reaching individuals who lack physical access to banks.

3. Financial Literacy: Dr. Rangarajan has emphasized the need for financial education and awareness programs. Educating people about banking services, savings, investments, and responsible borrowing empowers them to make informed financial decisions.

4. Microfinance Institutions: Recognizing the importance of microfinance institutions (MFIs) in reaching the unbanked, Dr. Rangarajan has emphasized their role in providing small loans and financial services to low-income individuals and small entrepreneurs.

5. Priority Sector Lending: He has highlighted the significance of priority sector lending by banks. Encouraging banks to allocate a certain percentage of their lending to sectors like agriculture, micro, small, and medium enterprises (MSMEs), and housing for the economically weaker sections helps promote financial inclusion.

6. Financial Inclusion Plans: Dr. Rangarajan has advocated for the formulation of comprehensive financial inclusion plans that involve various stakeholders, including banks, government agencies, and regulators. These plans should outline strategies for extending financial services to marginalized populations.

7. Credit Delivery Mechanisms: Ensuring that credit delivery mechanisms are efficient, transparent, and accessible is another aspect Dr. Rangarajan has highlighted. Simplified loan application procedures and faster disbursal of credit can improve access for those in need.

8. Inclusive Banking Services: He has stressed the need for banking products and services that cater to the specific needs of low-income and marginalized individuals. This includes products like no-frills accounts, small-ticket loans, and micro-insurance.

9. Collaboration: Dr. Rangarajan has emphasized collaboration between banks, microfinance institutions, self-help groups, and non-governmental organizations (NGOs) to collectively work towards the goal of financial inclusion.

10. Government Support: Lastly, he has underscored the role of government policies and support in promoting financial inclusion. Initiatives like the Jan Dhan Yojana, which aims to provide every household with a bank account, are examples of government efforts to enhance financial inclusion.

Dr. C. Rangarajan's approaches to financial inclusion emphasize a holistic and multi-faceted approach that combines technological advancements, policy measures, educational initiatives, and collaboration among various stakeholders to ensure that all segments of society have access to formal financial services.

7.19. Initiatives of Reserve Bank of India:

The Reserve Bank of India (RBI) has undertaken various initiatives to ensure the stability and development of the Indian financial system. Some key initiatives include:

1. Monetary Policy Framework: RBI implements monetary policies to control inflation and maintain price stability through tools like repo rates and reverse repo rates.

2. Digital Payment Initiatives: RBI has promoted digital payments through initiatives like UPI, BHIM, and the National Electronic Funds Transfer (NEFT) system, making transactions more efficient and accessible.

3. Financial Inclusion Efforts: RBI has launched schemes like Jan Dhan Yojana and Pradhan Mantri Mudra Yojana to provide banking and credit facilities to underserved sections of society.

4. Payment and Settlement Systems: RBI oversees payment and settlement systems to ensure smooth and secure financial transactions, reducing risks in the financial system.

5. Regulation and Supervision: RBI regulates banks and financial institutions, ensuring compliance with prudential norms and safeguarding financial stability.

6. Asset Quality Review (AQR): RBI initiated AQR to assess the true state of banks' non-performing assets (NPAs) and ensure transparency in reporting.

7. Prompt Corrective Action (PCA): RBI introduced PCA framework to monitor and take corrective measures for weak banks, ensuring their financial health and stability.

8. Financial Literacy and Awareness: RBI conducts campaigns to improve financial literacy and educate consumers about responsible financial behavior.

9. Banking Ombudsman Scheme: RBI offers a platform for consumers to resolve complaints against banks in a fair and efficient manner.

10. Currency Management: RBI manages currency issuance and distribution, maintaining the integrity of the Indian rupee.

11. Developmental Role: RBI supports the development of financial markets, regulatory frameworks, and infrastructure to foster economic growth.

12. External Commercial Borrowings (ECB) Policy: RBI regulates and monitors the borrowing of funds from foreign sources by Indian entities.

These initiatives collectively contribute to maintaining financial stability, promoting economic growth, and enhancing the efficiency of the Indian financial system.

7.20. In financial inclusion reserve bank of India's Initiatives:

The Reserve Bank of India (RBI) has taken several initiatives to promote financial inclusion in the country. Some of these include:

1. **Jan Dhan Yojana:** This is a government scheme aimed at providing every household access to a basic bank account, along with insurance and pension facilities.

2. **Pradhan Mantri Mudra Yojana:** This initiative offers financial support to micro and small businesses through loans from various banks and financial institutions.

3. **Payment Banks and Small Finance Banks:** RBI introduced these specialized banks to provide basic banking services to underserved and remote areas, increasing access to financial services.

4. **BHIM UPI:** The India Interface for Money (BHIM) Unified Payments Interface (UPI) is a digital payment system that allows easy and instant money transfers between bank accounts using smartphones.

5. **Financial Literacy Campaigns:** RBI conducts campaigns to enhance financial awareness and educate people about various banking and financial products.

6. **Customer Protection Measures:** RBI has implemented guidelines to protect the interests of customers, particularly in the digital and electronic banking space.

7. **Simplified KYC Norms:** The Know Your Customer (KYC) norms have been simplified to make it easier for individuals to open bank accounts and access financial services.

8. **Priority Sector Lending:** RBI mandates that a certain portion of banks' lending should be directed towards priority sectors like agriculture, education, and housing, ensuring better access to credit for marginalized sections.

9. Microfinance Institutions (MFIs): RBI regulates and supervises microfinance institutions to ensure responsible lending practices and to support financial inclusion.

10. Branch Expansion: RBI encourages banks to expand their branch network to cover rural and unbanked areas, thereby increasing access to banking services.

11. Business Correspondents (BCs): RBI permits banks to engage BCs, who act as intermediaries and provide basic banking services in areas where setting up brick-and-mortar branches is not feasible.

12. No-Frills Accounts: RBI introduced the concept of "no-frills" accounts, which are low-cost savings accounts designed to make banking accessible to low-income individuals.

13. Mobile Banking and Digital Payments: RBI promotes the use of mobile banking, digital wallets, and other electronic payment methods to improve financial accessibility.

7.21. Difference between Financial Inclusion and Financial Exclusion:

Financial Inclusion and Financial Exclusion are two contrasting terms that represent the availability and accessibility of financial services to different segments of the population. Here's the difference between the two:

7.22. Financial Inclusion:

Financial Inclusion refers to the process of ensuring that all individuals and communities, regardless of their socio-economic background, have access to a wide range of financial services and products. The goal of financial inclusion is to provide everyone with the means to manage their finances, save, invest, and participate in the formal financial system. This includes access to banking services, credit facilities, insurance, and other financial tools. Financial inclusion promotes economic growth, reduces poverty, and empowers individuals to improve their overall financial well-being.

7.23. Financial Exclusion:

Financial Exclusion refers to the situation where certain individuals or groups within society do not have access to adequate and affordable financial services. These individuals are marginalized and are unable to participate fully in the formal financial system. They often rely on informal and unregulated sources of finance, which can expose them to exploitative practices and limit their economic opportunities. Financial exclusion can contribute to income inequality and hinder socio-economic development.

Financial inclusion aims to provide universal access to financial services and promote economic empowerment, while financial exclusion refers to the lack of access to these services, resulting in socio-economic disadvantages for marginalized populations. Efforts to bridge the gap between financial inclusion and financial exclusion are crucial for achieving equitable and inclusive economic growth.

Chapter - 8

Business Correspondence Model of Bank, NBFC, and MFI in Indian Banking system

The Business Correspondent (BC) model is an important component of the financial inclusion efforts in the Indian banking system. It involves using intermediaries to extend banking services to areas and populations that lack easy access to traditional bank branches. Here's how the BC model works for banks, non-banking financial companies (NBFCs), and microfinance institutions (MFIs) in India:

8.1. Banks:

Banks engage Business Correspondents (BCs) who act as agents to provide basic banking services in areas where setting up physical bank branches is not feasible.

BCs can be individuals or entities like NGOs, microfinance institutions, post offices, etc.

They are equipped with handheld devices or mobile phones enabled with secure banking applications to perform various transactions on behalf of the bank.

BCs can help customers open accounts, deposit and withdraw money, transfer funds, provide loan application assistance, and offer other basic financial services.

8.2. Non-Banking Financial Companies (NBFCs):

NBFCs can also operate as BCs to provide financial services in underserved areas.

NBFCs, in collaboration with banks, can offer credit, insurance, and other financial products through their network of agents.

8.3. Microfinance Institutions (MFIs):

MFIs are specialized institutions that provide small loans and financial services to low-income individuals and groups.

In the BC model, MFIs can act as intermediaries to provide banking services to their clients.

This approach helps integrate microfinance services with mainstream banking, improving financial inclusion.

8.4. The BC model benefits both financial institutions and Customers:

Financial Institutions: The BC model enables financial institutions to expand their outreach without incurring the high costs of setting up and maintaining physical branches.

Customers: The model makes banking services more accessible to rural and remote areas, reducing the need for individuals to travel long distances to access banking facilities.

It's important to note that the BC model is subject to regulatory guidelines and oversight to ensure consumer protection, data security, and proper implementation. The Reserve Bank of India (RBI) issues guidelines and directions for the operation of the BC model to maintain transparency and accountability.

8.5. Bank Correspondent model:

The Banking Correspondent (BC) model, also known as the Business Correspondent model, is a strategy employed by banks to extend their reach and provide financial services to underserved and unbanked areas in a cost-effective manner. This model involves engaging intermediaries, known as Business Correspondents, to offer basic banking and financial services on behalf of the bank. Here's an overview of the BC model:

1. Role of Business Correspondents (BCs):

BCs are individuals or entities like NGOs, microfinance institutions, post offices, or other local organizations.

They act as intermediaries between banks and customers in areas where setting up traditional brick-and-mortar branches is not feasible due to logistical or economic constraints.

BCs are authorized to provide basic banking services like account opening, cash deposits, cash withdrawals, fund transfers, loan applications, and more.

2. Technology Integration:

BCs are equipped with handheld devices or mobile phones with secure banking applications.

They use these devices to perform various banking transactions securely, ensuring that customer data is protected.

3. Customer Accessibility:

The BC model brings banking services closer to customers, especially those residing in rural and remote areas.

It reduces the need for customers to travel long distances to access banking facilities.

4. Financial Inclusion:

The primary goal of the BC model is to promote financial inclusion by ensuring that even marginalized and underserved populations have access to basic banking services.

5. Services Offered:

BCs can facilitate account opening, deposit and withdrawal of funds, remittances, payment of utility bills, insurance premium collection, and more.

6. Regulatory Framework:

The Reserve Bank of India (RBI) governs and regulates the BC model to ensure compliance with customer protection, anti-money laundering (AML), and know your customer (KYC) norms.

7. Collaboration with Banks:

Banks partner with BCs through formal agreements.

BCs operate under the bank's brand and follow the bank's guidelines and standards.

8. Training and Support:

BCs receive training to effectively handle transactions, adhere to banking guidelines, and provide quality customer service.

The BC model has been instrumental in expanding the reach of banking services in India and promoting financial inclusion, especially in remote and underserved areas. It has enabled individuals who were previously excluded from the formal banking system to access essential financial services, fostering economic development and empowerment.

8.6. Who can be a business correspondent in Indian banking system?

In the Indian banking system, a Business Correspondent (BC) is an individual or entity that acts as an intermediary on behalf of banks to provide basic banking and financial services in areas where setting up traditional bank branches is not feasible or cost-effective. The Reserve Bank of India (RBI) has established guidelines for who can qualify as a BC. The following entities can potentially become Business Correspondents in the Indian banking system:

1. **Individuals:** Individuals with a suitable background, knowledge of the local community, and the ability to facilitate banking transactions can become BCs. They often work as agents who serve their communities by offering banking services.

2. **Non-Governmental Organizations (NGOs):** Registered NGOs with a history of community service and presence in rural and remote areas can be authorized as BCs. They can help in spreading financial literacy and providing banking services.

3. **Microfinance Institutions (MFIs):** Microfinance institutions that already serve low-income individuals and groups can act as BCs to provide banking services to their existing client base.

4. **Self-Help Groups (SHGs):** SHGs, which are community-based groups of women, can be authorized as BCs to assist their members in accessing banking services.

5. **Post Offices:** In some cases, post offices may act as BCs, especially in rural areas, to provide basic banking services along with postal services.

6. **Retailers:** Retail shops and establishments in rural and remote areas can become BCs, offering banking services to customers while they shop.

7. **Cooperatives:** Cooperative societies and organizations can also be authorized as BCs to extend banking services to their members.

8. **Rural Kiosk Operators:** Operators of common service centers or rural kiosks can be engaged as BCs to provide banking services in their localities.

It's important to note that becoming a Business Correspondent involves meeting specific criteria set by the RBI, including operational capacity, infrastructure, technological capabilities, security measures, and adherence to regulatory guidelines. BCs must operate within the framework provided by the RBI and maintain compliance with customer protection, anti-money laundering (AML), and know your customer (KYC) norms.

Entities interested in becoming BCs should approach banks and financial institutions with a proposal, outlining their capabilities and the value they can bring to extending financial services to underserved areas. The banks and financial institutions then enter into formal agreements with qualified BCs.

8.7. Scope of activities for BCs:

Business Correspondents (BCs) in the Indian banking system play a crucial role in extending financial services to underserved and unbanked areas. The scope of activities for BCs is defined by the Reserve Bank of India (RBI) and encompasses a range of basic banking and financial services. The exact scope may vary based on the specific agreement between the BC and the partnering bank or financial institution. Here are the typical activities that BCs are authorized to perform:

1. Account Opening:

BCs can help customers open bank accounts, including no-frills accounts, savings accounts, and other types of accounts.

2. Cash Deposits and Withdrawals:

BCs facilitate cash deposits and withdrawals for customers, allowing them to access banking services without traveling to a bank branch.

3. Fund Transfers:

BCs can assist customers in transferring funds between accounts within the same bank or to accounts in other banks using electronic payment methods.

4. Balance Inquiry and Mini Statements:

BCs provide customers with information about their account balances and mini statements of recent transactions.

5. Loan Application Assistance:

BCs can help customers with the process of applying for loans, including providing necessary documentation and guiding them through the application process.

6. Payments and Remittances:

BCs facilitate utility bill payments, government benefit transfers, and remittances on behalf of customers.

7. Mobile Banking and Aadhaar Services:

BCs may assist customers in using mobile banking applications and Aadhaar-based services, such as Aadhaar-enabled Payment Systems (AePS).

8. Financial Literacy and Awareness:

BCs educate customers about various banking services, financial literacy, and the benefits of using formal financial channels.

9. Insurance Services:

In some cases, BCs may offer insurance services, including premium collection for insurance policies.

10. Documentation and KYC Verification:

BCs assist customers with completing necessary documentation and verifying their identity as part of the Know Your Customer (KYC) process.

11. Customer Grievance Redressal:

BCs may help customers address basic issues and concerns related to banking services, forwarding more complex matters to the partnering bank.

It's important to note that BCs operate as representatives of the partnering bank or financial institution. They must adhere to regulatory guidelines set by the RBI, maintain customer privacy and data security, and ensure that transactions are conducted in a secure and transparent manner. The scope of BC activities is designed to enhance financial inclusion and improve access to basic banking services for individuals in remote and underserved areas.

8.8. Issues and Challenges of Financial Institutions in India:

Financial institutions in India, like those in other countries, face a range of issues and challenges that impact their operations, growth, and ability to serve customers effectively. Some of the key challenges faced by financial institutions in India include:

1. **Financial Inclusion:** Despite efforts to promote financial inclusion, a significant portion of the population in India remains unbanked or underbanked. Ensuring access to banking services for all segments of society, particularly in rural and remote areas, continues to be a challenge.

2. **Cybersecurity and Data Privacy:** With the increasing adoption of digital banking and technology-driven services, financial institutions must safeguard customer data and transactions from cyber threats and breaches. Maintaining strong cybersecurity measures and adhering to data protection regulations is critical.

3. **Non-Performing Assets (NPAs):** The issue of non-performing assets, or bad loans, remains a concern for banks. Economic downturns, defaulting borrowers, and factors affecting sectors like agriculture and industry contribute to the NPA problem.

4. **Regulatory Compliance:** Financial institutions must adhere to a complex web of regulatory guidelines, which can lead to operational challenges and increased compliance costs.

5. Fraud and Money Laundering: Preventing fraud and money laundering requires robust internal controls, advanced fraud detection systems, and continuous vigilance.

6. Technological Upgrades: Keeping up with technological advancements and implementing new digital solutions while ensuring a seamless customer experience can be challenging.

7. Credit Risk Assessment: Effective assessment of credit risk and managing lending portfolios while maintaining profitability is a constant challenge, particularly for banks dealing with diverse segments of customers.

8. Customer Experience: Financial institutions must balance the demand for modern, user-friendly digital services with providing personalized customer service that meets the needs of diverse customer segments.

9. Liquidity Management: Ensuring optimal liquidity levels while managing customer withdrawals and investments is crucial for maintaining financial stability.

10. Interest Rate Volatility: Changes in interest rates impact lending and borrowing costs, affecting profitability and investment decisions.

11. Infrastructure Challenges: Inadequate infrastructure in rural areas can hinder the expansion of banking services and limit the reach of financial institutions.

12. Talent Acquisition and Training: Recruiting and retaining skilled personnel in areas like risk management, compliance, and technology is a continuous challenge.

13. Competition from Fintech and Non-Bank Players: The rise of fintech companies and non-bank financial institutions has increased competition, compelling traditional financial institutions to adapt and innovate.

14. Capital Adequacy: Maintaining a strong capital base to meet regulatory requirements and withstand financial shocks is essential for financial stability.

15. Political and Economic Factors: Macroeconomic factors, government policies, and geopolitical uncertainties can impact the overall financial environment.

Financial institutions in India need to address these challenges proactively to ensure their sustainability, growth, and ability to provide reliable and secure services to their customers.

8.9. Issues and Challenges with Business Correspondent:

Business Correspondents (BCs) play a crucial role in extending banking services to underserved and remote areas in India. However, they also face a set of challenges and issues that can impact their effectiveness and the success of the financial inclusion efforts. Some of the key challenges faced by Business Correspondents include:

1. Infrastructure and Connectivity: Many areas where BCs operate lack reliable infrastructure and connectivity, making it challenging to conduct electronic transactions and provide seamless services.

2. Agent Viability: The economics of being a BC can be challenging. The commissions earned by BCs might not always cover their operational costs, especially in areas with low transaction volumes.

3. Risk Management: BCs handle cash transactions and sensitive financial data. Ensuring proper risk management practices to prevent fraud, theft, and security breaches is essential.

4. Customer Awareness: In rural and remote areas, customers may lack awareness about banking services and may be hesitant to use them. BCs need to invest in educating customers about the benefits of formal financial services.

5. Training and Capacity Building: BCs need to be adequately trained to handle transactions, adhere to regulatory norms, and provide quality customer service. Continuous training can be a challenge.

6. Regulatory Compliance: BCs must adhere to strict regulatory norms set by the Reserve Bank of India (RBI). Staying compliant while operating in remote areas with limited resources can be demanding.

7. Liquidity Management: Ensuring sufficient cash availability for customer transactions can be challenging, especially in areas with limited banking infrastructure.

8. Sustainability: Maintaining a sustainable business model that balances the costs of operations and revenue generation can be tough for BCs, especially in areas with low-income customers.

9. Interoperability: Ensuring interoperability between different banks' systems and services can be complex and impact the ease of transactions for customers.

10. Technology Challenges: BCs need to use technology effectively to process transactions and provide services. Technical glitches, lack of familiarity with technology, and connectivity issues can be barriers.

11. Incentive Structure: BCs are often compensated through commission-based models. Designing fair and effective incentive structures that motivate BCs while ensuring profitability can be a challenge.

12. Banking Culture: Encouraging a banking culture and building trust among customers who are unfamiliar with formal financial services can be an ongoing effort.

13. Market Competition: As the BC model gains popularity, competition among BCs and with other financial service providers increases, potentially affecting business viability.

14. Geopolitical and Socioeconomic Factors: External factors such as political instability, social dynamics, and local customs can impact BC operations.

Addressing these challenges requires a collaborative effort among financial institutions, regulators, and BCs themselves. Effective training, adequate support, technological solutions, and a customer-centric approach are key to overcoming these challenges and ensuring that the BC model continues to contribute to financial inclusion in India.

8.10. Multiple risk associated with BC model:

The Business Correspondent (BC) model, while instrumental in extending financial services to underserved areas, is associated with various risks that financial institutions, regulators, and BCs need to address to ensure its success and sustainability. Some of the multiple risks associated with the BC model include:

1. **Operational Risk:** This includes risks related to the day-to-day operations of BCs, such as errors in transactions, inadequate training, technology failures, and fraud.

2. **Compliance and Regulatory Risk:** BCs must adhere to regulatory guidelines set by the Reserve Bank of India (RBI). Non-compliance with KYC norms, AML regulations, and other legal requirements can result in penalties and reputational damage.

3. **Credit Risk:** BCs may provide small loans and credit facilities to customers. The risk of default and non-repayment poses credit risk to both the BC and the partnering financial institution.

4. **Reputation Risk:** Negative customer experiences, breaches of data security, or operational failures can damage the reputation of the BC, the partnering bank, and the financial system as a whole.

5. **Fraud and Security Risk:** BCs handle sensitive customer data and cash transactions. Inadequate security measures can lead to fraud, data breaches, and financial losses.

6. **Liquidity Risk:** Ensuring sufficient liquidity to meet customer demands for cash withdrawals can be challenging, especially in areas with limited banking infrastructure.

7. **Market Risk:** Fluctuations in economic conditions, interest rates, and local market dynamics can impact the business viability of BCs.

8. **Agent Viability and Sustainability:** BCs' financial sustainability can be challenging due to low transaction volumes, high operational costs, and limited revenue opportunities.

9. **Technology Risk:** Dependence on technology for transactions and data management exposes BCs to the risk of technical glitches, system failures, and cyber threats.

10. **Geopolitical and Socioeconomic Risk:** Local factors such as political instability, social dynamics, and cultural norms can impact BC operations.

11. **Risk of Over indebtedness:** BCs that provide credit facilities must ensure that borrowers do not become overindebted, which can lead to default and financial stress.

12. **Financial Literacy and Customer Risk:** Customers in underserved areas might lack financial literacy and awareness. BCs must educate customers to prevent mismanagement of funds or misuse of financial products.

13. **Intermediary Risk:** BCs act as intermediaries between customers and financial institutions. Failures on either side can impact the effectiveness of the BC model.

To mitigate these risks, financial institutions and regulators need to establish comprehensive risk management frameworks, provide ongoing training to BCs, implement strong internal controls, ensure technology security, and continuously monitor operations. BCs, on their part, need to adhere to regulatory guidelines, invest in customer education, maintain high ethical standards, and collaborate closely with partnering banks to manage risks effectively.

8.11. Difference between Business Correspondent and Business Facilitator:

Both Business Correspondents (BCs) and Business Facilitators (BFs) are intermediaries in the Indian banking system that play a role in extending banking services to underserved and remote areas. However, there are distinct differences in their roles, functions, and responsibilities. Here's a comparison between Business Correspondents and Business Facilitators:

8.12. Business Correspondent (BC):

1. Role and Function: BCs act as agents of banks and perform a variety of banking and financial services on behalf of the bank. They provide a range of services, including account opening, cash deposits, withdrawals, fund transfers, loan application assistance, and more.

2. Transactions: BCs are authorized to conduct both fund-based and non-fund-based transactions. This means they can handle cash transactions as well as assist customers with activities like balance inquiries and account statements.

3. Infrastructure: BCs are equipped with handheld devices or mobile phones enabled with secure banking applications to facilitate transactions and provide services to customers.

4. Banking Services: BCs offer more comprehensive banking services and are often engaged in areas where setting up traditional bank branches is not feasible.

5. Compliance and KYC: BCs must adhere to strict regulatory norms set by the Reserve Bank of India (RBI) and ensure proper Know Your Customer (KYC) documentation for customers.

8.13. Business Facilitator (BF):

1. Role and Function: BFs are also agents of banks but focus on a more limited set of activities. They primarily assist in identifying potential borrowers and help them in preparing loan applications.

2. Transactions: BFs are generally not authorized to handle cash transactions. Their role is primarily centered around facilitating the credit process, particularly for rural and underserved areas.

3. Credit Facilitation: BFs work to enhance financial inclusion by facilitating loans and credit services. They assist customers, especially in rural areas, in understanding loan requirements and completing application forms.

4. Banking Services: Unlike BCs, BFs do not typically provide a wide range of banking services beyond credit facilitation.

5. Compliance and KYC: BFs are also required to adhere to regulatory norms and ensure proper KYC documentation for loan applicants.

Business Correspondents are authorized to provide a broader range of banking services, including both fund-based and non-fund-based transactions. They serve as intermediaries for various banking activities. On the other hand, Business Facilitators focus primarily on facilitating credit and loan-related activities, assisting customers in rural areas with accessing credit services. Both BCs and BFs contribute to extending financial services to underserved areas and promoting financial inclusion in India.

8.14. Need of Collection Agency in Current Scenario:

Collection agencies play a crucial role in the current financial landscape by assisting businesses and financial institutions in recovering outstanding debts and managing delinquent accounts. Several factors highlight the need for collection agencies in the current scenario:

1. Economic Uncertainty: Economic challenges, such as those posed by the COVID-19 pandemic, can lead to financial difficulties for individuals and businesses. Collection agencies can help creditors recover owed funds during times of financial stress.

2. Business Sustainability: For businesses, especially small and medium-sized enterprises (SMEs), unpaid invoices and overdue payments can impact cash flow and hinder operational sustainability. Collection agencies aid in recovering these funds.

3. Financial Institutions' NPA Management: Banks and financial institutions face challenges related to non-performing assets (NPAs) and bad loans. Collection agencies can assist in managing NPAs and recovering loans that have turned delinquent.

4. Regulatory Compliance: Collection agencies are well-versed in compliance with debt collection laws and regulations, ensuring that debt recovery efforts adhere to legal standards and guidelines.

5. Time and Resource Efficiency: Pursuing overdue accounts can be time-consuming and resource-intensive for businesses. Outsourcing this task to collection agencies allows businesses to focus on core operations.

6. Expertise in Debt Recovery: Collection agencies specialize in debt recovery strategies and negotiation techniques. Their expertise increases the likelihood of successful recovery.

7. Customer Relations Management: Collection agencies often adopt respectful and professional approaches to debt recovery, aiming to preserve positive customer relations while recovering debts.

8. Consumer Protection: Professional collection agencies are experienced in adhering to consumer protection laws, ensuring fair treatment of debtors during the collection process.

9. Variety of Debts: Collection agencies can manage various types of debts, including consumer debts, commercial debts, medical debts, and more.

10. Legal Proceedings: If necessary, collection agencies can initiate legal proceedings to recover debts. They have the legal expertise to navigate these processes effectively.

11. Diverse Industries: Collection agencies serve a wide range of industries, from healthcare and finance to utilities and retail.

12. Cross-Border Collections: For international businesses, collection agencies offer the expertise needed to recover debts across different jurisdictions and regulatory environments.

Collection agencies provide a specialized and effective approach to debt recovery, offering their expertise in managing delinquent accounts and helping businesses maintain financial stability. However, it's essential to choose a reputable and ethical collection agency that prioritizes respectful communication and adheres to legal and regulatory standards.

8.15. Limitations of Collection Agency:

Collection agencies provide valuable services in recovering overdue debts, but they also have limitations and potential drawbacks. Here are some limitations to consider:

1. Reputation Risk: Collection agencies have been criticized for using aggressive or harassing tactics, which can damage the reputation of the original creditor. Choosing a reputable and ethical agency is crucial to avoid negative associations.

2. Customer Relations: The collection process can strain relationships between the debtor and the original creditor, especially if the collection agency employs aggressive tactics that might alienate customers.

3. Limited Success Rate: Collection agencies may not always be successful in recovering debts, especially if the debtor is facing severe financial hardship or is unresponsive.

4. High Costs: Collection agencies typically charge a percentage of the recovered debt as their fee. This cost can be substantial and may not always justify the amount recovered, especially for small debts.

5. Privacy Concerns: Collecting personal financial information requires compliance with data protection regulations. Mishandling customer data can lead to privacy breaches and legal issues.

6. Legal and Regulatory Challenges: The debt collection industry is subject to various laws and regulations. Failing to adhere to these regulations can result in legal actions against the collection agency.

7. Limited Scope: Some collection agencies specialize in specific types of debts or industries. Finding an agency with expertise in a particular debt type may be challenging.

8. Recovery Rate Variability: The success of debt recovery can vary based on factors such as the debtor's financial situation, willingness to cooperate, and the type of debt.

9. Timing: If a debt has already been sold to a collection agency, the original creditor may have limited control over the negotiation process or the terms of repayment.

10. Cultural and Language Differences: In cases involving international debt recovery, language barriers and cultural differences can complicate communication and negotiations.

11. Negative Perception: Some debtors may view collection agencies negatively, associating them with aggressive tactics, regardless of the agency's actual approach.

12. Legal Action Constraints: Collection agencies may not be authorized to initiate legal proceedings in all cases, limiting their options for recovering certain types of debts.

13. Complex Debts: Some debts may have complex terms or disputes associated with them, making the recovery process more challenging.

While collection agencies offer professional assistance in debt recovery, it's essential for businesses to carefully evaluate the benefits and drawbacks. Communication, transparency, adherence to ethical practices, and a balanced approach are key factors in ensuring a successful debt recovery process while maintaining positive customer relationships.

8.16. Challenges of collection agencies:

Collection agencies face several challenges that can impact their effectiveness and success in recovering overdue debts. Some of the key challenges faced by collection agencies include:

1. Compliance with Regulations: The debt collection industry is subject to various federal, state, and local regulations that dictate how collection agencies can interact with debtors, when they can contact them, and what tactics they can use. Ensuring compliance with these regulations is essential to avoid legal issues.

2. Consumer Protection Laws: Collection agencies must adhere to consumer protection laws, including the Fair Debt Collection Practices Act (FDCPA) in the United States, which outlines guidelines for fair and ethical debt collection practices. Violating these laws can result in legal action and damage to the agency's reputation.

3. Communication Challenges: Debtors may be unresponsive or difficult to reach, making effective communication a challenge. Balancing persistence with respecting debtors' rights and privacy is crucial.

4. Managing Delicate Situations: Collection agencies often deal with debtors who are facing financial hardship, health issues, or other personal challenges. Handling these situations with sensitivity and empathy while still pursuing debt recovery can be challenging.

5. Negotiation Skills: Successful debt recovery often involves negotiation with debtors to reach mutually acceptable repayment plans. Developing effective negotiation skills is essential for achieving optimal outcomes.

6. Limited Resources: Collection agencies need to allocate resources wisely to manage a large number of accounts. Prioritizing accounts that are more likely to yield successful recoveries is crucial.

7. Data Security: Collection agencies handle sensitive financial and personal information. Ensuring data security and protecting against data breaches is a significant challenge.

8. Technology Adoption: Keeping up with technological advancements for communication, data management, and analytics is crucial for efficient debt collection. However, implementing new technology can be complex and costly.

9. Reputation Management: Collection agencies often face negative stereotypes due to the actions of a few unethical agencies. Building and maintaining a positive reputation is challenging in such an environment.

10. Litigation Risks: In some cases, debtors may take legal action against collection agencies, claiming harassment or violation of their rights. Legal disputes can be costly and damaging to an agency's reputation.

11. Cultural Sensitivity: In international debt collection, cultural norms, language barriers, and varying legal frameworks can complicate the process.

12. Negotiating Settlements: Finding the right balance between recovering as much debt as possible and offering reasonable settlement terms to debtors can be challenging.

13. Economic Factors: Economic downturns or recessions can impact the ability of debtors to repay their debts, affecting collection agency operations.

14. Competitive Market: The debt collection industry is competitive, with many agencies vying for business. Agencies need to differentiate themselves and provide value-added services to clients.

To navigate these challenges, collection agencies must invest in training, adopt ethical practices, stay informed about regulations, and focus on building strong relationships with both clients and debtors. Adapting to changing industry dynamics and embracing innovative approaches are also essential for long-term success.

8.17. Risk with collection agencies:

Collection agencies are exposed to various risks as they engage in the process of debt recovery and managing overdue accounts. These risks can impact their operations, reputation, and financial stability. Here are some of the key risks associated with collection agencies:

1. **Regulatory and Compliance Risk:** Collection agencies must adhere to a complex web of federal, state, and local regulations governing debt collection practices. Non-compliance with these regulations can result in legal actions, fines, and reputational damage.

2. **Legal Risk:** Debtors may file lawsuits against collection agencies for perceived violations of their rights, including claims of harassment, privacy breaches, or unfair practices.

3. **Reputation Risk:** Negative perceptions of collection agencies as aggressive or unethical can damage the agency's reputation, leading to reduced business opportunities and mistrust from clients and debtors.

4. **Privacy and Data Security Risk:** Collection agencies handle sensitive personal and financial information. Data breaches or mishandling of customer data can lead to privacy violations and legal repercussions.

5. **Operational Risk:** Errors in communication, documentation, or transaction processing can result in lost opportunities and tarnished relationships with clients and debtors.

6. **Financial Risk:** Collection agencies often work on a contingency fee basis, meaning they only get paid when debts are recovered. An unsuccessful collection effort can lead to financial losses for the agency.

7. **Economic Downturn Risk:** During economic downturns, debtors may have even more difficulty repaying their debts, which can impact the agency's success rate and profitability.

8. **Client Expectations Risk:** Client expectations for recovery rates and outcomes may not align with the reality of debt collection, leading to dissatisfaction and potential termination of contracts.

9. **Litigation Risk:** Debtors may initiate legal action against collection agencies, leading to legal expenses and potential settlements.

10. Technological Risk: Dependence on technology for communication, data management, and security exposes collection agencies to the risk of technical glitches, cyberattacks, and data breaches.

11. Market Risk: The competitive landscape of the debt collection industry can impact an agency's ability to secure contracts and clients.

12. Ethical Risk: The pursuit of debt recovery must be conducted ethically and professionally to avoid negative perceptions and potential legal challenges.

13. Disputes and Miscommunication Risk: Miscommunication or disputes between the agency, debtor, and client can lead to delays in resolution and hinder the recovery process.

14. Operational Scalability Risk: Scaling operations to handle a larger number of accounts and diverse debtors can lead to challenges in maintaining consistent quality.

15. Macroeconomic Risk: Macroeconomic factors such as interest rates, inflation, and economic instability can impact debtors' ability to repay and the overall success of collection efforts.

To mitigate these risks, collection agencies need to invest in robust compliance programs, prioritize ethical practices, adopt stringent data security measures, train employees effectively, and maintain open communication with both clients and debtors. Establishing strong relationships with clients, operating transparently, and providing value-added services can help collection agencies build trust and navigate potential risks successfully.

Chapter – 9

Microfinance Implications and Impact

9.1. Impact of Microfinance:

Microfinance, a powerful and transformative financial tool, has significantly impacted individuals, communities, and economies worldwide. This innovative approach to providing financial services to low-income individuals has far-reaching implications for poverty reduction, gender empowerment, economic development, and financial inclusion.

Microfinance institutions, ranging from grassroots community-based organizations to formal financial institutions, extend small loans, savings accounts, and insurance products to those who are often excluded from traditional banking systems. These microloans, typically provided without the need for collateral, enable individuals to start or expand small businesses, invest in education and healthcare, and create pathways out of poverty.

Women, in particular, have been a central focus of microfinance initiatives. By providing financial resources and support, microfinance has empowered women economically and socially, elevating their roles within households and communities. This gender-inclusive approach has led to a ripple effect of positive change, as empowered women tend to invest in the well-being of their families and communities.

Microfinance's impact extends to local economies, where microenterprises fuelled by these small loans contribute to job creation, stimulate economic activity, and foster economic growth, especially in rural areas. Moreover, it enhances financial literacy and improves access to financial services for underserved populations, promoting broader financial inclusion.

While microfinance has brought about numerous benefits, it's essential to recognize that its impact can vary depending on program design, region, and socio-economic context. Challenges such as high-interest rates, over-indebtedness, and sustainability concerns have been raised. Ongoing research, responsible practices, and the incorporation of impact assessments are vital for maximizing the positive effects of microfinance while addressing potential pitfalls.

In this exploration of the impact of microfinance, we will delve deeper into its multifaceted effects, examining poverty reduction, women's empowerment, economic development, and financial inclusion in detail. We will also consider the challenges and ethical considerations associated with microfinance, offering a comprehensive overview of its role in shaping a more inclusive and equitable world.

Microfinance Implications and Impact refer to the consequences and outcomes resulting from the practice of microfinance. This includes examining both the intended and unintended effects of providing small loans and financial services to individuals and communities with limited access to traditional banking. The impact can encompass various dimensions such as economic, social, and empowerment effects on borrowers and their communities. Researchers and practitioners often analyse these implications to assess the effectiveness and sustainability of microfinance programs and their contribution to poverty alleviation and economic development.

9.2. Microfinance has had a significant impact on individuals, communities, and economies, primarily in developing regions. Some key impacts mentioned here:

1. Poverty Reduction: Microfinance provides access to financial services, such as small loans and savings accounts, to low-income individuals.

This helps them start or expand small businesses, generate income, and ultimately lift themselves out of poverty.

2. **Women's Empowerment:** Microfinance has often targeted women, empowering them economically and socially. By giving women access to financial resources and training, it has enhanced their decision-making power within households and communities.

3. **Economic Growth:** Microenterprises fueled by microfinance contribute to local economic development. They create jobs, stimulate economic activity, and contribute to overall economic growth, especially in rural areas.

4. **Financial Inclusion:** Microfinance institutions expand access to financial services for underserved populations who are often excluded from traditional banking systems. This promotes financial inclusion and improves overall financial literacy.

5. **Social Impact:** Microfinance can have broader social impacts, including improved health and education outcomes. Access to credit can help families afford healthcare and send their children to school.

6. **Risk Mitigation:** For vulnerable populations, microinsurance products offered by microfinance institutions can provide a safety net against unexpected events like illness or natural disasters.

7. **Entrepreneurship:** Microfinance encourages entrepreneurship and innovation by enabling individuals to start or expand small businesses, fostering economic diversification.

8. **Community Development:** Microfinance can strengthen communities by fostering social capital, encouraging savings, and supporting local infrastructure development.

9.3. Objective of Impact assessment in Microfinance:

The objective of impact assessment in microfinance is to systematically evaluate and measure the effects and outcomes of microfinance programs and initiatives. This process serves several important purposes:

1. **Effectiveness Evaluation:** Impact assessment helps determine how well microfinance programs are achieving their stated goals and objectives. It provides insights into whether these programs are effectively reaching their target populations and making a positive difference in the lives of the borrowers.

2. **Poverty Alleviation:** Assessing the impact of microfinance allows organizations to gauge its contribution to poverty alleviation. It helps answer questions about whether access to financial services is helping individuals and communities move out of poverty or improve their livelihoods.

3. **Sustainability:** Impact assessment helps identify the sustainability of microfinance programs. It examines whether these programs can continue to operate effectively in the long term and whether they are financially viable without relying on external subsidies.

4. **Risk Assessment:** Evaluating the impact also involves assessing any potential risks and negative consequences of microfinance. This includes examining whether borrowers are falling into debt traps or facing other adverse outcomes as a result of their participation in microfinance programs.

5. **Policy and Program Improvement:** Impact assessment provides valuable information for policymakers and microfinance institutions to make informed decisions. It can highlight areas where program design, delivery, or regulations may need adjustments to enhance positive outcomes and minimize negative impacts.

6. **Empowerment and Social Change:** Impact assessment can measure the extent to which microfinance contributes to empowerment, especially for women and marginalized groups. It looks at changes in social dynamics and gender relations within households and communities.

7. **Learning and Knowledge Sharing:** The results of impact assessments can be used to share knowledge and best practices within the microfinance sector. This facilitates learning and helps organizations adapt their strategies to better serve their clients.

8. Accountability: Impact assessment holds microfinance institutions accountable for their actions and results. It ensures transparency and helps build trust among stakeholders, including donors, investors, and clients.

9. Resource Allocation: Organizations can use impact assessment findings to allocate resources more efficiently and effectively. This includes deciding where to invest or expand microfinance programs based on their demonstrated impact.

9.4. Concept of impact assessment in Microfinance:

Impact assessment in microfinance refers to the systematic evaluation of the social, economic, and environmental effects of microfinance programs and initiatives on individuals, households, communities, and the broader society. The primary goal of impact assessment is to measure and understand the outcomes and consequences of microfinance interventions, helping organizations make informed decisions, improve program effectiveness, and ensure responsible practices. Here are some key concepts related to impact assessment in microfinance:

1. Measuring Outcomes: Impact assessment seeks to measure both intended and unintended outcomes of microfinance interventions. These outcomes may include changes in income, poverty reduction, increased access to financial services, women's empowerment, job creation, and improved living standards.

2. Quantitative and Qualitative Data: Impact assessment uses a combination of quantitative data (numbers and statistics) and qualitative data (narratives and stories) to provide a comprehensive view of the impact. Surveys, interviews, focus groups, and case studies are commonly used methods.

3. Baseline and Endline Data: A typical approach involves collecting data before the microfinance intervention (baseline) and after some time has passed (endline). Comparing these datasets helps determine the impact of the program over time.

4. Control Groups: In impact assessment, control groups are often used to compare the outcomes of individuals or communities that receive microfinance services with those that do not. This helps isolate the specific effects of microfinance.

5. Attribution and Causality: Establishing a causal link between microfinance and observed outcomes can be challenging. Impact assessments aim to attribute changes to microfinance interventions while considering other factors that may influence the outcomes.

6. Social Performance Indicators: Microfinance institutions often use social performance indicators (SPIs) to track and assess their impact on social objectives, such as poverty reduction and gender equality. SPIs help measure progress toward broader social goals.

7. Client Protection: Impact assessment also considers the potential risks and negative consequences of microfinance, including over-indebtedness and client protection issues. Ensuring responsible lending and risk management is part of the assessment.

8. Learning and Improvement: The findings of impact assessments are not only for reporting but also for learning and program improvement. Microfinance organizations use the results to refine their strategies and policies.

Impact assessment in microfinance is a critical process that helps stakeholders understand the real-world effects of microfinance programs and make informed decisions to maximize positive outcomes while mitigating potential negative consequences. It plays a vital role in the responsible and sustainable development of microfinance initiatives.

9.5. Impact monitoring in Microfinance:

Impact monitoring in microfinance refers to the ongoing and systematic process of tracking and assessing the social, economic, and environmental effects of microfinance programs and initiatives over time. Unlike impact assessment, which typically involves collecting data at specific points (baseline and endline), impact monitoring is a continuous effort that allows microfinance institutions and organizations to keep a close eye on the progress and outcomes of their programs. Here's a more detailed explanation of impact monitoring in microfinance:

1. **Continuous Tracking:** Impact monitoring involves the regular collection of data and information on various indicators related to the performance and outcomes of microfinance interventions. This data collection occurs throughout the life of the program, not just at specific evaluation points.

2. **Real-time Feedback:** By monitoring impact continuously, microfinance organizations can receive real-time feedback on their programs. This enables them to identify issues, challenges, or opportunities as they arise and make timely adjustments to program design and implementation.

3. **Key Performance Indicators (KPIs):** Impact monitoring often focuses on specific KPIs that are relevant to the objectives of the microfinance program. These could include loan repayment rates, changes in income levels, poverty reduction, women's empowerment indicators, and more.

4. **Adaptive Management:** Microfinance institutions use the insights gained from impact monitoring to practice adaptive management. They can adapt their strategies, products, and services based on the evolving needs and circumstances of their clients and the communities they serve.

5. **Risk Management:** Impact monitoring helps in identifying potential risks, such as over-indebtedness among clients, and allows organizations to take proactive measures to mitigate these risks.

6. **Accountability and Reporting:** Regular impact monitoring ensures that microfinance institutions remain accountable to their stakeholders, including donors, investors, and regulators. It provides a basis for transparent reporting on the outcomes and impacts of their programs.

7. **Learning and Improvement:** Just like impact assessments, the findings from impact monitoring are valuable for learning and program

improvement. Microfinance organizations use this information to refine their practices and enhance their effectiveness.

Impact monitoring in microfinance is a dynamic and ongoing process that allows organizations to stay informed about the progress and effects of their interventions. It is a critical component of responsible and sustainable microfinance, ensuring that programs remain aligned with their objectives and contribute positively to the well-being of clients and communities.

9.6. Tools used to measure impact of microfinance and poverty assessment:

Measuring the impact of microfinance and conducting poverty assessments involves a variety of tools and methodologies. These tools help collect data and analyze outcomes to understand the effects of microfinance interventions and their impact on poverty. Here are some commonly used tools for impact measurement and poverty assessment in microfinance:

1. Household Surveys: These surveys collect data from targeted households and individuals, covering aspects such as income, consumption, assets, and access to financial services. Surveys may use structured questionnaires and interviews.

2. Baseline and Endline Studies: Baseline studies are conducted before the microfinance program begins, while endline studies are carried out after a specific period to assess changes in economic conditions, poverty levels, and other relevant indicators.

3. Randomized Control Trials (RCTs): RCTs involve randomly assigning eligible participants to either a control group or a treatment group that receives microfinance services. By comparing the outcomes of the two groups, researchers can attribute changes to the microfinance intervention.

4. Qualitative Research: Qualitative methods, such as focus group discussions and in-depth interviews, help capture nuanced insights into the experiences and perceptions of microfinance clients. They can provide context to quantitative data.

5. Financial Diaries: Financial diaries involve tracking the daily financial transactions and activities of selected households over an extended period. This provides a detailed picture of how microfinance impacts clients' financial lives.

6. Poverty Scorecards: Poverty scorecards are tools that assess the poverty level of individuals or households based on a set of indicators. They are often used as a quick and simple way to determine eligibility for microfinance programs.

7. Impact Assessment Software: Various software solutions and platforms are available to streamline data collection, analysis, and reporting for impact assessment and poverty measurement. They often include built-in tools for statistical analysis.

8. Composite Indices: Researchers may use composite indices, like the Multidimensional Poverty Index (MPI) or the Progress out of Poverty Index (PPI), to measure poverty and well-being based on multiple indicators.

9. Social Performance Management (SPM) Tools: Microfinance institutions may use SPM tools to assess their social impact, including financial and non-financial performance indicators related to poverty reduction, gender equality, and client protection.

10. Institutional Data: Microfinance institutions often maintain records of client demographics, loan disbursements, repayments, and financial transactions, which can be analyzed to assess the impact of their services.

11. External Evaluators: Independent evaluators or research organizations may be engaged to conduct impact assessments and poverty evaluations, providing impartial and rigorous analysis.

9.7. Indicators of Impact Assessment in Microfinance:

Impact assessment in microfinance involves evaluating various indicators to determine the effects of microfinance programs on individuals, households, and communities. These indicators help measure the program's success in achieving its goals and objectives. Here are some common indicators used in microfinance impact assessment:

1. Income and Employment:

- Increase in household income.
- Change in employment status (e.g., job creation, self-employment).

2. Poverty Reduction:

- Decrease in the poverty headcount ratio.
- Reduction in the depth and severity of poverty.

3. Financial Inclusion:

- Increased access to financial services (savings accounts, credit).
- Growth in the number of clients served.

4. Loan Repayment Performance:

- Portfolio at risk (PAR) or delinquency rates.
- Percentage of loans repaid on time.

5. Women's Empowerment:

- Enhanced economic decision-making power among women.
- Increase in women's participation in income-generating activities.

6. Savings and Asset Accumulation:

- Growth in savings balances.
- Accumulation of assets, such as land or housing.

7. Entrepreneurship and Business Development:

- Number of new businesses started.
- Growth in the size and profitability of existing businesses.

8. Education and Healthcare Access:

- Increased investment in education for children.
- Improved access to healthcare and nutrition.

9. Social Capital and Networking:

- Strengthening of social networks and community participation.
- Collaborative activities among microfinance clients.

10. Gender Equality:

- Reduction in gender-based disparities in income and resources.
- Increase in women's ownership of productive assets.

11. Food Security:

- Improvement in food consumption and nutrition.
- Reduction in the frequency of food shortages.

12. Client Satisfaction:

- Client feedback and satisfaction surveys.
- Perception of the value and quality of microfinance services.

13. Financial Health:

- Improved financial well-being and resilience.
- Reduction in financial stress and vulnerability.

14. Risk Mitigation:

- Access to microinsurance and its utilization.
- Coping strategies for dealing with unexpected events.

15. Client Protection and Ethical Practices:

- Compliance with client protection principles.
- Reduction in over-indebtedness and coercive lending practices.

16. Environmental Impact:

- Assessment of the program's environmental sustainability.
- Reduction in negative environmental effects, if applicable.

9.8. Impact Assessment in Microfinance

Impact assessment in microfinance is a systematic process of evaluating and measuring the social, economic, and environmental effects of microfinance programs and initiatives. It is conducted to understand the outcomes and consequences of these programs on individuals, households, communities, and the broader society. Impact assessment helps microfinance institutions, policymakers, and stakeholders make informed decisions, improve program effectiveness, and ensure responsible and sustainable microfinance practices.

9.9. Key elements and considerations of impact assessment in microfinance include:

1. **Objectives and Goals:** Clearly defining the objectives and goals of the impact assessment is essential. This could involve assessing poverty reduction, income generation, financial inclusion, women's empowerment, or other specific outcomes.

2. **Indicators:** Identifying relevant indicators that align with the assessment's objectives. These indicators could include changes in income, poverty levels, access to financial services, employment, or education.

3. **Data Collection:** Collecting both quantitative and qualitative data through methods such as surveys, interviews, focus groups, and document reviews. Baseline data is often collected before the microfinance program begins, and follow-up data is collected at subsequent intervals (endline).

4. **Control Groups:** Establishing control groups, which are groups of individuals or communities that do not receive microfinance services, to compare outcomes and determine the impact of the program.

5. **Data Analysis:** Analyzing collected data using appropriate statistical and analytical techniques to measure the impact and draw conclusions. This may involve regression analysis, propensity score matching, and other statistical methods.

6. Attribution: Determining the extent to which observed changes can be attributed to the microfinance program, considering other factors that may influence outcomes.

7. Ethical Considerations: Ensuring that the impact assessment is conducted ethically, with consideration for client protection, informed consent, and privacy.

8. Reporting and Communication: Presenting the findings of the impact assessment in a clear and transparent manner to stakeholders, including microfinance clients, donors, investors, and regulators.

9. Learning and Improvement: Using the assessment's findings to inform program design and decision-making. Impact assessments should lead to actionable insights and improvements in microfinance practices.

10. Long-Term Perspective: Recognizing that the impact of microfinance may evolve over time and conducting follow-up assessments to assess longer-term effects.

Impact assessment in microfinance is crucial for ensuring that microfinance programs are making a positive difference in the lives of their clients and communities. It helps in identifying successes and challenges, refining program strategies, and promoting responsible and sustainable microfinance practices. Additionally, it contributes to the broader understanding of the role of microfinance in poverty reduction and economic development.

Chapter - 10

Recent Evolution of Microfinance in India

10.1. Introduction:

The development of microfinance has been a transformative force in the global landscape of financial services, particularly in emerging economies and underserved communities. This remarkable evolution represents a pivotal shift from traditional banking practices, aiming to empower individuals and small businesses at the grassroots level by providing access to affordable and tailored financial solutions. Over the years, microfinance has grown into a multifaceted field, encompassing a wide range of services, technologies, and strategies. This introduction sets the stage to delve deeper into the fascinating journey of microfinance, exploring its origins, key players, pivotal moments, and the profound impact it has had on poverty alleviation, financial inclusion, and economic development worldwide.

The recent evolution of microfinance in India, as of March 31, 2023, provides a fascinating snapshot of the industry's growth and impact. In this overview, we delve into key data points sourced from Equifax, Reserve Bank of India (RBI), and government bodies to understand the state of microfinance in the country. It's important to note that while these statistics offer valuable insights, it's essential to cross-reference them with official sources for accuracy.

1. Overall Microfinance Industry Size:

As of March 31, 2023, the microfinance industry in India has reached impressive milestones. The total loan portfolio (outstanding) stands at Rs 3,48,339 Crores, with a noteworthy YoY growth of 22.0%. There are 13.0 Crores active loan accounts, benefiting 6.6 Crores unique borrowers. Notably, the DPD 180+ portfolio amounts to Rs 29,828 Crores.

2. Leading Microfinance Providers:

Within the microfinance landscape, different types of financial institutions play significant roles. Notably, 82 NBFC-MFIs lead the sector with a loan amount outstanding of Rs 1,38,310 Crores, followed closely by 13 Banks with Rs 1,19,133 Crores. Small Finance Banks (SFBs) account for Rs 57,828 Crores, NBFCs for 8.5%, and Other MFIs (including non-profit MFIs) for 1.0% of the universe.

3. SHG Bank Linkage Programme (SBLP):

In addition to MFIs, the National Rural Livelihood Mission (NRLM) contributes significantly through its SHG Bank Linkage Programme. As of March 2023, around 83.4 lakhs Self-Help Groups (SHGs) have an outstanding portfolio of Rs 1,98,918 Crores. This translates to approximately 8.3 Crores members benefiting from an average loan portfolio of Rs 23,851 per member.

4. Regional Distribution:

The regional distribution of microfinance borrowers and portfolio is notable. Around 63% of the portfolio is concentrated in the East & North East and South regions of India. The top 10 states, led by Bihar, Tamil Nadu, and Uttar Pradesh, constitute 83.9% of the Gross Loan Portfolio (GLP).

5. State Distribution:

Microfinance operations extend across 729 districts, covering 28 states and 8 union territories. With a significant presence, 211 entities serve

6,64,45,839+ unique borrowers through 12, 95, 53,251+ loan accounts, totaling a GLP of 3,44,393 Crores+.

6. Performance Indicators:

Microfinance institutions have seen improved portfolio quality as measured by PAR (>30 days), reflecting the sector's resilience and risk management efforts.

7. Portfolio Securitization:

Portfolio securitization is an avenue for microfinance institutions to manage risk and access additional funding sources. It can play a pivotal role in the sector's growth and stability.

In conclusion, the recent evolution of microfinance in India showcases its significant role in financial inclusion and poverty alleviation. The industry continues to grow, diversify, and adapt to changing economic landscapes, making it a vital component of India's financial ecosystem. However, it is essential to remain vigilant and verify data with official sources for a comprehensive understanding of this dynamic sector.

10.2. Recent developments in the Indian microfinance sector:

1. Digital Lending Platforms: The use of digital lending platforms and apps has expanded, enabling easier access to microloans.

2. UPI Integration: Many microfinance institutions have integrated with the Unified Payments Interface (UPI) for seamless transactions.

3. Small Finance Banks: Several microfinance institutions have transformed into small finance banks, offering a broader range of financial services.

4. Credit Scoring Technology: Advanced credit scoring models are being used, incorporating non-traditional data sources for risk assessment.

5. Regulatory Reforms: The Reserve Bank of India (RBI) has introduced regulatory reforms to ensure the stability and sustainability of microfinance institutions.

6. Fintech Partnerships: Microfinance organizations are partnering with fintech companies to improve service delivery and customer experience.

7. Self-Help Groups (SHGs): The promotion of SHGs continues to be a key strategy for microfinance in India.

8. Rural and Remote Expansion: Microfinance institutions are expanding their reach to remote and underserved areas, promoting financial inclusion.

9. Microinsurance Growth: The microinsurance sector is growing to offer risk protection to microfinance clients.

10. Women-Centric Initiatives: Specialized microfinance programs targeting women entrepreneurs and borrowers are on the rise.

11. Aadhaar Integration: The Aadhaar system has been integrated into many microfinance operations to verify the identity of clients.

12. Rural Entrepreneurs: Microfinance institutions are supporting rural entrepreneurs in sectors like agriculture, handicrafts, and small-scale industries.

13. Sustainable Practices: There is a growing focus on environmentally sustainable microfinance practices and products.

14. Data Security Measures: With increased digitization, data security measures have been strengthened to protect client information.

15. Education and Training: Microfinance institutions are providing financial literacy and training programs to empower clients.

16. Repayment Flexibility: Flexibility in loan repayment schedules has been introduced to accommodate borrowers' cash flows.

17. COVID-19 Response: Microfinance institutions played a crucial role during the pandemic by offering loan moratoriums and relief measures to clients.

18. Partnerships with NGOs: Collaborations with non-governmental organizations (NGOs) are helping microfinance organizations expand their reach.

19. Government Initiatives: Government-backed microfinance programs like MUDRA have gained prominence.

20. Mobile Wallets: The integration of mobile wallets into microfinance services has increased convenience for clients.

21. India's Central Bank (RBI) Digital Currency: RBI's approach to a digital currency up to that point:

Motivation: The primary motivation behind RBI's interest in a CBDC is to modernize the payment system, enhance financial inclusion, reduce the cost of cash management, and potentially provide a more efficient and secure form of digital payment.

Research and Development: The RBI had initiated research and development efforts to explore the possibility of issuing a digital rupee. They were examining various aspects of CBDC, including technology, security, regulatory concerns, and potential use cases.

Pilot Projects about to launch: At that time, the RBI was considering pilot projects and conducting proof-of-concept studies to test the feasibility of a CBDC in a controlled environment.

Regulatory Framework: The RBI is established a regulatory framework for the issuance and use of a digital rupee, including guidelines for banks and financial institutions.

International Collaboration: The RBI was also monitoring developments in CBDCs globally and collaborating with international organizations to stay updated on best practices and potential challenges.

Digital Payment Ecosystem: The introduction of a digital rupee would likely integrate with India's existing digital payment ecosystem, which includes Unified Payments Interface (UPI) and mobile wallets.

Privacy and Security: Ensuring the privacy and security of digital transactions would be a top priority for the RBI, as digital currencies raise concerns about data protection and fraud prevention.

Financial Inclusion: The RBI aimed to use CBDC to further financial inclusion by providing easier access to digital payment services, especially in remote and underserved areas.

10.3. The National Rural Livelihoods Mission (NRLM)

Is a poverty alleviation program launched by the Government of India. Here's a brief overview of the NRLM mission:

1. Objective: The primary goal of the NRLM is to reduce poverty and improve the livelihoods of rural households, particularly those belonging to marginalized communities.

2. Implementation: NRLM is implemented by the Ministry of Rural Development, Government of India. It operates at both the national and state levels, with state governments playing a key role in its execution.

Key Components of NRLM:

1. Self-Help Groups (SHGs): NRLM promotes the formation and strengthening of SHGs, which are small community-based organizations of rural women. These groups help women come together for collective decision-making, resource mobilization, and income-generation activities.

2. Livelihoods Promotion: NRLM focuses on providing financial support, training, and capacity-building to SHGs and their members. It aims to enhance their skills and income-generating abilities through various livelihood activities such as agriculture, animal husbandry, crafts, and non-farm enterprises.

3. Financial Inclusion: NRLM encourages financial inclusion by linking SHGs to formal banking institutions. This enables SHG members to access credit, savings, insurance, and other financial services.

10.4. SRLM stands for State Rural Livelihood Mission

And it is a poverty alleviation program in India. Each Indian state has its own SRLM, and they are implemented by state governments. Here's a brief overview of SRLM:

1. Objective: The primary objective of the State Rural Livelihood Mission (SRLM) is to reduce poverty and improve the livelihoods of rural households, particularly those belonging to marginalized communities, at the state level.

2. Implementation: SRLMs are implemented at the state level, and each state has its own mission. These missions are usually autonomous bodies or agencies created by the respective state governments.

Key Components:

1. Self-Help Groups (SHGs): Like the National Rural Livelihoods Mission (NRLM), SRLMs also promote the formation and strengthening of SHGs. SHGs are community-based organizations of rural women that facilitate collective decision-making, resource mobilization, and income-generation activities.

2. Livelihoods Promotion: SRLMs focus on providing financial support, training, and capacity-building to SHGs and their members. The goal is to enhance their skills and income-generating abilities through various livelihood activities such as agriculture, animal husbandry, crafts, and non-farm enterprises.

3. Financial Inclusion: SRLMs work on improving financial inclusion by linking SHGs to formal banking institutions. This enables SHG members to access credit, savings, insurance, and other financial services.

4. Community Institutions: Apart from SHGs, SRLMs also promote the formation of higher-level community institutions such as Village Organizations (VOs) and Cluster-Level Federations (CLFs). These institutions facilitate collective decision-making, resource pooling, and better governance at the community level.

5. Social Mobilization and Capacity Building: SRLMs invest in building the social and human capital of rural communities by providing training and capacity-building programs. This empowers them to actively participate in local development processes.

6. Microfinance: Similar to NRLM, SRLMs facilitate access to microfinance services for SHG members to help them meet their financial needs and invest in income-generating activities.

7. Inclusion of Vulnerable Communities: SRLMs emphasize the inclusion of Scheduled Castes (SCs), Scheduled Tribes (STs), and other marginalized communities in their activities to reduce social disparities.

8. Monitoring and Evaluation: SRLMs include monitoring and evaluation mechanisms to assess the impact and effectiveness of their interventions at the state level.

9. Key Outcomes: SRLMs have contributed to the formation and strengthening of SHGs at the state level and have played a significant role in improving the socio-economic status of rural women and marginalized communities within each state. They have helped rural households gain financial independence, access education and healthcare, and actively participate in local governance.

The specific initiatives, impact, and focus areas of each state's SRLM can vary, so for the most up-to-date and state-specific information about SRLMs, it's advisable to refer to official government sources or the SRLM website of each respective state.

Chapter - 11

Veterans of Microfinance along with Indian Microfinance Leaders

"In this chapter, titled 'Veterans of Microfinance along with Indian Microfinance Leaders,' I'm to shed light on the notable figures in the microfinance field. While it is regrettable that I cannot encompass the entirety of their remarkable contributions within these pages, I extend my apologies to those not featured in this volume. I am committed to expanding this exploration in the forthcoming second volume of this book, where I hope to include more veterans and their invaluable insights and experiences."

11.1. Prof. Dr. Muhammad Yunus:

Prof. Dr. Muhammad Yunus is a renowned Bangladeshi social entrepreneur and economist who pioneered the concept of microfinance. His groundbreaking work has had a profound impact on poverty alleviation and financial inclusion.

Background:

Dr. Muhammad Yunus is credited with being the inspiration for the Grameen Foundation and a founding member of its Board of Trustees.

He began his work in microfinance in 1976, experimenting with providing small loans to impoverished individuals, particularly women, in rural Bangladesh.

Founding of Grameen Bank:

In 1983, Dr. Yunus founded the Grameen Bank to formalize and expand his microcredit initiative.

His innovative approach challenged traditional banking by offering small loans without requiring collateral from borrowers.

The primary goal of the Grameen Bank was to empower the poor, especially women, by providing them with access to credit for income-generating activities like small businesses and farming.

Nobel Peace Prize:

In recognition of his pioneering work in microfinance and poverty alleviation, Dr. Yunus and the Grameen Bank jointly received the Nobel Peace Prize in 2006.

They were honoured for their efforts in promoting economic and social development through microcredit.

Impact of Grameen Bank:

Under Dr. Yunus's leadership, the Grameen Bank has grown significantly, providing collateral-free loans to 7.5 million clients in rural Bangladesh, with 97% of them being women.

Over the years, Grameen Bank has loaned out more than $6.5 billion to the poorest of the poor, maintaining a repayment rate consistently above 98%.

Global Influence:

Dr. Yunus's innovative approach to poverty alleviation has inspired a global microcredit movement, reaching millions of impoverished women, from rural South Africa to inner-city Chicago.

Autobiography:

He has authored the autobiography "Banker to the Poor: Microlending and the Battle Against World Poverty," which has been translated into multiple languages.

11.2. Madam Ela Bhatt:

Madam Ela Bhatt, whose full name is Ela Ramesh Bhatt, was a distinguished Indian social activist known for her work in empowering self-employed female textile workers in India.

Early Life:

Madam Ela Bhatt was born on September 7, 1933, in Ahmedabad, India.

She graduated from Sarwajanik Girls High School in Surat in 1948.

She attended MTB (Maganlal Thakordas Balmukunddas) Arts College in Surat and earned a bachelor's degree in English in 1952.

In 1954, she graduated from Sir L.A. Shah Law College in Ahmedabad, where she received a gold medal for her achievements in Hindu law.

Career and Achievements:

In 1955, Madam Ela Bhatt joined the legal department of the Textile Labour Association (TLA), India's oldest union for textile workers, which was established after a textile workers' strike led by Mahatma Gandhi.

Inspired by Gandhi's principles, she founded the Self-Employed Women's Association (SEWA) in 1972 and served as the union's secretary-general until her retirement in 1996.

Under her leadership, SEWA established a cooperative bank in 1974 to provide small loans to impoverished women, enabling them to start their own businesses. The union also offered financial and business counselling.

In 1979, she co-founded Women's World Banking (WWB), a global network of microfinance organizations focused on assisting poor women. She served as WWB's chairperson from 1984 to 1988.

Madam Ela Bhatt was appointed to the Rajya Sabha (Council of States), the upper house of India's parliament, by the President of India in 1986. She served until 1989 and chaired the National Commission on Self-Employed Women during her tenure, which aimed to investigate the conditions of poor women workers.

She also served as an adviser to international organizations such as the World Bank on matters related to microfinance, banking, and poverty alleviation.

In 2007, Madam Ela Bhatt became a member of the Elders, a group of global leaders founded by Nelson Mandela to advocate for human rights and peace. She became an emeritus member in 2016.

Throughout her life, she received numerous honorary degrees and prestigious awards, including the Ramon Magsaysay Award for Community Leadership (1977), the Right Livelihood Award for Changing the Human Environment (1984), and the Padma Shri (1985) and Padma Bhushan (1986), which are among India's highest civilian honours.

Madam Ela Bhatt's remarkable contributions to empowering marginalized women through SEWA and her advocacy for microfinance and women's rights left an indelible mark on India and the world. Her work continues to inspire efforts to promote economic and social justice. She passed away on November 2, 2022, in Ahmedabad, India.

11.3. Madam Vijay Lakshmi Das:

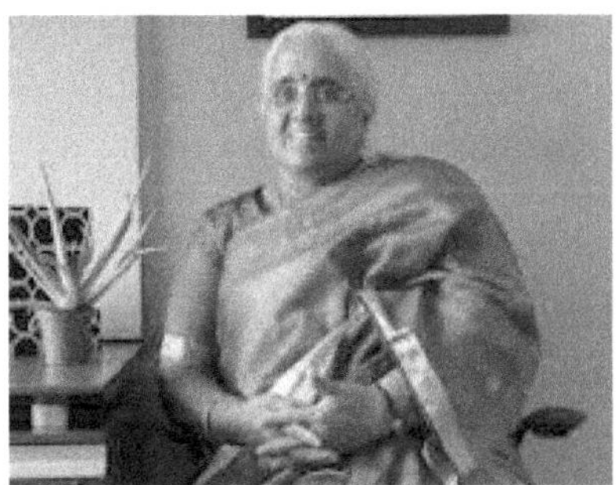

Madam Vijay Lakshmi Das is a pioneering figure in the field of Indian microfinance and has been instrumental in breaking gender stereotypes in finance.

Early Career and Education:

Madam Vijay Lakshmi Das earned a postgraduate degree in Economics from Madras University.

In the 1970s, at a time when women's roles were predominantly confined to domestic duties, she ventured into the world of finance, shattering gender stereotypes.

Professional Achievements:

She served as a Board Member at Micro Pension and as the Managing Director at Ananya.

One of her significant roles was as the Chief Executive of FWWB (Foundation for Women's World Banking), India. During her tenure, she played a pivotal role in FWWB's strategic development, including the formulation of the organization's first business plan, team building, and capital base expansion.

Madam Vijay Lakshmi Das also contributed her expertise as a member of the Project Advisory Group at CGAP (Consultative Group to Assist the Poor).

She is a current member of the Board of Trustees of Sa-Dhan, the Association of Community Development Finance Institutions, where she continues to play an active role in the microfinance sector.

As one of the founding Trustees, she has been associated with the Indian School of Microfinance for Women (ISMW), a school established in partnership with Citigroup.

Ms. Madam Vijay Lakshmi Das is a non-executive director on the board of IIMPS (Indian Institute of Management for Production and Services).

Her journey from breaking gender norms to her significant contributions to microfinance in India demonstrates her commitment to financial inclusion and women's empowerment. Ms. Madam Vijay Lakshmi Das is widely respected as a trailblazer in the microfinance industry and a champion for women's economic independence.

Madam Vijay Lakshmi Das Known as the mother of Indian Microfinance, Das shattered stereotypes way back in the '70s when she took up a job in finance—after a degree in economics—when women's roles were mostly limited to domestic duties.

Madam Vijay Lakshmi Das served as a Board Member at Micro Pension. She also served as Managing Director at Ananya. She is the former Chief Executive of FWWB, India. She joined the organization at a crucial stage of FWWB's growth and worked on the strategic positioning of the institution by formulating the first business plan, building a committed team and its capital base. She has also served as a member of Project Advisory Group-CGAP. She currently is a member of the Board of Trustees of Sa-Dhan, the Association of Community Development Finance Institutions. She is one of the founding Trustees of Indian School of Microfinance for Women (ISMW) - a school started in partnership with Citi group. Ms. Das is a Post Graduate in Economics from Madras University. She is a non-executive director on the board of IIMPS.

11.4. Mr. Vijay Mahajan:

Early Life:

Vijay Mahajan was born in India in October 1954.

He pursued a bachelor's degree in technology, specializing in Electrical Engineering, from the Indian Institute of Technology, Delhi, in 1970.

In 1981, he graduated with a master's degree in business management from the Indian Institute of Management, Ahmedabad (IIMA).

In 1988, he attended the Woodrow Wilson School of Public and International Affairs at Princeton University, USA, as a Mid-Career Fellow for a year.

Career Highlights:

Philips:

Vijay's career began at the multinational electronics company Philips, where he worked in marketing positions.

He travelled extensively in the small towns and rural areas of Northeastern India, gaining valuable exposure to different regions.

PRADAN:

After his MBA from IIMA, inspired by renowned professors and leaders, Vijay joined a Gandhian NGO named ASSEFA in Bihar in 1982.

At ASSEFA, he worked on settling landless poor people on gifted land (Bhoodan) and initiated projects related to land and water development, agriculture, and allied activities.

This work led to the founding of PRADAN (Professional Assistance for Development Action), an Indian non-government organization (NGO), in 1983, funded by the Ford Foundation.

Vijay Mahajan was served as the first executive director of PRADAN.

VikaSoko:

In 1991, Vijay, along with his Princeton classmates Thomas Fisher and Geoffrey Onegi-Obel, established VikaSoko Development Exchange, a US-registered non-profit NGO.

VikaSoko focused on development consulting, research, and training, primarily concerning livelihoods.

BASIX:

In 1996, Vijay conceptualized BASIX, a social enterprise group aimed at promoting livelihoods for the poor and women sustainably.

BASIX founded Bhartiya Samruddhi Finance Ltd (BSFL), one of the early microfinance companies globally to attract commercial debt and equity investments.

BASIX offered various services, including savings, insurance, agricultural and non-farm enterprise development, and institutional development for rural producers.

Vijay worked alongside colleagues like BL Parthasarathy, Ashok Singha, Sankar Datta, M S Sriram, and D Sattaiah.

Institution and Sector Building Roles:

Co-founder of Sa-Dhan, the association of community development financial institutions, in 1999.

Founding President of Microfinance Institutions Network (MFIN) of India in 2009.

Elected Vice-Chair of the Global Agenda Council on Social Entrepreneurship of the World Economic Forum (WEF) in 2010.

Chair of the Board of the World Bank's Consultative Group to Assist the Poor (CGAP) in 2012.

Policy Advisory and Board Roles:

Member of various committees and boards, including those related to financial sector reforms, financial inclusion, and livelihoods.

Principal Advisor to the Government of Rajasthan on Livelihoods.

Awards and Recognitions:

Listed in "60 Outstanding Social Entrepreneurs" by the Schwab Foundation for Social Entrepreneurship at the World Economic Forum in 2002.

Recognized as "India's 50 Most Powerful People" by BusinessWeek in 2009.

Received numerous awards, including the HSBC Access award, Skoch Foundation Award, and the MFIN Award for outstanding contribution to the microfinance sector.

Vijay Mahajan's remarkable journey from a corporate career at Philips to his impactful work in the development sector, including the founding of PRADAN and BASIX, has left a lasting legacy in promoting livelihoods and financial inclusion for the marginalized communities in India. His leadership roles in various organizations and advisory capacities have further strengthened his influence in the field of social entrepreneurship and development.

11.5. Mr. Nachiket Mor:

Nachiket Mor is a distinguished Indian banker known for his contributions to financial inclusion and his inventions of financial devices aimed at delivering banking services to rural villages.

Full Name: Nachiket Mor

Early Life and Education:

Birth: Nachiket Mor was born into a farming family in Yavatmal, Maharashtra, India.

Education: He holds a bachelor's degree in Physics from Mumbai University, a master's degree in Management from the Indian Institute of

Management Ahmedabad (IIM-A), and a PhD in Economics from the University of Pennsylvania. His PhD specialization is in Finance from the Wharton School.

Career Highlights:

Early Career: After completing his MBA, Nachiket Mor began his career with a non-governmental organization called Pradan, where he worked with mushroom farmers. Later, he joined ICICI Bank in 1987 under the recruitment of K.V. Kamath.

Academic Pursuit: In the mid-1990s, he pursued his PhD at the Wharton School and eventually returned to ICICI Bank.

Foundation for Inclusive Growth: In late 2007, he left ICICI Bank to lead the newly established ICICI Foundation for Inclusive Growth, focusing on rural development.

Intuit India Advisory Board: In May 2009, Mor joined the India advisory board of Intuit, a financial software company.

SughaVazhvu: In September 2010, he left the foundation to work with SughaVazhvu, an organization dedicated to improving healthcare in villages.

Reserve Bank of India (RBI): In May 2013, Nachiket Mor was appointed as a director on the Central Board of the Reserve Bank of India (RBI) and its local board in the eastern area.

Committee on Comprehensive Financial Services: In September 2013, Mor chaired the Committee on Comprehensive Financial Services for Small Businesses and Low-Income Households, making significant contributions to financial inclusion initiatives.

RBI Panel: He was also a member of a 4-member RBI panel led by Bimal Jalan that examined applications for new bank licenses in October 2013.

Bill and Melinda Gates Foundation: In March 2016, Nachiket Mor assumed the role of head at the Bill and Melinda Gates Foundation's India country office, where he served until March 2019.

Current Role: As of now, Nachiket Mor holds the position of National Director for the Bill and Melinda Gates Foundation, where he continues to work towards solving India's financial inclusion challenges.

Nachiket Mor's extensive career in the banking and financial inclusion sectors, along with his innovative contributions, has made him a significant figure in India's efforts to address financial inclusion and empower rural communities.

11.6. Mr. Vikram Akula:

Vikram Akula is an American banker and social entrepreneur known for his significant contributions to the field of microfinance and financial inclusion.

Early Life and Education:

Birth: Vikram Akula was born on November 7, 1968, in Ryakal Village, Medak district, Telangana, India.

Nationality: He holds American citizenship.

Family: His parents are Akula V. Krishna and Padma Krishna.

Vikram Akula's educational journey is characterized by a diverse range of experiences:

He completed his undergraduate studies at Tufts University, graduating with a double major in philosophy and English with honours in 1990.

He pursued a Master of Arts (M.A.) in International Relations at Yale University.

Akula was awarded a Fulbright scholarship in 1994-95 for an action-research microfinance project in India.

He obtained his Ph.D. in Political Science from the University of Chicago in 2004.

In 2019-20, he served as a Distinguished Career Fellow at Stanford University.

Career:

Vikram Akula's career began with his involvement in grassroots rural development. After his Fulbright scholarship, he worked with the Deccan Development Society, a small rural non-profit organization in India.

He then worked as a researcher at the World watch Institute in Washington D.C., where he focused on poverty and sustainable development.

While at the University of Chicago as a Ph.D. student, Akula developed a business plan for a for-profit microfinance company.

In 1997, he returned to India to set up Swayam Krishi Sangam (SKS) as a non-profit organization initially.

SKS later converted into a for-profit microfinance institution, known as SKS Microfinance, in 2005.

The company attracted significant investments, including an equity investment of $11.5 million in March 2007 led by Sequoia Capital and a $75 million equity investment in November 2008.

In 2010, SKS Microfinance went public with an IPO on the Bombay Stock Exchange, raising $350 million.

Akula resigned from his role as Executive Chairperson in November 2011 and relinquished his role as a promoter of SKS in May 2014.

Influences:

Vikram Akula was inspired by the work of Muhammad Yunus, the founder of Grameen Bank in Bangladesh and a Nobel laureate, when founding SKS Microfinance.

He advocated for the idea that going public is essential for microfinance institutions to raise sufficient funds to provide micro-loans to impoverished individuals globally.

Controversy:

In 2010, SKS Microfinance faced controversy when the state government of Andhra Pradesh accused microfinance companies, including SKS, for the suicides of poor residents in the state.

Investigations revealed allegations of illegal practices, including harassment and coercion by SKS employees in debt recovery.

These events led to criticism of SKS's approach to microfinance.

Awards and Recognition:

Vikram Akula received numerous awards and recognition for his work in microfinance, including being named one of TIME magazine's 100 Most Influential People in the World in 2006.

He was honoured as the Social Entrepreneur of the Year in India in 2006 and received the Ernst & Young Entrepreneur of the Year awards in 2006 and 2010.

Akula also received awards such as the Godfrey Phillips National Bravery Award, the World Economic Forum's Young Global Leader award, and more.

Vikram Akula's journey in microfinance has been marked by his efforts to promote financial inclusion and alleviate poverty, even though it has faced both acclaim and criticism along the way. His contributions to the field have earned him recognition as a significant figure in the world of microfinance and social entrepreneurship.

11.7. Prof. David S. Gibbons:

Microfinance work and achievements of David S Gibbons and the microfinance institution CASHPOR Microcredit (CMC) in India.

Name: David S Gibbons

Background and Career:

In the 1990s, David S Gibbons embarked on a journey into the field of microfinance after studying the pioneering methodology of the Grameen Bank.

Before venturing into India, he successfully incubated AIM, a microfinance institution (MFI) in Malaysia, demonstrating his commitment to the microfinance sector.

In India, Gibbons founded CASHPOR Microcredit (CMC), an MFI focused on providing financial services to impoverished women.

CMC chose to operate in Uttar Pradesh (UP) and Bihar, two of India's poorest states, despite the challenges and reputation for lawlessness in these regions.

Over time, CMC has grown significantly and currently serves more than 300,000 poor women in UP and Bihar.

CMC has ambitious plans to extend its outreach further by aiming to reach 2.5 million poor women in the next five years.

Gibbons' approach to microfinance straddles two distinct schools of thought: the Welfarist School, emphasizing poverty lending and social impact, and the Institutionist School, focusing on building financial systems and sustainability.

His vision for CMC is to achieve the "double bottom line," which involves balancing social impact and financial sustainability, making CMC a financially sustainable MFI for the poor.

Achievements and Approaches:

Professor Gibbons has been instrumental in addressing various challenges faced by CMC during its initial years, including establishing credibility, navigating legal and regulatory complexities, and experimenting with lending methodologies.

To achieve the double bottom line, CMC has pursued strategies such as seeking subordinated debt and commercial loans instead of grants, initially charging higher-than-market interest rates and subsequently reducing them.

CMC has maintained a strict "No Tolerance for Arrears" policy to ensure timely repayments and financial sustainability.

The institution employs tools like the CASHPOR Housing Index (CHI) and assets tests to identify poor clients and prevent any deviation from their social objectives in pursuit of financial goals.

CMC has adapted its microfinance model, drawing inspiration from both the ASA (Bangladesh) and Grameen models, to suit the local conditions and needs of its clients.

David S Gibbons' work through CASHPOR Microcredit (CMC) reflects his dedication to microfinance as a means of improving the lives of impoverished women in India. His efforts to balance social impact and financial sustainability exemplify his commitment to the "double bottom line" approach in microfinance. This biography highlights his significant contributions to the field.

11.8. Madam Padmaja Reddy:

Padmaja Reddy is a highly accomplished entrepreneur and a passionate advocate for women's rights. With a career spanning over two decades in the financial services and development sectors, she has established herself as a visionary leader.

Full Name: Padmaja Reddy

Career Highlights:

Founder and Managing Director: Padmaja Reddy co-founded Spandana Sphoorty Financial Limited in January 2002 and served as its Managing Director for nearly 20 years until October 2021. During her tenure, she transformed Spandana from a not-for-profit entity into one of India's largest Microfinance Institutions (MFIs).

Leadership at Keertana Financial Limited: In November 2021, Padmaja Reddy took on the role of Managing Director at Keertana Financial

Limited, where she continues to contribute her expertise in the financial sector.

Recognition and Awards: Padmaja Reddy's contributions have not gone unnoticed. She has been recognized as a Women Achiever of the Year by ABP News, acknowledging her dedication to women's empowerment and social impact.

Global Engagement: Padmaja Reddy is actively involved in global initiatives as a member of the United Nations Global Compact and UN Women. Her commitment to sustainability, responsible business practices, and gender equality is evident in her participation in these organizations.

Accolades: In further recognition of her leadership and potential, Padmaja Reddy was honoured with 'The Economic Times Most Promising Women Leaders 2021' award powered by Femina. This accolade underscores her reputation as a determined and forward-thinking businesswoman.

Educational Background: Padmaja holds a master's degree in Business Administration, equipping her with the necessary knowledge and skills for her successful career.

Microfinance Expertise: She has pursued specialized training in Microfinance from esteemed institutions such as Naropa University, Durham University Business School, and Harvard Business School, further enhancing her expertise in the microfinance sector.

Padmaja Reddy's journey is characterized by her unwavering determination and foresight. Her dedication to empowering marginalized communities, particularly women, through financial inclusion and sustainable development, reflects her strong commitment to making a meaningful difference in the world.

11.9. Mr. M Uday Kumar:

M. Uday Kumar is a distinguished figure in the field of financial inclusion with over 35 years of dedicated experience. As the founder and Managing Director of Share Microfin Limited (SML), he has played a pivotal role in advancing financial inclusion and sustainable development financing in India.

Full Name: M. Uday Kumar

Professional Background:

Founder and Managing Director: M. Uday Kumar is the visionary founder and serves as the Managing Director of Share Microfin Limited (SML). His leadership and extensive expertise have been instrumental in guiding the growth of the company and its mission to promote financial inclusion.

Decades of Experience: With over three decades of hands-on experience, M. Uday Kumar possesses an in-depth understanding of financial inclusion, sustainable development financing, and the intricate dynamics of the microfinance sector.

Key Role in Regulatory Changes: He played a significant role during the challenging period when the Andhra Pradesh Microfinance Institutions Ordinance 2010 had a profound impact on microfinance entities operating in Andhra Pradesh. His leadership skills were crucial in navigating the regulatory changes.

Geographic Presence: Based in Hyderabad, Telangana, India, M. Uday Kumar operates in a region that has been at the forefront of India's microfinance and financial inclusion efforts.

M. Uday Kumar's unwavering commitment to financial inclusion and sustainable development financing has established him as a prominent figure in the microfinance sector. As the founder and Managing Director of Share Microfin Limited, he continues to lead the organization's endeavours to empower underserved communities through increased access to financial services. His extensive experience and dedication have made significant contributions to the advancement of financial inclusion in India.

11.10. Mr. Anup Singh:

Anup Kumar Singh is a respected pioneer in India's microfinance sector, boasting a career spanning over two decades. With extensive experience and expertise, he currently serves as the Managing Director on the Board of Sonata Finance Pvt. Ltd., a company he founded in 2006 with the goal of making microfinance self-sustainable and economically viable.

Key Highlights:

Founding Sonata Finance: Anup Kumar Singh established Sonata Finance in 2006 with the vision of creating a sustainable and economically viable microfinance institution. As the Managing Director, he is responsible for crafting innovative business models and strategies, assessing opportunities and risks, guiding day-to-day operations, and overseeing the overall functioning of the company to realize its mission and vision.

Achieving Sustainability: Under his capable leadership and mentorship, Sonata Finance has successfully achieved its goals and built a robust, sustainable, and value-creating business. While financial success is noteworthy, the true source of pride lies in the improvement of the income-generating capacity of numerous households, a testament to the company's positive social impact.

Grameen Bank Training: Before embarking on his journey with Sonata Finance, Anup Kumar Singh received training with the renowned Grameen Bank in Bangladesh, gaining insights and expertise in the microfinance domain.

Cashpor Group of Companies: Anup Singh's career includes over eight years of association with the Cashpor group of Companies, where he held significant roles. His tenure culminated in him serving as an ex-officio Chief Executive, making him one of the top executives within the Cashpor group of companies.

Educational Background: Anup Singh holds a Master's degree in Economics & Sociology, a Postgraduate Diploma in Rural Development and Management, and an MBA in Finance. His educational qualifications reflect his strong foundation in economics, rural development, and finance.

Personal Background: Born and raised in Uttar Pradesh, India, Anup Kumar Singh currently resides in Allahabad with his wife and three children.

Anup Kumar Singh's remarkable career is a testament to his commitment to microfinance, rural development, and economic empowerment. As a pioneer in the sector, he continues to make significant strides in improving the livelihoods of countless households and driving the microfinance industry towards sustainability and positive social impact.

11.11. Mr. Samit Ghosh:

Samit Ghosh is a prominent figure in the field of finance and microfinance, known for his contributions to financial inclusion in India.

Early Life and Education:

Samit Ghosh was born in 1949 in Dhanbad, India, to father Dr. Sailendra Kumar.

He spent a significant part of his early years in Dhanbad, where his father, a doctor, established government hospitals in coal mining areas.

Tragically, he lost his father at the age of 10, and his mother was a professor at Sri Shikshyatan College.

Ghosh completed his undergraduate degree in economics from St. Xavier's College in Kolkata.

He pursued a Master of Business Administration (MBA) with a specialization in finance from The Wharton School of Business at the University of Pennsylvania, United States.

Career:

Samit Ghosh boasts a distinguished banking career spanning over 30 years, with expertise in retail banking.

He commenced his career at Citibank in 1975.

Between 1980 and 1985, Ghosh served as the vice president for investment and corporate banking at Arab Bank in Bahrain.

In 1985, he returned to India and rejoined Citibank, where he was part of the team that launched retail banking in India in 1985.

Ghosh held the position of vice-president at Citibank from 1975-1980 and again from 1985-1993.

From 1993 to 1996, he served as the regional head of personal banking for South Asia and the Middle East at Standard Chartered Bank in Dubai.

Before founding Ujjivan, he served as the CEO at Bank of Muscat.

In November 2005, he founded Ujjivan Financial Services in Bengaluru as a non-deposit taking, non-banking financial company (NBFC), with a primary focus on microfinance, providing loans to women in urban and semi-urban areas.

In 2013, Ujjivan Financial Services obtained registration with the Reserve Bank of India (RBI) as a non-banking financial company - microfinance institution (NBFC-MFI).

From February 1, 2017, he held the position of Managing Director & CEO at Ujjivan Small Finance Bank until his retirement on November 30, 2019.

Currently, Ghosh serves as a Non-Executive, Non-Independent Director at Ujjivan Small Finance Bank.

Other Roles:

He has held leadership roles in various microfinance organizations, including serving as the president of Microfinance Institutions Network (MFIN) and chairman of Association of Karnataka Microfinance Institutions (AKMI).

Since April 2020, he has been serving as a CSI Partner at the Nudge Centre for Social Innovation, and as a Non-Executive Director at Parinaam Foundation since September 2020.

Awards and Honors:

In 2011, Ujjivan Financial Services, under his leadership, was awarded as Microfinance Organization of the Year.

Samit Ghosh received the Social Impact Entrepreneur of the Year Award in 2015 by Forbes India.

In 2019, he was honored for his contribution to advancing financial inclusion at the Inclusive Finance India Awards.

Samit Ghosh's journey from a banking career to the founding and leadership of Ujjivan Financial Services reflects his commitment to providing financial services to underserved communities, particularly women, and his significant impact on the microfinance sector in India. His accolades and leadership roles underscore his dedication to advancing financial inclusion and social impact.

11.12. Mr. R. Baskar Babu:

Baskar Babu is a notable figure in the financial services sector, particularly in the realm of small finance banks.

Overview:

Full Name: R. Baskar Babu
Primary Job Title: Co-Founder & Chief Executive Officer
Primary Organization: Suryoday Small Finance Bank
Location: Pune, Maharashtra, India
Regions: Asia-Pacific (APAC)

Career Highlights:

Baskar Babu co-founded Suryoday Micro Finance Private Limited in 2008 and currently serves as its Chief Executive Officer.

He has accumulated 17 years of experience in the financial services industry, holding leadership positions in various renowned organizations.

His previous roles include working with Cholamandalam-DBS, HDFC Bank, and GE Commercial Finance in various leadership capacities.

Career Timeline:

Suryoday Small Finance Bank: Co-Founder & Chief Executive Officer (December 2008 - Present)

GE Commercial Finance: Vice President & Head- Quality & Ops (July 2003 - July 2006)

HDFC Bank: Head-Products & Sales- CV Finance (January 2002 - July 2003)

Cholamandalam: Chief Marketing Officer (November 1992 - December 2001)

Education:

Baskar Babu pursued his MBA at Pondicherry University from 1990 to 1992.

Baskar Babu's career has been marked by his significant contributions to the financial services sector, particularly in microfinance. As the co-founder and CEO of Suryoday Small Finance Bank, he has played a pivotal role in shaping the institution's growth and impact. His extensive experience and leadership positions in notable organizations underscore his expertise in the field.

11.13. Mr. Rakesh Dubey:

Rakesh Dubey is a seasoned professional in the field of microfinance, known for his extensive experience and contributions to the industry.

Overview:

Full Name: Mr. Rakesh Dubey

Primary Job Title: CEO

Primary Organization: SV Creditline

Education:

Mr. Rakesh Dubey holds a Master's degree in Business Administration.

He also possesses a Post Graduate Diploma in Rural Development Management.

Career Highlights:

Mr. Dubey has more than 22 years of experience in the microfinance domain.

He specializes in setting up both domestic and international microfinance institutions, showcasing his expertise in this field.

Before joining SV Creditline, he co-founded SONATA Finance Pvt. Limited.

He was a founding team member of CASHPOR, a prominent Micro Finance Institution.

Both of these microfinance companies have made significant impacts by serving more than 1 million households in the heartland.

Additional Roles:

Mr. Rakesh Dubey served as the President of MFIN (Self-Regulatory body of Microfinance Institutions Network) from 2017 to 2018.

Currently, he is a member of the board of MFIN.

Training and Education:

He has undergone specialized training with INSEAD FRANCE in the Executive Leader Forum on "Enterprise Leaders in a VUCA World."

Mr. Dubey has attended the HBS-ACCION Strategic Leadership for Microfinance Practitioners program from the Harvard Business School.

Rakesh Dubey's career has been marked by his dedication to microfinance and his leadership in establishing and nurturing microfinance institutions, both nationally and internationally. His educational background and extensive experience make him a notable figure in the field of microfinance.

11.14. Mr. HP Singh:

Mr. HP Singh is a distinguished figure with a remarkable career and an impressive legacy in the field of microfinance and social innovation. With a law degree and a fellowship from The Institute of Chartered Accountants of India since 1984, his journey has been characterized by a deep commitment to improving the lives of countless individuals and families across India.

Early Career and Pioneering Contributions: Mr. Singh's career in microfinance spans over three decades, during which he made pioneering contributions that have left a lasting impact on the industry. One of his most notable innovations was the introduction of the concept of daily collection of loan repayments, making loan repayment more flexible and convenient for borrowers. This innovation revolutionized the microfinance sector, enabling access to financial services for millions of unserved families.

Versatile Expertise: Beyond his expertise in lending and microfinance, Mr. Singh possesses a wealth of knowledge and experience in various domains, including auditing, accounts, project financing, advisory services, and company law matters. This well-rounded skill set has been instrumental in his ability to drive strategic and operational success in his ventures.

Educational Pursuits: Mr. Singh's commitment to personal and professional growth is evident through his participation in prestigious programs. He attended the Harvard Business School's Action Program on Strategic Leadership for Microfinance in 2009, gaining insights and skills crucial to his leadership in the sector. In 2011, he furthered his leadership capabilities by participating in a program organized by Women's World Banking at Wharton Business School, University of Pennsylvania.

SATIN: A Visionary's Dream Realized: Mr. Singh's journey as a first-generation entrepreneur has been closely intertwined with SATIN, a microfinance institution he co-founded in 1990. His passion for social engineering and dedication to financial inclusion have guided SATIN to reach over 3.5 million Indian families, positively impacting their livelihoods. Under his visionary leadership, SATIN has become one of India's leading microfinance companies, with assets under management (AUM) of approximately `7,139 crore (as of August 31, 2019). The company has received recognition as a Fortune The Next 500 Company, a testament to Mr. Singh's strategic acumen.

Innovation and Expansion: Mr. Singh's commitment to innovation is evident in SATIN's evolution. The company has diversified its offerings through subsidiaries like Taarashna, Satin Housing Finance, and Satin Finserv, expanding its reach and impact. SATIN has also ventured into the fintech space with the launch of "Loan Dost," a digital platform for retail lending aimed at millennials, a pioneering move in the microfinance industry.

Social Impact Beyond Business: Mr. Singh's dedication to social change extends beyond the corporate world. In 2015, he founded the Global Social (India) Foundation (GSIF), a not-for-profit organization with a vision to create a better India. GSIF focuses on critical areas such as education, healthcare, poverty alleviation, and child labor eradication. His contributions have led to the inception of projects like iHero and Bachcha Party, aimed at fostering positive change in society.

Recognition and Awards: Mr. Singh's outstanding contributions have been acknowledged through prestigious awards. He received the 'Social Innovator' award at the Global HR Excellence Awards in February 2017 and the 'Exemplary Leader Award' in April 2018 in Kuala Lumpur, Malaysia.

Continued Leadership: Throughout SATIN's journey, Mr. Singh has remained at the helm, shaping the company's operations and long-term strategy. His guidance is expected to play a pivotal role in establishing SATIN as a differentiated and influential financial institution in India, furthering its mission of financial inclusion and social impact.

Mr. HP Singh's life and career epitomize the transformative power of visionary leadership, innovation, and a steadfast commitment to making a positive difference in the lives of millions. His legacy will continue to inspire generations to come.

11.15. Mr. Manoj Kumar Nambiar:

Manoj Kumar Nambiar is a prominent figure in the microfinance industry, known for his extensive experience and leadership.

Overview:

Full Name: Manoj Kumar Nambiar

Current Position: Managing Director of Arohan Financial Services Limited

Board Member: MFIN (Microfinance Institutions Network)

Career Highlights:

Manoj Kumar Nambiar possesses over 28 years of experience in consumer finance and retail banking.

He embarked on his career with Modi Xerox in 1988.

Over the years, he ventured into various roles in consumer financial services with GE Countrywide (1995), retail banking with ANZ Grindlays (1997), and retail assets & business development with ABN Amro Bank NV India (2000).

In 2002, he assumed the position of Head of Retail Banking at National Bank of Oman, overseeing operations in Oman, UAE, and Egypt.

Subsequently, he served as the Chief Operating Officer of Alhamrani-Nissan Finance Company, KSA in 2004.

In 2008, he returned to Oman as the Deputy CEO of Ahli Bank SAOG.

Education:

Manoj Kumar Nambiar completed his Mechanical Engineering degree from VJTI (Veermata Jijabai Technological Institute) in 1986.

He pursued an MBA in Marketing from JBIMS (Jamnalal Bajaj Institute of Management Studies) in 1988, both from Mumbai University.

He holds tertiary qualifications in insurance from the Insurance Institute of India.

Notable Accomplishments:

Manoj Kumar Nambiar completed the "Strategic Leadership in Microfinance" course from Harvard Business School, Boston.

He also participated in the "Strategy meets Leadership" course at INSEAD, France.

Leadership Roles:

Mr. Nambiar is currently the Managing Director of Arohan Financial Services Limited.

He is a Director on the boards of IntelleCash Microfinance Network Company (P) Limited, Aavishkaar Venture Management Services (P) Limited, and Intellecap Software Technologies (P) Limited.

Association with MFIN:

Mr. Manoj Kumar Nambiar joined the governing board of MFIN (Microfinance Institutions Network) in early 2013.

He served as the President of the MFIN Board in FY15-16, FY19-20, FY20-21.

Manoj Kumar Nambiar's career has been marked by his dedication to the microfinance sector and his leadership in various key positions. His extensive experience and education make him a respected figure in the field of microfinance.

11.16. Mr. Uday Kumar Hebbar:

Udaya Kumar Hebbar is a prominent figure in the microfinance industry, known for his extensive experience and leadership.

Overview:

Current Position: Managing Director & CEO of CreditAccess Grameen Limited (CA Grameen)

Chairperson: Microfinance Institutions Network (MFIN)

Career Highlights:

Udaya Kumar Hebbar is a veteran in the microfinance industry and is recognized for establishing the success of inclusive finance through a market-based model.

He boasts a remarkable career spanning over 35 years with a diverse background encompassing operations, rural banking, agriculture, and micro-banking.

Before assuming his role at CA Grameen, he held several leadership positions, including the role of Head of Commercial Banking and Payment Operations at Barclays Bank PLC.

He also had successful stints of over a decade each at Corporation Bank and ICICI Bank, where he likely gained substantial banking and financial experience.

Education:

Udaya Kumar Hebbar holds a Master's degree in Commerce from Karnatak University, Dharwad.

He is a certificated associate from the Indian Institute of Bankers.

Additionally, he holds a diploma from Vanderbilt University.

Leadership Roles:

Mr. Hebbar currently serves as the Managing Director & CEO of CreditAccess Grameen Limited, where he has played a pivotal role in establishing the company as a leading microfinance institution in India.

Association with MFIN:

Udaya Kumar Hebbar serves as the Chairperson of the Microfinance Institutions Network (MFIN), demonstrating his commitment to the microfinance sector and its growth.

Udaya Kumar Hebbar's career trajectory reflects his profound expertise in banking and microfinance. His leadership at CA Grameen and as the Chairperson of MFIN underscores his dedication to the industry's development and financial inclusion in India.

11.17. Mr. Govind Singh:

Mr. Govind Singh is a distinguished figure in the banking and finance sector, renowned for his extensive experience and leadership in various facets of the industry. As the Managing Director and Chief Executive Officer of Utkarsh Small Finance Bank, he has played a pivotal role in shaping the institution's growth and success. His career journey is marked by a commitment to financial inclusion and innovation.

Educational Background: Mr. Govind Singh's journey began with a strong foundation in education. He holds a bachelor's degree in commerce from Delhi University. In addition to his academic achievements, he is a certified associate of the Indian Institute of Bankers, reflecting his dedication to professional development and expertise in the field.

Banking and Finance Expertise: With a career spanning over 30 years, Mr. Singh possesses a wealth of knowledge and experience in various aspects of banking and finance. His career trajectory includes significant roles at prestigious financial institutions:

ICICI Bank: Prior to his leadership at Utkarsh Small Finance Bank, Mr. Singh served at ICICI Bank, one of India's largest private sector banks. During his tenure, he held several critical positions, including Business Head for Micro Banking. In this role, he oversaw the largest microfinance portfolio among commercial banks in India, managing relationships with over 100 Microfinance Institutions (MFIs) and overseeing the Business Correspondent and Bulk Jewel Loan businesses.

Varied Experience: Mr. Singh's career at ICICI Bank was diverse, encompassing roles such as Business Head for Rural and Agri Liabilities, Trust, Societies, Associations, and Clubs (TASC) segment. He also gained extensive experience with the Retail Liabilities group and Retail Infrastructure Group at the bank.

Other Financial Institutions: Mr. Singh's career extends beyond ICICI Bank, with stints at institutions like UTI Bank Ltd. (now Axis Bank), Bank International Indonesia, Surya Fincap Limited, Allahabad Bank, and State Bank of Patiala (which later amalgamated with State Bank of India). His broad exposure to various facets of banking and finance has contributed to his comprehensive expertise.

Contributions to Financial Inclusion: Mr. Singh's commitment to financial inclusion is evident in his work. He was nominated by ICICI Bank to serve on the boards of Cashpor Micro Credit and Asmitha Microfin Ltd. He also participated in RBI's Working Group to Review the Business Correspondent Model, showcasing his dedication to improving financial services access for underserved communities.

Leadership at Utkarsh Small Finance Bank: As the founder and Managing Director & CEO of Utkarsh Small Finance Bank Limited, Mr. Govind Singh has led the institution with vision and dedication. Utkarsh Small Finance Bank has emerged as a significant player in the microfinance sector under his leadership. His innovative approach and strategic guidance have positioned the bank for growth and success.

Professional Associations: Mr. Singh is associated with various professional organizations, including the Indian Institute of Bankers (IIBF), where he earned his certification. His commitment to continuous learning and professional development is a testament to his dedication to the banking and finance industry.

Legacy and Recognition: Throughout his career, Mr. Govind Singh's contributions have been recognized and celebrated. Notably, he received the "Award of Excellence for Apy Big Believers (ABB) 4.0" from the Pension Fund Regulatory and Development Authority in Fiscal 2022.

Mr. Govind Singh's remarkable journey in the banking and finance sector reflects his unwavering commitment to financial inclusion, innovation, and excellence. His leadership at Utkarsh Small Finance Bank continues to make a significant impact on the industry and the lives of the communities it serves.

11.18. Mr. Vivek Tiwari:

Mr. Vivek Tiwari is a prominent figure in the field of microfinance and development, known for his visionary leadership and significant contributions to financial inclusion and social entrepreneurship. With a diverse educational background and nearly two decades of experience in the sector, he has been instrumental in driving innovation and responsible lending within the microfinance industry.

Educational Background: Mr. Tiwari holds a Post Graduate Degree in Rural Development & Management from the Institute of Engineering & Rural Technology at Allahabad. This academic foundation laid the groundwork for his career dedicated to improving the lives of underserved communities.

Certified Professional: He is not only well-educated but also a certified professional, having completed the Concentration in Management Program from Boulder Microfinance Training in Italy. This certification reflects his commitment to continuous learning and development in the field of microfinance.

Leadership in Microfinance: With over 20 years of experience in the Microfinance and Development Sector, Mr. Vivek Tiwari has been a driving force behind several transformative initiatives. His expertise and leadership extend to various aspects of microfinance, including responsible lending, financial inclusion, social entrepreneurship, and impact investing.

MFIN Vice Chairperson: Mr. Tiwari's dedication to the microfinance sector is further highlighted by his role as the Vice Chairperson of MFIN (Microfinance Institutions Network), an influential association representing the microfinance sector in India. This position underscores his commitment to the industry's growth and development.

Recognition: Mr. Tiwari's outstanding contributions have not gone unnoticed. He was honoured as one of the "Promising Entrepreneurs of India 2021" by The Economic Times, recognizing his significant impact on the micro-lending space and his visionary thinking.

Founding SATYA: Under Mr. Tiwari's far-sighted leadership, SATYA has emerged as one of the fastest-growing MFIs (Microfinance Institutions) in the country. Even in the face of formidable challenges like Demonetization, the IL & FS Crisis, and the COVID-19 Pandemic, he has successfully built a robust network with over 3,000 employees operating across 22 states. His strategic vision prioritizes expansion, ethical practices, and the development of entrepreneurship opportunities for the economically marginalized, particularly those at the Bottom of the Pyramid.

Role at SATYA: Mr. Tiwari serves as the Founder, CEO, CIO, and Managing Director of Satya MicroCapital, a testament to his multifaceted leadership within the organization.

Previous Contributions: Prior to founding SATYA, Mr. Tiwari played a significant role in the transformation of Satin Credit Care Network Ltd (SCNL) as the Chief Operating Officer. Under his leadership, SCNL's portfolio grew from INR 50 crore to INR 4,000 crore, contributing significantly to the financial inclusion movement.

Awards and Recognition: His contributions have earned him prestigious awards such as the BFSI Leadership Award and the "India Jyoti Award" by India International Friendship Society, further highlighting his invaluable role in advancing financial inclusion and microfinance.

Mr. Vivek Tiwari's career is characterized by a deep commitment to improving the lives of marginalized communities through innovative microfinance solutions. His leadership, vision, and dedication have left an indelible mark on the microfinance industry in India and continue to drive positive change for those in need.

11.19. Mr. Shirish Chandra Panda:

Mr. Shirish Chandra Panda is a highly accomplished professional with a distinguished career in the financial services industry, particularly in microfinance and retail banking. He has a wealth of experience spanning over 23 years and has held key positions in various organizations. Currently, he serves as the Business Head, Microfinance at Tata Capital, one of India's leading financial institutions.

Professional Journey:

Tata Capital: As the Business Head, Microfinance at Tata Capital, Mr. Panda plays a pivotal role in overseeing and managing microfinance operations within the organization. His leadership and expertise contribute to Tata Capital's continued growth and success in the microfinance sector.

Arohan Financial Services Limited: He also held the position of Head of Business and Executive Vice President at Arohan Financial Services Limited, further demonstrating his commitment to the microfinance sector.

Satin Creditcare Networks Limited: Mr. Panda has a notable history with Satin Creditcare Networks Limited, where he served in multiple capacities. These roles included Head of Internal Audit and Risk Management, Deputy Chief Operating Officer, and Vice President of Operations. His contributions were instrumental in the company's success and expansion.

IFMR KGFS: Shirish Chandra Panda was the Chief Operating Officer of IFMR KGFS, where he played a crucial role in setting up two business units, including Puddhuaru KGFS in Tamil Nadu and Dhanei KGFS in Odisha.

BASIX: He began his career at BASIX, starting as a Field Executive and advancing to the position of Unit Head between 2001 and 2007, laying the strong foundation for his work in microfinance.

Educational Background:

Mr. Panda's educational qualifications include an Advanced Diploma in Strategy for Leaders from the Indian Institute of Management, Lucknow. This educational foundation has complemented his practical experience in financial services.

Professional Expertise:

Throughout his career, Mr. Shirish Chandra Panda has honed his skills in various aspects of microfinance, retail banking, credit, and risk management. His leadership and strategic thinking have been key drivers of success in the organizations he has served.

Current Position: As of the latest available information, Mr. Panda is actively contributing to Tata Capital's microfinance initiatives as the Business Head, Microfinance.

Mr. Panda's extensive experience, strategic acumen, and commitment to the financial services industry have made him a respected figure in the microfinance sector. His role at Tata Capital underscores his dedication to driving financial inclusion and empowering individuals and small businesses through microfinance solutions.

11.20. Mr. Shalabh Saxena:

Mr. Shalabh Saxena is a seasoned professional in the Consumer Banking and Life Insurance industry with a remarkable career spanning over 28 years. He currently serves as the Managing Director and CEO of Spandana Sphoorty, one of the country's leading microfinance institutions. His extensive expertise and accomplishments within the sector have made him a prominent figure in the financial world.

Background and Education: Mr. Shalabh Saxena holds a degree in Economics and completed his MBA in Marketing from B K School of Management, Ahmedabad. His educational background laid a solid foundation for his subsequent achievements in the business world.

Career Highlights: Throughout his illustrious career, Mr. Saxena has held several pivotal roles in renowned organizations, showcasing his versatility and leadership abilities. Notable positions he has held include:

Managing Director & CEO at India Financial Inclusion Limited (BFIL): Before joining Spandana Sphoorty, Mr. Saxena served as the MD & CEO of BFIL, a significant microfinance institution in India.

Chief Operating Officer at HSBC Life Insurance: He held the role of Chief Operating Officer at HSBC Life Insurance, contributing to the growth and operational excellence of the company.

Roles at ING Life Insurance & Standard Chartered Bank: Mr. Saxena's career also includes key roles at ING Life Insurance and Standard Chartered Bank, where he gained valuable experience and insights into the financial and insurance sectors.

Expertise: Mr. Saxena's expertise spans various domains, including distribution and sales management in large business environments, marketing, strategic planning, information technology, alliances, and acquisitions. His well-rounded skill set has played a pivotal role in driving growth and success in the organizations.

New Leadership at Spandana Sphoorty: Mr. Shalabh Saxena took on the crucial role of Managing Director and CEO at Spandana Sphoorty, a significant microfinance institution. His appointment came at a critical time for the organization, following changes in leadership and concerns over a potential sale to Axis Bank.

Mr. Shalabh Saxena's extensive experience and strong leadership have positioned him as a key figure in the financial services industry, and his appointment at Spandana Sphoorty, gives stability to company.

11.21. Mr. Devesh Sachdev:

Devesh Sachdev is a seasoned professional with a rich background in the service industry and a strong entrepreneurial spirit. Here's a brief overview of his career and accomplishments:

Overview:

Current Position: Co-Founder & CEO of Fusion Microfinance

Chairperson: Governing board of Microfinance Institutions Network (MFIN)

Investor Type: Individual/Angel

Career Highlights:

Devesh Sachdev holds a Post Graduate degree from XLRI and has amassed 25 years of experience in the service industry before venturing into microfinance with Fusion Microfinance in 2009-10.

He commenced his career with Citigroup, where he was a part of the Credit Card Operations team in Delhi for 4 years.

His entrepreneurial journey began with BSA, a logistics company, where he played a pivotal role in the company's growth. He transformed BSA from a single-city operation with limited-service offerings to a nationwide presence, establishing it as the market leader in its segment.

Devesh Sachdev's expertise encompasses various aspects of business, including strategic management, relationship management, and cost-efficient team management.

Educational Background:

Devesh Sachdev has completed a Strategic Leadership Program at Harvard Business School, showcasing his commitment to continuous learning and leadership development.

Leadership Role at MFIN:

Devesh Sachdev serves as the Chairperson of the governing board of the Microfinance Institutions Network (MFIN), a Self-Regulatory Organization for NBFC-MFIs in India. MFIN collaborates closely with regulators and stakeholders to contribute actively to the financial inclusion dialogue through microfinance.

Devesh Sachdev's career trajectory reflects his diverse experience in the service industry, his entrepreneurial acumen, and his dedication to promoting financial inclusion through microfinance in India. His role as Chairperson at MFIN underscores his commitment to the industry's growth and development.

11.22. Mr. Pathangi Narasimhan Vasudevan (PN):

Vasudevan Pathangi Narasimhan (PN) has had a distinguished career in the financial services sector and currently serves as the Managing Director (MD) and Chief Executive Officer (CEO) of Equitas Small Finance Bank Limited.

Background and Career Highlights:

PN Vasudevan was initially appointed as the MD of Erstwhile Equitas Finance Limited, which has since transitioned into a bank, on July 23, 2016.

He holds a bachelor's degree in science (physics) from the University of Madras.

Additionally, he is a qualified company secretary certified by the Institute of Company Secretaries of India.

Vasudevan has accumulated extensive experience in the financial services sector, spanning over two decades.

He began his career as a management trainee in Cholamandalam Investment and Finance Company Limited, which is part of the Murugappa Group. During his tenure, he held various roles and eventually resigned as the Vice President and Head of Vehicle Finance.

Vasudevan further expanded his expertise by serving as the Executive Vice President and Head of Consumer Banking Group in Development Credit Bank Limited for a period of over one and a half years.

His contributions also extend to industry associations, as he held the position of Chairman of the Managing Committee of the South India Hire Purchase Association for the fiscal year 2006.

Reappointment as MD & CEO of Equitas Small Finance Bank:

The board of directors of Equitas Small Finance Bank Limited approved the proposal to reappoint Vasudevan PN as the MD & CEO for an additional three-year term, effective from July 23, 2022, to July 22, 2025. This decision is subject to RBI (Reserve Bank of India) and shareholders' approval.

Vasudevan's career journey reflects his deep-rooted expertise in financial services and his substantial contributions to the sector. His reappointment as the MD & CEO of Equitas Small Finance Bank signifies his continued leadership in the organization.

11.23. Mr. Chandra Shekhar Ghosh:

Chandra Shekhar Ghosh is a prominent figure in the financial industry known for his role as the Founder, Managing Director, and CEO of Bandhan Bank. He has dedicated over three decades to the fields of microfinance and development, contributing significantly to financial inclusion in India.

Early Life and Education:

Chandra Shekhar Ghosh was born on August 8, 1960, in Bishalgarh, Tripura, India.

His father, Late Haripada Ghosh, operated a sweet shop in Tripura, and Ghosh assisted his father at the shop during his student years.

Ghosh pursued his education and later joined BRAC, Bangladesh's largest non-government organization (NGO).

After returning to India, he worked with several NGOs and eventually founded Bandhan-Konnagar, a not-for-profit organization in West Bengal, dedicated to providing microfinance services to marginalized individuals, thus promoting financial inclusion. Ghosh holds a Master's degree in Statistics.

Career:

In 2001, Chandra Shekhar Ghosh initiated Bandhan-Konnagar, an NGO focused on offering micro-credit to marginalized women, empowering them to become entrepreneurs.

In 2009, the microfinance portfolio of Bandhan-Konnagar was transferred to a Non-Banking Financial Company (NBFC) that Bandhan had acquired in 2006.

Gradually, the organization expanded its operations across various states in India, and by 2010, Bandhan had become the largest microfinance institution in India.

In 2014, Bandhan received approval in principle from the Reserve Bank of India (RBI) to establish a universal bank. The final license was granted in June 2015.

Bandhan Bank commenced its operations on August 23, 2015, marking the first instance of an Indian microfinance institution transforming into a universal bank. It is also the first bank established in Eastern India since Independence.

Chandra Shekhar Ghosh has held prestigious positions such as the Chairman of The Confederation of Indian Industry (CII), Eastern Region, and the President of Bengal Chamber of Commerce & Industry (BCC&I). He is associated with various other industry bodies.

Awards and Recognitions:

Ghosh received the 'Senior Ashoka Fellow' award in 2007 from the Ashoka Foundation, recognizing his contributions to social entrepreneurship.

He was honoured as the 'Entrepreneur with Social Impact' in 2014 at the Forbes India Leadership Awards.

In 2014, The Economic Times named him 'Entrepreneur of the Year'.

Chandra Shekhar Ghosh was recognized as the 'Banker of the Year' for 2018-19 by Business Standard.

In 2016, he received the CNN-IBN 'Indian of the Year' award in the Business category.

Personal Life:

Chandra Shekhar Ghosh's journey from a small-town background to becoming a trailblazer in microfinance and banking showcases his dedication to improving financial inclusion and empowering marginalized communities in India.

11.24. Mr. V S Radhakrishn:

V S Radhakrishn is the founder and CEO of Microfinance India, a non-profit organization that provides microloans to rural and urban poor individuals and small businesses. He has been instrumental in promoting microfinance as a tool for poverty alleviation and financial inclusion in India. Under his leadership, Microfinance India has disbursed over $100 million in microloans to over 1 million borrowers across the country.

11.25. Mr. Dibyajyoti Pattanaik:

Dibyajyoti Pattanaik is a notable individual recognized for his contributions to microfinance and micro-enterprise development. He has been acknowledged by Forbes India as one of "India's 100 Great People Managers 2021."

Dibyajyoti Pattanaik is an alumnus of the Entrepreneurship Development Institute of India (EDII). He is the director of Annapurna Finance Pvt Ltd, a company based in Bhubaneswar, Odisha, India. With over 16 years of experience, he has worked extensively in the fields of microfinance, micro-enterprise development, and development sector consulting.

His journey in microfinance began when he joined "People's Forum," a non-governmental organization, after completing the Post Graduate Programme in Management (Batch 2002-03). People's Forum focused on providing credit services to individuals at the bottom of the economic pyramid.

In 2005, Dibyajyoti Pattanaik, in collaboration with the founder of People's Forum, established Annapurna Finance. The mission of Annapurna Finance was to empower women and promote financial independence. It aimed to provide resources and support in critical areas such as women's empowerment, sanitation, health, child protection, and more. Over the years, Dibyajyoti has played a significant role in empowering millions of underprivileged individuals.

Under his leadership, Annapurna Finance Pvt. Ltd. evolved into one of the top 10 Non-Banking Financial Companies-Microfinance Institutions (NBFC-MFIs) in the industry. Additionally, Dibyajyoti Pattanaik serves as the President of the Odisha Association of Financial Inclusion, an organization dedicated to advancing financial inclusion in Odisha and serving the needs of the economically disadvantaged through responsible finance.

Dibyajyoti Pattanaik's work in the microfinance sector and his commitment to empowering marginalized communities have earned him recognition as a great people manager and leader in India. His efforts have contributed to the financial inclusion and empowerment of countless individuals and communities in Odisha and beyond.

11.26. Mr. Vineet Chattree:

Vineet Chattree is a highly experienced professional with over 25 years of expertise in Operations and Management Consulting, having worked in various regions including India, the USA, and the Middle East. He currently serves as the Managing Director of Svatantra Microfin and Svatantra Micro Housing Finance.

Vineet's career has been marked by his deep commitment to serving the financially excluded segment, and his strategic thinking has been instrumental in driving accelerated, differentiated, and sustainable growth for both Svatantra Microfin and Svatantra Micro Housing. These organizations have earned recognition as impactful and respected entities in their respective fields.

Vineet strongly believes that an organization can achieve sustainable growth only if it makes a meaningful difference in the lives of its customers. He emphasizes the importance of aligning all aspects of business, including 'People, Product, and Processes,' with the needs of customers to achieve this goal.

As a dedicated lifelong learner, Vineet holds a degree in chemical engineering and has pursued post-graduate studies in Business Administration. He is currently working on a post-graduate degree in Business Laws and has also attended an executive program at The Wharton School.

Vineet Chattree serves on the board of both Svatantra Microfin Pvt. Ltd. and Svatantra Micro Housing Finance Corporation Ltd. He has also contributed to the microfinance industry by serving on the board of MFIN, which is a Self-Regulatory Organization (SRO) for the microfinance sector.

11.27. Mr. Mukul Jaiswal

Mukul Jaiswal is a distinguished professional in the field of microfinance, holding the esteemed position of Managing Director at Cashpor Micro Credit.

Full Name: Mukul Jaiswal

Professional Journey:

Current Role: Mukul Jaiswal has been serving as the Managing Director at Cashpor Micro Credit since June 2009. His leadership and expertise have played a pivotal role in the organization's success.

A Visionary Leader: Mukul Jaiswal's tenure as Managing Director at Cashpor Micro Credit reflects his commitment to the microfinance sector. He has been instrumental in guiding the organization's strategies and operations, contributing to its growth and impact.

Corporate Affiliations: Mukul Jaiswal is associated with multiple companies, showcasing his versatile leadership. He holds the position of

Director at Cashpor Financial And Technical Services Private Limited and Aayushya Foundation, further underlining his dedication to financial inclusion and development initiatives.

Past Engagements: Prior to his current roles, Mukul Jaiswal was associated with three other companies: Jeevanshree Inclusive Finance India Private Limited, Bhartiya Micro Credit, and Satya Microcapital Limited. His extensive experience and contributions in these roles have contributed to his standing in the microfinance industry.

Geographic Presence: Mukul Jaiswal resides in Varanasi, Uttar Pradesh, India, and his professional endeavors are closely tied to the region.

Mukul Jaiswal's career is characterized by his dedication to microfinance and financial inclusion. As Managing Director at Cashpor Micro Credit, he continues to make a meaningful impact on the lives of underserved communities while driving the organization's mission forward. His contributions to various companies in the sector underscore his commitment to creating positive change through financial services and development initiatives.

11.28. Mr. Gyan Mohan:

Mr. Gyan Mohan is a seasoned professional who has held various significant positions in his career, with notable involvements in the finance and banking sectors. As of the latest available information, he is associated with the following organizations:

1. **Adi Chitragupta Finance Ltd:** Mr. Mohan holds the position of Director at Adi Chitragupta Finance Ltd., where he likely plays a role in overseeing the company's operations and decision-making processes.

2. **Century Metal Recycling Ltd:** Additionally, Mr. Gyan Mohan serves as an Independent Director on the board of Century Metal Recycling Ltd. This role reflects his expertise and contributions to the company's governance and strategic direction.

Past Career Highlights:

Throughout his career, Mr. Gyan Mohan has accumulated valuable experience in various roles:

The Investment Trust of India Ltd: He served as an Associate at The Investment Trust of India Ltd., where he may have been involved in investment-related activities.

Power Exchange India Ltd: Mr. Mohan worked as an Associate for Power Exchange India Ltd., indicating his involvement in the energy exchange industry.

State Bank of India: He has been associated with the State Bank of India, one of India's largest and most prominent banks, likely contributing to the banking sector in various capacities.

IDBI Capital Markets & Securities Ltd: Mr. Mohan also worked as an Associate of IDBI Capital Markets & Securities Ltd., where he might have been involved in capital market activities and securities trading.

Education: Mr. Gyan Mohan holds a degree from Patna University, which has likely provided him with a strong foundation for his career in finance and related fields.

Membership: He is also a Member of the Indian Institute of Banking & Finance, indicating his commitment to professional development and the financial sector.

As an experienced professional with a diverse background in finance and banking, Mr. Gyan Mohan brings a wealth of knowledge and expertise to the organizations he is associated with. His role as an Independent Director and Director in various companies demonstrates his ongoing contributions to the Microfinance and corporate sector.

11.29. Mr. Sadaf Sayeed:

Mr. Sadaf Sayeed: Empowering Communities through Financial Inclusion

Mr. Sadaf Sayeed is a distinguished figure in the world of finance, known for his relentless dedication to expanding financial access and opportunities for individuals and communities in need. As the Chief Executive Officer of Muthoot Microfin, he has played a pivotal role in driving positive change and enabling financial empowerment.

Educational Background and Early Career:

Sadaf Sayeed holds a Bachelor of Commerce (Honours) degree from the prestigious University of Delhi, a testament to his strong academic foundation. He furthered his education by obtaining a Master of Business Administration degree from Guru Gobind Singh Indraprastha University.

With a solid educational background, Sadaf embarked on a remarkable career journey that spans over 22 years in the banking and financial services industry. His wealth of experience and expertise in this field has positioned him as a dynamic leader capable of effecting significant change.

Association with Muthoot Pappachan Group:

Sadaf Sayeed's association with the Muthoot Pappachan Group for the last 12 years speaks volumes about his commitment and loyalty to the organization. During his tenure, he has not only demonstrated his prowess in financial management but has also made substantial contributions to the group's growth and diversification.

His journey within the Muthoot Group includes a significant role as the Chief Operating Officer of the microfinance division at Muthoot Fincorp Limited. In this capacity, he played a crucial role in expanding the company's reach and impact, particularly in the microfinance sector.

A Visionary Leader at Muthoot Microfin:

As the Chief Executive Officer of Muthoot Microfin, Sadaf Sayeed has been at the helm of an organization committed to fostering financial inclusion, particularly among rural women. Under his visionary leadership, Muthoot Microfin has embarked on a mission to support the entrepreneurial aspirations of disadvantaged women, empowering them to achieve financial independence and self-sufficiency.

The organization's focus extends beyond traditional finance, encompassing a range of services, including microloans, personal loans, insurance, and more. Sadaf's unwavering dedication to this cause is rooted in the belief that financial support can be a powerful tool for positive change, especially in disadvantaged communities.

Contributions to Financial Inclusion:

Sadaf Sayeed's work aligns with the broader vision of the Muthoot Group, which is renowned for its gold loan services and is one of the largest gold loan NBFCs in India. Beyond gold loans, the group diversifies into various financial services, such as housing finance, money transfer, foreign exchange, and non-convertible debentures (NCD).

Through his leadership, Sadaf has contributed significantly to expanding the Muthoot Group's footprint and impact, thereby reaching more individuals and communities in need of financial assistance and guidance.

Sadaf Sayeed is a finance luminary with a heart for empowering communities through financial inclusion. His journey, marked by dedication, expertise, and a commitment to making a positive impact, showcases his remarkable contributions to the world of finance. As the CEO of Muthoot Microfin, he continues to be a beacon of hope, working tirelessly to provide disadvantaged women with the financial support they need to thrive and succeed. In the ever-evolving landscape of financial services, Sadaf Sayeed stands as a symbol of positive change and empowerment.

11.30. Mr. K. M. Vishwanathan:

Mr. K M Vishwanathan is a seasoned professional in the Banking, Financial Services, and Insurance (BFSI) sector with an illustrious career spanning 33 years. His extensive experience covers various aspects of banking and financial management, making him a well-rounded expert in the field. Here's a brief biography highlighting his remarkable journey:

Educational Background: Mr. Vishwanathan holds a Master's degree in Financial Management from the prestigious Jamnalal Bajaj Institute of Management Studies, Mumbai University. His educational foundation has undoubtedly contributed to his comprehensive understanding of financial management and banking principles.

Career Highlights:

Karnataka Bank Ltd: Mr. Vishwanathan began his career at Karnataka Bank Ltd., where he gained valuable experience in branch banking, retail assets, and credit management. This early exposure laid the groundwork for his successful career in the BFSI sector.

Cholamandalam Finance: He transitioned to Cholamandalam Finance, where he honed his skills in NBFC lending. This experience in the non-banking financial sector broadened his understanding of diverse financial products and services.

HDFC Bank Ltd: Mr. Vishwanathan's career reached new heights during his tenure at HDFC Bank Ltd., where he spent approximately 10 years. He held the position of Vice President and played a pivotal role in the Credit function of the Commercial & Business Banking Group. Notably, he was a founding member of the Commercial business team and was instrumental in building and managing a substantial book of approximately Rs 6,500 Crores. This achievement underscores his leadership and contribution to HDFC Bank's success.

Microfinance Expertise: While his career predominantly focused on traditional banking and financial services, Mr. Vishwanathan transitioned into the microfinance sector, bringing with him a wealth of experience and expertise. He currently serves as the MD & CEO of M Power Micro Finance Pvt. Ltd., where he has spent a decade as a microfinance practitioner.

Comprehensive BFSI Experience: Mr. Vishwanathan's career spans retail branch banking, retail assets, business banking, credit management, and risk management. His diverse background in the BFSI sector positions him as a valuable asset with a deep understanding of various financial domains.

Throughout his career, Mr. K M Vishwanathan has demonstrated exceptional leadership, strategic thinking, and a commitment to excellence in the financial services industry. His journey reflects a continuous pursuit of knowledge and a dedication to delivering value to the organizations he has been a part of.

CEOs of Microfinance along with mfin team members (Photo courtesy mfin):

11.32. Mr. Alok Prasad

Alok Prasad is a distinguished professional with a rich background in the banking and financial services sector, characterized by over 34 years of experience.

Full Name: Alok Prasad

Education:

Alok Prasad pursued his higher education at the University of Delhi, where he earned a master's degree in arts.

Career Journey:

Reserve Bank of India (RBI):

Alok Prasad embarked on his professional journey with the Reserve Bank of India (RBI) in 1976. He joined the prestigious institution as a member of the elite senior staff officer cadre (Grade B direct recruit).

During his tenure at RBI, he served with distinction in various central office departments, contributing to the institution's critical functions.

National Housing Bank (NHB):

Alok Prasad transitioned to the National Housing Bank (NHB) in 1989, where he continued to make significant contributions to the financial sector.

At NHB, a statutory body wholly owned by RBI, he played a pivotal role in formulating policies aimed at developing the housing finance sector.

Microfinance Institutions Network (MFIN):

Alok Prasad assumed the position of CEO at the Microfinance Institutions Network (MFIN), a self-regulatory organization of RBI-regulated NBFC-Microfinance Institutions NBFC-MFIs.

MFIN is the primary representative body for these institutions and focuses on promoting responsible lending, client protection, good governance, and a supportive regulatory environment.

Under Alok Prasad's leadership, MFIN has played a crucial role in the development and regulation of the microfinance sector in India.

Private Sector Experience:

Alok Prasad's career also includes valuable experience in the private sector. He served as the Country Director for Citi Microfinance Group in India, where he played a pivotal role in Citi's exponential growth in the microfinance sector.

He was a member of the board of directors of CitiFinancial and Citicorp Maruti Finance Ltd.

Board Memberships:

Alok Prasad has served on the board of directors of several companies, including Gang-Jong Development Finance Private Limited and Fincare Small Finance Bank Limited.

Leadership and Contributions:

Alok Prasad's extensive experience, which includes both public and private sectors, has established him as a veteran banker in the Indian financial landscape. His contributions to the RBI, NHB, and microfinance sector have been instrumental in shaping policies and promoting responsible financial practices. His leadership at MFIN reflects his dedication to the robust development of the microfinance sector in India.

Alok Prasad's career is marked by a commitment to financial inclusion, regulatory excellence, and responsible lending practices. His vast experience and expertise continue to benefit the Indian financial industry.

11.33. Ms. Ratna Viswanathan:

Ratna Viswanathan is a seasoned professional who has made significant contributions to the microfinance industry in India.

Full Name: Ratna Viswanathan

Career Overview:

Ratna Viswanathan served as the CEO of the Microfinance Institutions Network (MFIN), a self-regulatory organization (SRO) representing microfinance institutions (MFIs) in India. During her tenure, she played a vital role in shaping the microfinance sector in the country.

Leadership at MFIN:

Ratna Viswanathan assumed the role of CEO at MFIN during a crucial period of transformation in the microfinance industry. Her leadership was marked by a strong commitment to promoting responsible lending practices and ensuring the welfare of microfinance clients.

Under her guidance, MFIN initiated various regulatory changes in the microfinance sector, contributing to its growth and development. Ratna Viswanathan recognized the challenges and opportunities faced by the industry, particularly as some MFIs transitioned into small finance banks.

Industry Growth and Outlook:

During her tenure, Ratna Viswanathan emphasized the positive outlook for the microfinance industry, highlighting its potential for sustained high double-digit growth. She acknowledged the changes in the sector, including the shift of some major MFIs towards becoming banks, such as Bandhan.

Despite these changes, Ratna Viswanathan believed that there was ample space for growth and investment in the microfinance sector. She noted that the Reserve Bank of India (RBI) had raised MFI lending limits, paving the way for more capital inflow into the sector.

Impact of Small Finance Banks:

Ratna Viswanathan addressed the impact of MFIs transitioning into small finance banks. She anticipated that a significant number of MFIs would apply for small bank licenses, leading to a positive outcome for the sector. Small finance banks were expected to cater to the credit demand of small enterprises, complementing the role of MFIs.

Advocacy and Regulatory Changes:

Ratna Viswanathan's tenure at MFIN was marked by collaborative efforts with regulatory bodies like the RBI. She emphasized the need for further regulatory actions, including addressing micro regulations related to small savings accounts under Jan Dhan Yojana. She advocated for client-friendly banking practices, particularly for MFI clients who often required access to higher transaction limits.

Funding and Investment in Microfinance:

Ratna Viswanathan observed the growth of private equity (PE) investments, especially among MFIs with diversified portfolios. Bank funding also played a significant role in supporting MFIs, with a substantial percentage of funding coming from banks.

Throughout her tenure, Ratna Viswanathan's leadership and strategic insights contributed to the resilience and growth of the microfinance sector in India. Her work at MFIN underscored her commitment to the welfare of microfinance clients and the sustainable development of the industry.

11.34. Mr. Harsh Shrivastava

Harsh Shrivastava is a seasoned professional with extensive experience in policy advisory, corporate affairs, and leadership roles in various organizations.

Full Name: Harsh Shrivastava

Career Overview:

Harsh Shrivastava has amassed over two decades of experience, primarily advising businesses and governments on policy matters. His career has encompassed leadership positions in diverse sectors, including finance, infrastructure, and microfinance.

Leadership at MFIN:

Harsh Shrivastava served as the CEO of Microfinance Institutions Network (MFIN), a pivotal organization that both advocates for and regulates microfinance lending companies in India. During his tenure, he played a crucial role in shaping the microfinance landscape and promoting responsible lending practices within the industry.

Corporate Affairs and Communication:

Before his role at MFIN, Harsh Shrivastava held the position of Head of Corporate Affairs and Communication at Feedback Infra, a leading provider of infrastructure services in India. In this capacity, he managed key aspects of corporate communication and engagement.

Experience in Finance and Infrastructure:

Harsh Shrivastava's professional journey also includes senior roles in organizations such as Reliance Capital, Confederation of Indian Industry (CII), and Srei Infrastructure and Finance. His multifaceted experience across these sectors has enriched his understanding of policy and business dynamics.

Education and Authorship:

Harsh Shrivastava is an alumnus of the prestigious Indian Institute of Management (IIM) Ahmedabad, reflecting his strong educational foundation. He is also the author of India's first book on Corporate Social Responsibility (CSR), highlighting his commitment to responsible corporate practices.

Government and Planning Commission:

Harsh Shrivastava's career includes a significant stint in the Prime Minister's Office, where he served as Deputy Speechwriter during the tenure of Prime Minister Atal Bihari Vajpayee. He contributed to shaping the government's communication and messaging.

Additionally, he played a vital role in the formulation of India's 12th plan while working as a consultant with the Planning Commission, further demonstrating his involvement in shaping national policies.

Current Roles and Contributions:

Presently, Harsh Shrivastava offers advisory services to governments, businesses, and entities, leveraging his extensive knowledge of public policy and governance. He also serves as an independent director on the boards of company boards, contributing to strategic decision-making.

Furthermore, Harsh Shrivastava is an accomplished author, public speaker, and commentator on various policy-related issues, reflecting his dedication to driving positive change through informed discourse.

Harsh Shrivastava's career journey showcases his commitment to policy advocacy, corporate responsibility, and leadership in both the public and private sectors. His multifaceted experiences have made him a respected figure in India's policy and business landscape.

11.35. Dr. Alok Mishra:

Dr. Alok Misra is a distinguished professional with an impressive career spanning 30 years in the fields of international development, rural finance, microfinance, inclusive finance, and research. His work has encompassed both policy development and on-the-ground implementation.

Full Name: Dr. Alok Misra

Educational Background:

Dr. Alok Misra's academic qualifications reflect his commitment to excellence in the field of development studies and finance:

PhD in Development Studies from Victoria University of Wellington

Master's in Development Management (Gold Medallist) from the Asian Institute of Management, Manila

Recipient of the ADB-Government of Japan scholarship for the Master's in Development Management (MDM) program

Awarded the NZAID scholarship for his PhD studies

Career Journey:

Dr. Alok Misra's career has been marked by significant contributions and leadership roles in various key organizations:

National Bank for Agriculture and Rural Development (NABARD):

Dr. Misra began his career in 1992 at NABARD, India's apex rural development bank. His responsibilities included financial sector supervision, institutional development, microfinance, agricultural and rural finance, and rural livelihoods and MSME finance.

Setting up India's First Online Demutualized Commodities Exchange (NCDEX):

From 2003 to 2004, Dr. Misra was a part of a multi-institutional task force responsible for establishing India's first online demutualized commodities exchange, NCDEX.

Global Microfinance Rating and Policy Analysis:

In 2008, he transitioned to a global microfinance rating, policy analysis, and technical advisory agency, where he contributed significantly to the microfinance sector at an international level.

Management Development Institute (MDI), Gurgaon:

Before assuming his role as CEO & Director at MFIN, Dr. Misra served as Professor and Chairperson of the School of Public Policy & Governance at Management Development Institute (MDI), Gurgaon.

Board Memberships and Strategic Groups:

Dr. Misra has served as a board member of MFIN and Vaya Finserv. He has also been a member of NABARD's strategic group on microfinance.

International Involvement:

He has been actively involved in international initiatives such as the Smart Campaign and SPTF (Social Performance Task Force). His work has taken him to 24 countries across Asia, Africa, Europe, and the Pacific.

Authorship and Research:

Dr. Misra has contributed extensively to the field of inclusive finance through numerous articles, reports, and authored the "Inclusive Finance India report" for two years.

Training and Fellowships:

He received specialized training at Harvard Business School in "Strategic Leadership for Microfinance" and was a Fellow in the Fletcher Leadership Program for Financial Inclusion at Tufts University.

Professional Associations:

Dr. Alok Misra is actively engaged in various professional associations and working groups, including being a member of the Inclusive Finance India Group of Advisors and the Digital Finance Working Group constituted by ITU, Geneva.Dr. Alok Misra's career reflects a deep commitment to the advancement of inclusive finance and development, both at the national and international levels. His extensive experience, academic achievements, and leadership roles have made him a respected authority in the field.

11.36. Late. Mr. Pillarisetti Satish:

Late Mr. Pillarisetti Satish, often referred to as P. Satish, was a distinguished figure in the field of microfinance and financial inclusion in India. His remarkable contributions to the industry and his leadership roles in various key organizations have left a lasting impact.

Full Name: Late Mr. Pillarisetti Satish

Background:

P. Satish was a visionary leader in the microfinance sector, with a profound commitment to improving financial access and services for underserved communities in India.

Career Achievements:

Throughout his career, Late Mr. P. Satish held pivotal positions and played a crucial role in shaping the landscape of microfinance and financial inclusion in India:

Sa-Dhan (Network of Microfinance Institutions):

Position: CEO (Chief Executive Officer) and Executive Director

P. Satish served as the CEO and Executive Director of Sa-Dhan, the network of all Microfinance Institutions in India. This network comprises over 220 member institutions and is recognized by the Reserve Bank of India as the Self-Regulatory Organization for MFIs in India.

Under his leadership, Sa-Dhan played a crucial role in promoting self-regulation and best practices among microfinance institutions in India.

India Post Payments Bank (IPPB):

Position: Director on the Board

P. Satish also served as a Director on the Board of India Post Payments Bank, contributing his expertise to the development of accessible and inclusive financial services through India's extensive postal network.

Reserve Bank of India (RBI):

P. Satish was a member of RBI's Financial Inclusion Advisory Committee, demonstrating his involvement in shaping India's financial inclusion policies.

National Bank for Agriculture and Rural Development (NABARD):

Position: Member of the SHG-Bank Linkage Programme Strategic Advisory Board

P. Satish's expertise was recognized at NABARD, where he served as a member of the Strategic Advisory Board for the Self-Help Group (SHG)-Bank Linkage Programme.

Ministry of Housing and Urban Development, Government of India:

Position: Steering Committee Member of PMSvaNidhi Scheme

He contributed to the Steering Committee of the Pradhan Mantri Street Vendor's Atmanirbhar Nidhi (PMSvaNidhi) Scheme under the Ministry of Housing and Urban Development, Government of India.

Bankers Institute of Rural Development (BIRD), Lucknow:

Position: Member of the Governing Council

P. Satish was a member of the Governing Council of Bankers Institute of Rural Development (BIRD) in Lucknow.

MUDRA (Micro Units Development and Refinance Agency Ltd.):

Position: Director on the Board

He served as a Director on the Board of MUDRA, which focuses on providing financial support to micro-enterprises.

IRDAI (Insurance Regulatory and Development Authority of India):

Position: Member of IRDAI's Insurance Advisory Council

He also contributed to IRDAI's Insurance Advisory Council, where he provided valuable insights into the insurance sector.

Late Mr. P. Satish's extensive experience, leadership, and dedication to financial inclusion have left an indelible mark on the microfinance industry in India. His legacy continues to inspire individuals and organizations committed to making financial services accessible to all segments of society.

11.37. Mr. Jiji Mammen

Mr. Jiji Mammen Executive Director & CEO Mr. Jiji Mammen has been appointed Executive Director & CEO of Sa-Dhan with effect from June 17, 2022. An industry veteran with over 36 years of experience in microfinance, agriculture and rural development, Mr. Mammen was earlier the Managing Director of NABFINS, an NBFC MFI promoted by NABARD. He was the founder MD & CEO of Micro Units Development and Refinance Agency Ltd. (MUDRA), an NBFC formed to support the flagship programme of Govt. of India viz. Pradhan Mantri Mudra Yojana for three years from

2015. He has been CGM at NABARD, heading the regional offices in Rajasthan, Andhra Pradesh and Telengana. Mr. Mammen was also the country head of Department of Refinance in NABARD. A post Graduate from the Indian Agricultural Research Institute, New Delhi, Mr. Mammen also holds a degree in law and is a Certified Associate of Indian Institute of Banking and Finance (IIBF). He has been a faculty member at Bankers Institute of Rural Development, Mangaluru. He is widely travelled and has attended several international conferences/seminars.

11.38. Dr. Aqueel Ahmed Khan:

Dr. Aqueel Ahmed Khan: A Visionary Leader in Development and Finance

Dr. Aqueel Ahmed Khan is a remarkable individual who has dedicated his life to creating positive change on both local and global scales. His diverse career spans the fields of development and finance, where he has made significant contributions to the well-being of communities and individuals around the world.

Early Career and Commitment to Development:

Dr. Khan's journey in the realm of development and social change began over 29 years ago. During this time, he worked tirelessly at various levels, from grassroots initiatives to national and international organizations. His work has focused on critical issues, including child rights, community development, and the capacity building of development organizations and actors.

Before establishing the Association for Stimulating Know-how (ASK), a not-for-profit development support organization, Dr. Khan honed his expertise and deepened his commitment through collaborations with renowned institutions. He notably served with the United Nations High Commission for Refugees (UNHCR) and Child Fund India, an American development agency with a mission to empower children and communities.

Global Impact and Collaboration:

Dr. Aqueel Ahmed Khan's influence extends well beyond national borders. He has had the privilege of working with esteemed multilateral institutions, including the Asian Development Bank (ADB), World Bank (WB), and the International Finance Corporation (IFC). His involvement with these organizations underscores his commitment to effecting change on a global scale.

Dr. Khan's dedication has seen him collaborate with numerous bilateral and development organizations in various countries. His ability to navigate complex international landscapes and build partnerships has been instrumental in driving positive outcomes for communities and underserved populations.

Pioneering Inclusive Financial Services:

Dr. Khan's passion for social change led him to his current role as the Founder and Managing Director of Mitrata Inclusive Financial Services Pvt Ltd. In this capacity, he continues to be a force for empowerment and progress. Mitrata Inclusive Financial Services is at the forefront of creating financial inclusion opportunities for marginalized communities. Under Dr. Khan's visionary leadership, the organization is dedicated to enabling individuals to lead more secure and prosperous lives through improved access to financial resources and services.

Recognition and Influence:

Dr. Aqueel Ahmed Khan's impact is evident not only in his extensive body of work but also in his influence within the development and finance sectors. His dedication to positive change has earned him recognition and respect among peers and colleagues.

Dr. Aqueel Ahmed Khan is a visionary leader who has dedicated his life to advancing the causes of social justice, community development, and financial inclusion. His journey from grassroots activism to global collaborations showcases his unwavering commitment to making the world a better place for all. As a Founder, Director, and Managing Director, his work continues to inspire and uplift communities, leaving a lasting legacy of positive change.

Chapter - 12

Microfinance Companies, NBFC's, SFB's & Banks in India at a glance

India's financial landscape is a diverse and dynamic ecosystem, driven by a myriad of financial institutions catering to the needs of a vast and varied population. From the bustling streets of its megacities to the remote corners of its rural heartland, India's financial sector plays a crucial role in empowering individuals and fostering economic growth. This chapter, titled "Microfinance Companies, NBFC's, SFB's & Banks in India," is a journey into this multifaceted world.

12.1. Microfinance Industry Trends:

There are around 211 lenders in the microfinance segment. This group comprises NBFC-MFIs, Banks, Small Finance Banks (SFBs), and others, including non-profit entities. As of 31 March 2023, the microfinance industry provided credit to over 6.6 Cr customers pan India with a gross loan portfolio of Rs 3,48,339 crore. NBFC-MFIs were the largest provider of microcredit, accounting for 39.7% of total industry portfolio. Banks held the second largest share of Micro-credit which was 34.2% of the total micro-credit universe.

12.2. Microfinance Industry Performance in FY 22-23

A. Sector:

Clients (Cr) - 6.6
Loan Accounts (Cr.) - 13
Total Loan Portfolio (Rs Cr.) - 3,48,339
Loan Disbursed (during the year, Cr.) - 2.3
Loan Amount Disbursed (during the year, Rs Cr.) - 1,00,800

B. NBFC-MFIs:

Performance of NBFC-MFIs in FY 22-23 is given below:
Indicator As on 31 March 2023:
Branches - 18,739
Employees - 1,61,010
Clients (Cr.) – 3.9
Loan accounts (Cr.) – 4.6
Asset Under Management (Rs Cr.) - 1,31,163
Loans disbursed (during the year, Cr.) - 3.1
Loan amount disbursed (during the year, Rs Cr.) - 1,30.563

12.3. Pan India (India) Presence of NBFC-MFIs:

In terms of regional distribution of portfolio (AUM), East and Northeast accounts for 32% of the total NBFC-MFI portfolio, South 26%, North 17%, West 15% and Central contributes 10%.

Five top states in terms of loan amount outstanding are Bihar, Tamil Nadu, Uttar Pradesh, Karnataka and Madhya Pradesh. They account for 54.9% of AUM and Top 10 states account for 83.6% of the total loan amount outstanding.

12.4. OUTREACH:

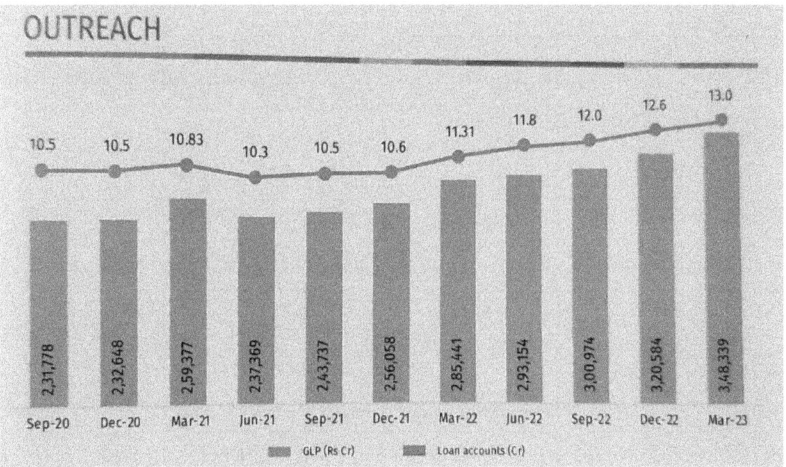

As on 31 March 2023, aggregated GLP (own + managed) of NBFC-MFIs stood at Rs 1,31,163 Cr, growth of 38.7% in comparison to 31 March 2022 and 15.7% over the quarter ending 31 December 2022, Managed portfolio is Rs 29,411 Cr, which includes Rs 5,480 Cr of On-balance sheet managed portfolio (due to IndAS) and Rs 23,931 Cr of Off-balance sheet managed portfolio. Within the managed portfolio, portfolio created under Business Correspondent (BC) partnership has 15.9% share amounting to Rs 4,685 Cr. PTC & DA contributes 17.1% and 67.0% of total managed portfolio. As on 31 March 2023, Top 10 MFIs accounted for 75.1% of the industry portfolio.

12.5. Debt Funding & Securitization (Rs. Cr.):

During FY 22-23, NBFC-MFIs received a total of Rs 74,787 Cr in debt funding (from Banks and other Financial Institutions) which is an increase of 59.2% as compared to FY 21-22. 69% of debt funding for Large MFIs was from Banks. Medium and Small MFIs received 54% and 48% of their debt funding from Banks respectively.

12.6. Portfolio Quality:

PAR >30 has decreased significantly to 4.0% as on 31 March 2023 as compared to 9.7% as on 31 March 2022. It signifies gradual and sustained improvement in portfolio quality.

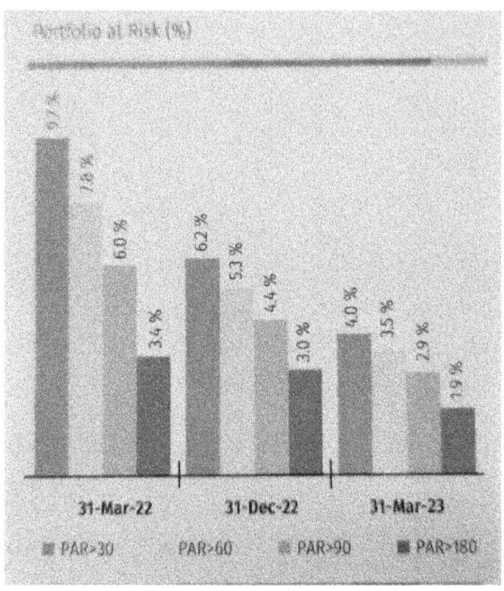

12.7. Productivity Ratios:

On an average, a loan officer caters to 372 clients with a portfolio of Rs 1.2 Cr. Similarly, on an average a branch caters to 2,093 clients with a portfolio of Rs 7.0 Cr.

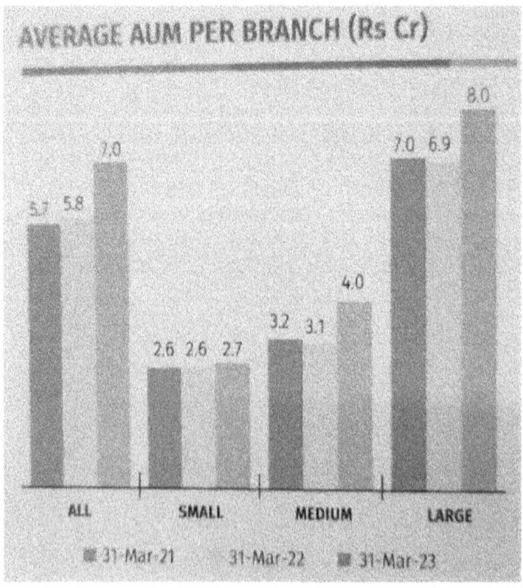

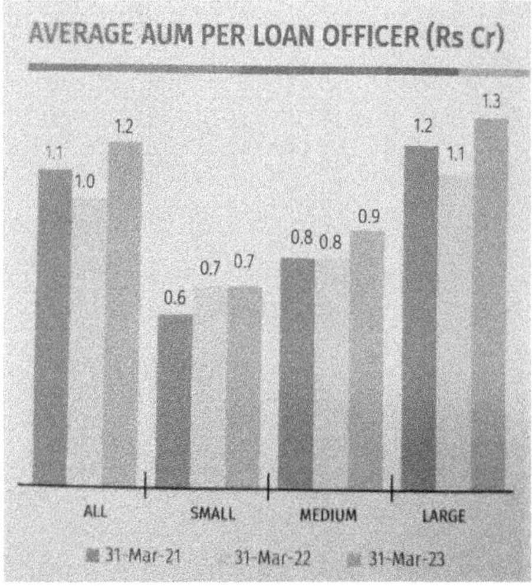

12.8. List of Members of mfin:

Institution/Website:

1 - Adhikar Microfinance Pvt. Ltd./www.adhikarIndia.in
2 - Adi Chitragupta Finance Ltd./www.acfl.co.in
3 - Agora Microfinance India Ltd./www.amil.co.in
4 - Annapurna Finance Pvt. Ltd./www.annapurnafinance.in
5 - Arohan Financial Services Ltd./www.arohan.in
6 - Arth Finance/www.arthfinance.com
7- ASA International India Microfinance Ltd./www.asaIndia.in
8 - Asirvad Microfinance Ltd/www.asirvadmicrofinance.co.in
9 - Avanti Finance Ltd./www.avantifinance.in
10 - Aviral Finance Pvt. Ltd./www.aviralfinance.com
11 - Belstar Microfinance Ltd./www.belstar.in
12 - BWDA Finance Ltd./www.bwda.in?page_id=82
13 - Chaitanya India Fin Credit Pvt. Ltd./www.chaitanyaIndia.in
14 - Credit Access Grameen Ltd./www.creditaccessgrameen.com
15 - Fino Finance Pvt. Ltd./www.finofinance.in
16 - Fusion Micro Finance Ltd./www.fusionmicrofinance.com
17 - Grameen Shakti Microfinance Services Pvt. Ltd/www.grameenshakti.co.in
18 - Hindusthan Microfinance Pvt. Ltd./www.hindusthanmfi.com

19 - Humana Financial Services Pvt. Ltd./www.humanafinancial.com
20 - Inditrade Microfinance Ltd./www.inditrade.com
21 - Jagaran Microfin Pvt. Ltd./www.jagaranmf.com
22 -Janakalyan Financial Services Pvt. Ltd./www.janakalyan.net
23 - Light Microfinance Pvt. Ltd./www.lightmicrofinance.com
24 - Madura Microfinance Ltd./www.maduramicrofinance.com
25 - Magenta Financial Services Pvt. Ltd./www.magentafinance.co.in
26 - Midland Microfin Ltd./www.midlandmicrofin.com
27 - Mitrata Inclusive Financial Services Pvt. Ltd./www.mitrata.in
28 - M Power Micro Finance Pvt. Ltd./www.mpowermicro.com
29 - MSM Microfinance Ltd./www.msmmicrofinance.com
30 - Muthoot Microfin Ltd./www.muthootmicrofin.com
31 - Namra Finance Ltd./www.namrafinance.com
32 - Nightingale Finvest Pvt. Ltd./www.nightingalefinvest.in
33 - Saija Finance Pvt. Ltd./www.saija.in
34 - Samasta Microfinance Ltd./www.samasta.co.in
35 - Samavesh Finserv Pvt. Ltd./www.samaveshmfi.com
36 - Sarala Development & Microfinance PM. Ltd./www.sarala.co.in
37 - Sarwadi Finance PM. Ltd./www.sarwadi.in
38 - Satin CreditCare Network Ltd./www.satincreditcare.com
39 - Satya MicroCapital Ltd./www.satyamicrocapital.com
40 - SAVE MicroFinance Pvt. Ltd./www.savemicrofinance.com
41 - Share Microfin Ltd./www.sharemicrofin.com
42 - Sindhuja Microcredit Pvt. Ltd./www.sindhujamicrocredit.com
43 - Sonata Finance Pvt. Ltd./www.sonataIndia.com
44 - South India Finvest Pvt. Ltd./www.southIndiafinvest.com
45 - Spandana Sphoorty Financial Ltd./www.spandanasphoorty.com
46 - SV Creditline Ltd./www.svcl.in
47 - Svamaan Financial Services Pvt. Ltd./www.svamaan.in
48 - Svasti Microfinance Pvt. Ltd./www.svasti.in
49 - Svatantra Microfin Pvt. Ltd./www.svatantramicrofin.com
50 - Unacco Financial Services Pvt. Ltd./www.unacco.in
51 - Unnati Finserv Pvt. Ltd./www.unnatimfi.com

52 - Vaya FinServ Pvt. Ltd./www.vayaIndia.com
53 - Vector Finance Pvt. Ltd./www.vectorfinance.in
54 - Village Financial Capital Ltd./www.village.net.in
55 - Vruksha Microfin Pvt. Ltd./www.vrukshamicrofin.com

List of Associates of mfin (All these become a member of mfin in place of associate):

1 - AU Small Finance Bank Ltd./www.aubank.in
2 - Axis Bank Ltd./www.axisbank.com
3 - Buldana Urban Management Services Pvt. Ltd./www.burnspl.org
4 - Care Health Insurance Ltd./www.careinsurance.com
5 - CSB Bank Ltd./www.csb.co.in
6 - Craft Silicon Pvt. Ltd./craftsolicon.com
7 - Davinta Financial Services Pvt. Ltd./www.davintafinserv.com
8 - DBS Bank Ltd./www.dbs.com
9 - Dvara KGFS/www.dvarakgfs.com
10 - Equifax Credit Information Services Pvt. Ltd./www.equifax.co.in
11 - ESAF Small Finance Bank Ltd./www.esafbank.com
12 - Equitas Small Finance Bank Ltd./www.equitasbank.com
13 - Experian Credit Information Company of India/www.experiamn.in
14 - Fincare Small Finance Bank Ltd./www.fincarebank.com
15 - Fortune Credit Capital Ltd./www.itiorg.com/entities.php
16 - Fullerton India Credit Company Ltd./www.fullertonIndia.com
17 - Hinduja Leyland Finance Ltd./www.hindujaleylandfinance.com
18 - ICICI Bank Ltd./www.icicibank.com
19 - IDFC First Bank Ltd./www.idfcfirstbank.com
20 - IDFC First India Ltd./www.idfcIndia.com
21 - Indusind Bank Ltd./www.indusind.com
22 - Jana Small Finance Bank Ltd./www.janabank.com
23 - Jeevan Utthan Financial Services Private Limited/www.jeevanutthan.in
24 - Kaleidofin Pvt. Ltd./www.kaleidofin.com
25 - Kamal Fincap Pvt. Ltd.)/www.kamalkfc.com
26 - Kotak Mahindra Bank Ltd./www.kotak.com

27 - L&T Financial Services Ltd./www.ltfs.com
28 - MAS Financial Services Ltd./www.mas.co.in
29 - M-Insure Services Pvt. Ltd/www.m-insure.in
30 - New Opportunity Consultancy Pvt. Ltd./www.nocpl.in
31 - Northern Arc Capital Ltd./www.northernarc.com
32 - Piramal Capital & Housing Finance Pvt. Ltd/www.piramalfinance.com
33 - RBL Bank Ltd./www.rbibank.com
34 - RBL FinServe Ltd./www.rbifinserve.com
35 - SAGGRAHA Management Services Pvt. Ltd./www.saggraha.com
36 - Sub-K Impact Solutions Ltd./www.subk.co.in
37 - Suryoday Small Finance Bank Ltd./www.suryodaybank.com
38 - Tata Capital Financial Services Ltd./www.tatacapital.com
39 - TransUnion CIBIL Ltd./www.transunioncibil.com
40 - Ujjivan Small Finance Bank Ltd./www.ujjivansfb.in
41 - Unity Small Finance Bank Ltd./www.theunitybank.com
42 - Utkarsh Small Finance Bank Ltd./www.utkarsh.bank
43 - Vivriti Capital Pvt. Ltd./www.vivriticapital.com
44 - Water.Org/www.water.org
45 - Yes Bank Ltd./www.yesbank.in

"All the associates of MFIN are now honorable members of MFIN, as MFIN's name is also going to change."

"There are many more MFIs that have the license with RBI but are not members of MFIN, so their names are not mentioned here. All those MFI names will be mentioned in Volume 2 of this book."

"Please refer to the book 'Navigating Microfinance: Insights and Implementation,' Volume 2, to continue your learning journey."

"Navigating Microfinance: Insights and Implementation" Volume 2

Volume 2 Highlights:

Operational Aspects of Microfinance

Chapter 1: Financial Products and Services

Minimalist vs. Integrated Financial Services
Credit Services
Remittance Services
Micro-Insurance
Micro Pension
Non-Financial Services
Fundamentals of Designing Products
Credit Product
Sustainable Interest Rate

Chapter 2: Financial Accounting and Reporting

Characteristics of Financial Statements
Components of Financial Statements
The Accounting Equation
The Chart of Accounts
Financial Reporting Formats
Some Special Transactions
Mechanics of Accounting

Chapter 3: Revenue Models of Microfinance, Profitability, Efficiency, and Productivity

The Revenue Model of an MFI
CVP Analysis
Measuring Operating Efficiency and Productivity in MFIs
Factors Affecting Operating Expenses
Operating Efficiency - The Negative Side
Strategies for Improved Efficiency
Risk Management

Chapter 4: Risk Management

Introduction to Risk Management
Risk Management Process
Types of Risks for MFIs
Managing Credit Risk
Setting Up a Risk Organization
Assets Liabilities Management
Risk Exposure Analysis
Open Position
Duration & Modified Duration
Convexity RAROC
Auditing Risk Management
Understanding Basel Accord and Its Implications

Chapter 5: Basics of Banking

Financial System including RBI, PFRDA, and IRDA
Functions of Banks
Types of Customers and Their Accounts and Operations

Chapter 6: Compliance to Various Regulations

Compliance to State Acts like AP Act
Priority Sector Guidelines Compliance
Compliance to RBI Guidelines on NBFC-MFIs

Concept of Self-Regulation

Microfinance (Development and Regulation) Bill

Chapter 7: Annexures and References for both Volume 1 & 2.

Chapter 8: Conclusion

"I kindly request you to consider sharing this book with your friends and family members who are part of the financial sector or share an interest in the transformative world of microfinance. Your recommendation can help spread knowledge and empower others on this impactful journey."

"Stay tuned for the forthcoming Volume 2 of 'Navigating Microfinance: Insights and Implementation.' Please note that the author and publisher are not liable for any numerical inaccuracies. We urge readers to verify all data using credible references and authoritative sources."

"It's a journey; see you soon and take care...

Pradeep Kumar Singh

www.ingramcontent.com/pod-product-compliance
Lightning Source LLC
LaVergne TN
LVHW021135160826
845679LV00023B/1914

* 9 7 9 8 8 9 1 3 3 6 8 5 8 *